Bibliography of the Sequence Novel

Bibliography of the Sequence Novel

by ELIZABETH MARGARET KERR

OCTAGON BOOKS

A DIVISION OF FARRAR, STRAUS AND GIROUX

New York   1973

Copyright 1950 by the University of Minnesota

Reprinted 1973
by special arrangement with the University of Minnesota Press

OCTAGON BOOKS
A Division of Farrar, Straus & Giroux, Inc.
19 Union Square West
New York, N. Y. 10003

Library of Congress Catalog Card Number: 70-153637
ISBN 0-374-94568-3

Printed in U.S.A. by
NOBLE OFFSET PRINTERS, INC.
New York, N.Y. 10003

Acknowledgments

To all those who generously aided me in all stages of gathering material and preparing this bibliography for publication, I express my sincere gratitude.

For the term sequence novel and for encouragement in the project of compiling a bibliography of sequence novels, I am indebted to Joseph Warren Beach, professor emeritus of English of the University of Minnesota. Harold G. Russell, reference librarian of the University of Minnesota, advised me on data to be included in the bibliography. Margaret S. Harding, director of the University Press, and her staff have been of great assistance in working out a practical form for entries.

The staffs of the libraries of the University of Minnesota and the University of Chicago have been unfailingly helpful in the detective work of tracking down elusive data.

Completion of this bibliography would have been impossible without the aid of authorities in foreign languages and literature who translated titles, furnished information, and gave me leads to helpful critical works. I am especially indebted to Konstantin Reichardt, professor of Germanic philology, Yale University, for helping me with the German, Scandinavian, and Russian sections. The following members of foreign language departments of the University of Minnesota were consulted for the languages indicated: Jacques Fermaud, French; Elizabeth Nissen, Italian; Walter T. Pattison, Spanish; Frederick L. Pfeiffer and Gina Wangsness, German; and Alrik Gustafson, Scandinavian. Hans Nestlbichler, of Milwaukee State Teachers College, helped me with final preparation of the Russian section and with the last additions to the German section. In collection of data on Polish novels and in translation of titles I was greatly assisted by Edmund Zawacki, assistant professor of Slavic of the University of Wisconsin; John Dulka, of Milwaukee State Teachers College; and Salomea K. Stapko, of the Milwaukee Public Library.

I hope that all those who so kindly lent their services will feel that their labors are in part rewarded by whatever use they may be able to make of the bibliography.

Elizabeth Margaret Kerr

Table of Contents

INTRODUCTION TO THE SEQUENCE NOVEL.	3
KEY TO BIBLIOGRAPHY	9
BRITISH AND AMERICAN.	11
ROMANCE LANGUAGES	
FRENCH	39
ITALIAN.	63
SPANISH AND PORTUGUESE	66
TEUTONIC LANGUAGES	
DUTCH.	77
GERMAN AND LOW GERMAN.	78
SCANDINAVIAN	
DANISH.	102
ICELANDIC	106
NORWEGIAN	107
SWEDISH	112
SLAVIC AND UGRIC LANGUAGES	
BULGARIAN.	116
CZECH.	116
HUNGARIAN.	117
POLISH	117
RUSSIAN.	121

Introduction to the Sequence Novel

The term sequence novel is used to designate a series of closely related novels that were originally published as separate, complete novels but that as a series form an artistic whole, unified by structure and themes that involve more than the recurrence of characters and some continuity of action. The sequence may have a series title in addition to a separate title for each part and may be published ultimately in one volume under the series title. Since such publication is often a commercial rather than an artistic matter, many sequences do not achieve it.

Characteristics of content and form are more significant than external features. The sequence novel has its origin in the writer's desire to expand the scope of the novel without destroying the form. It is characteristically distinguished by a deep and serious purpose and an active concern with technical and esthetic problems created by the inclusion of a broader social scene, a more intensive study of psychology, or a longer span of family history than can be accommodated in the ordinary novel. Although in specific novels it is sometimes hard to draw a line between sequels and sequences, the general distinction between them lies in this serious purpose of the sequence and in the consequent emphasis upon such elements as social values and thematic structure, instead of upon exciting action and a gallery of striking characters, such as sustain interest in the ordinary sequel. Sequels are like the charming and romantic songs in an operetta, gaining little individually by being linked with others and together forming no unified pattern. But the true sequence, being more than the sum of its parts, is like a symphony, an artistic whole with each part contributing its own tone and character.

Two well-known examples may make this distinction clear. John Galsworthy's Forsyte Saga is a typical sequence. Although Galsworthy had not envisaged the series when he wrote The Man of Property, on the foundation of that first book he built a trilogy that is much more than the story of Soames Forsyte or even of the Forsyte family. The crumbling of the Forsyte way of life and of the whole Victorian age began in the first volume with the failure of the sense of property to secure for Soames the intangible satisfactions of life and to protect the family from social change, and it is completed in To Let, with the house on Bayswater Road, the symbol of the Forsytes and their class, "to let." The strength of Galsworthy's picture of the dissolution of Forsyteism depends upon the contrast between the palmy days of the Victorian Forsytes, with which the trilogy begins, and their decline, a kind of bourgeois Götterdämmerung. The Forsyte Saga is both the history of the disintegration of a family and a chapter in social history.

Any one volume of The Forsyte Saga has as much interest and significance as an ordinary novel dealing with similar material, but the series as a whole has an added significance that depends upon continuity of theme and structure and upon the comprehensive view of social life and change, not merely upon the recurrence of characters. Despite his tardy conception of the sequence plan, Galsworthy achieved sound sequence form in this trilogy and the two that followed it.

Exceeding Galsworthy by one volume, Mazo de la Roche has written eleven volumes about a family and its ramifications, the Whiteoaks of Jalna. Dealing with a somewhat smaller group, she would seem to have a simpler problem. But after introducing the family, in Jalna, she continued the history without developing any central theme that would unify the series. For those who have read the previous books in the series, the interest is increased by former acquaintance with the characters, but that is all. The only external links are the titles, referring to the family or to individual members, and the family tree at the beginning of each volume. But external links are not essential; more serious is the lack of an evident structural pattern uniting the volumes, of a well-defined structure within volumes, of basic themes. The family does not represent any social class or even typical family relationships, the emphasis being on eccentricities rather than on universalities.

INTRODUCTION TO THE SEQUENCE NOVEL

Comparison with G. B. Stern's Matriarch novels may make these last points clearer. Miss Stern deals with equally eccentric characters, dominated, like the Whiteoaks, by a matriarch. But she also presents a vast panorama of European society, with the tribe of Rakonitzes reflecting cosmopolitan life and change. She traces the recurrent matriarch characteristics through several generations. And she works out well-defined themes in each volume, with themes in one volume reappearing as minor motifs in another. The series is really autobiographical, and hence the continuation down to the present is implicit in the material, the definite fund of memory and experience being extended just as straight autobiography may be kept up to date. Despite greater scope in time, place, and characters, the Matriarch novels have a closer texture, a surer movement, a greater unity than the Jalna books.

The facts of publication of the Jalna books also indicate that the author has continued the series from time to time without a preconceived fund of material. The first book, chronologically the fifth in the series, was Jalna; it won the Atlantic Monthly prize contest in 1927 and was very popular. It dealt with contemporary life, with events taking place only a few years before the actual writing. At two-year intervals the next three books appeared, Whiteoaks of Jalna, Finch's Fortune, and Master of Jalna, bringing the family history up to date, with the center of interest shifting from Finch to Renny. But Young Renny, 1935, goes back to 1906, seventeen years before the beginning of the first book, and is now third in the series. Whiteoak Harvest, 1936, chronologically ninth in the series, covers 1934-35, but Whiteoak Heritage, 1940, is chronologically fourth, filling in the gap between Young Renny and Jalna. Wakefield's Course, 1941, continues the action from Whiteoak Harvest down to World War II. The next book is chronologically the first, The Building of Jalna, 1944. The next to the last Jalna book, Return to Jalna, 1946, is now the final one in the series, covering the last part of World War II. But it has been followed by Mary Wakefield, 1949, which is chronologically second in the series. And the end may not yet be in sight. The publication data seem to reveal chiefly a desire to capitalize on the popularity of the characters by alternately continuing to the present and, while time marches on bringing new things, filling in the gaps in family history until a new chapter in current history can be written. Now that Miss de la Roche has covered the logical beginning of the series, she will have to content herself, it would seem, with keeping one jump behind the present.

The reader familiar with the series from the beginning is at a distinct disadvantage in trying to get an orderly and coherent view of the whole history, with this backing and filling method. Few other readers are likely to read the whole series in chronological order, with all eleven stretching ahead of them. Obviously Miss de la Roche was not concerned with a unified concept, for herself or her readers. In the absence of external or internal evidence of coherent plan and structure, as well as in the lack of substance and serious purpose, the Jalna books, though superior to many of their kind, are typical of sequels rather than of sequences.

The difference between the continuation of the Whiteoaks history, which could logically go on as long as the author will write and the public read, and the bringing of a sequence up to date may be seen by returning to Galsworthy. Galsworthy covered postwar events and social history in his second and third trilogies, thus approximating the performance, in bulk, of Miss de la Roche. But each trilogy has its own theme, each volume has its individual theme related to the trilogy theme, and each series forms a complete whole, with no possibility of tacking on additions.

In the second trilogy, A Modern Comedy, for example, the Forsyte theme is continued through Soames, but the title refers to Wilfrid Desert's philosophy (Wilfrid is a leading character in the third trilogy), reflecting the attitude of youth in the 1920s. The disillusionment of the young generation is represented by the White Monkey, who has squeezed life dry; the dissolution of the old order is seen in the failure of the Silver Spoon of wealth and position to bring its possessors a secure and happy life; the Swan Song of the older Forsytes, of the love of Soames for Irene and of Fleur for Jon, echoes in the death of Soames. These symbols serve as titles of the three novels. The third trilogy shifts to other branches of the Forsytes and their group in the postwar period. This superficial analysis of the trilogies ignores minor themes and the very competent technique that insures the recognition of a larger plan behind the separate volumes. The inferiority of the last trilogies to the first is in interpretation and grasp of subject rather than in sequence form.

Galsworthy and Miss de la Roche wrote approximately the same number of books about a family. Galsworthy, by the time he had written one novel, conceived a plan that would give

INTRODUCTION TO THE SEQUENCE NOVEL 5

his material artistic form and social significance; Miss de la Roche goes on telling new stories about the same people, and little more. Whatever weight her series has, greater than that of individual volumes, lies only in the extension of the story of the characters and the pleasant sense of familiarity with them. But even Galsworthy's less successful trilogies have a seriousness of purpose and a technical excellence that put them above the merely entertaining novels of Miss de la Roche and that make them as typical of the sequence form as the Jalna books are typical of sequels.

The sequel generally has its origin in the popularity of earlier books and makes the reader ask, "What happens next?" The sequence generally has its origin in a serious purpose that cannot be achieved in one novel and in an esthetic ideal that refuses to sacrifice artistic form even to the most excellent matter. The sequence makes the reader ask, "Why does it happen, and what does the pattern mean?" The sequence aims at greatness; the sequel aims at popularity; either may achieve the quality aimed at by the other, but the sequence novel is more likely to be popular than the sequel to be great.

Because a number of series are difficult to classify, being more than sequels but perhaps less than sequences, and because specific examples of sequences are more familiar than the genre, it has been necessary to set up some criteria by which the genre may be recognized in its manifold forms. Even sequence novelists are often unaware of the characteristics of the genre; critics are no more helpful than novelists in establishing general standards of sequence form. Therefore one must rely upon external or internal evidence or both in distinguishing between sequels and sequences, and when the combined evidence is inconclusive, the classification must be arbitrary. The inclusion or omission of some series in this bibliography may be open to question, but usually examination of a specific series with reference to the following criteria will suggest the reason for its classification.

The most definite and reliable external evidence, though it is not infallible, is the author's explicit statement that he is writing or has written a trilogy, tetralogy, or cycle. Such statements have to be accepted on faith if it is not possible to examine the books or if the author does not go on to explain his plan in unmistakable terms. If the author is reticent, the publisher may be less so, and may give advance publicity to forthcoming novels continuing a series or may refer to those already published. Publishers, like novelists, are not infallible and do not always use such terms as trilogy accurately — especially if trilogies happen to be the literary fashion. Better evidence than a casual epithet is the combination of series and volume titles, as in The Forsyte Saga, or a clear relationship between volume titles, as in Vardis Fisher's tetralogy, all four titles of which come from a single quotation from Meredith and refer to dominant themes. (Here publishers worked in reverse, as it were; the title of the first book was changed in the English edition, obscuring the relation between it and the following three.) Library catalog cards are often helpful in confirming such evidence, sometimes citing statements by the author. But even Library of Congress cards are not consistent in indicating sequence relationships. National trade catalogs of current publications and books in print are often useful, but not always, in furnishing external evidence.

Short of reading the books themselves and all that the author may have written about them, there is sometimes no sure way of recognizing a sequence novel. In the absence of an explicit statement by the author, there may be implicit evidence of his intention in such details as dates of publication. If the author publishes a second novel continuing the life of a character or an account of a historical period so soon after the first that he must have written them in rapid succession without waiting for returns on the first, the chances are that from the beginning he had some definite plan for a series. There is an implicit continuity in some kinds of subjects, such as a clearly defined historical period like that of the Civil War, or autobiographical or biographical material with emphasis on character development, or a sociological case study of a family. If a writer does not cover, in his first volume, the scope suggested by his subject, there is presumptive evidence, on the appearance of later novels, that the continuation was intended from the beginning. On the basis of such clues, one can recognize possible sequences and verify suspicions by examining the books themselves, if they are available. If an author with the sequence habit produces these suspicious successive novels, they are likely to show internal signs of sequence structure.

The one sure test is a unified structure running through the entire series, plus the ability of individual books to stand alone, with their own artistic unity. In The Past

INTRODUCTION TO THE SEQUENCE NOVEL

Recaptured, the end of the long sequence Remembrance of Things Past, Proust ties the end to the beginning by explaining the psychological basis of the sequence in relation to themes and motifs already familiar to the reader. Symphonic structure is one of the distinctive achievements of the sequence novel and is better evidence of sequence form than any of the external indications. Although it is rarely true that major sequences are to be detected only by reading the novels, there are a number of interesting sequences distinguishable from sequels only on the basis of internal evidence.

Since the line between sequels and sequences is ill defined and some limits must be imposed that will exclude at least the greater number of related novels that do not show characteristic sequence form, it may be helpful to define by exclusion. The term sequence novel does not include: (1) ordinary sequels; (2) series connected only by recurrent characters; (3) adventure and detective stories, such as John Buchan's Richard Hannay books or Dorothy Sayers' Lord Peter Wimsey stories; or (4) historical series connected only by the chronological sequence of events. Neither does it include the many omnibus volumes of such adventure or detective stories, though they may resemble the one-volume editions of sequences such as The Bounty Trilogy by Nordhoff and Hall.

One general distinction between sequences and some of the most popular sequels is that the latter are likely to depend upon exciting action for interest and are connected only by recurrent characters, whereas the sequence depends upon character development or themes or both and is not episodic. Each volume of a sequence is inherently bound to those that precede and follow it; although it is intelligible in itself, it gains appreciably when it is considered in relation to the rest of the series.

Sequence novels do not properly include series loosely connected by time or place, and these series are included in this bibliography only if the author or publisher has described or published them as trilogies, tetralogies, or cycles, and if there is some shadow of an excuse for accepting the term. Sequence novels do not include the old-fashioned novel in several volumes, of which there are a few modern survivors; the separate volumes are not independent and were not intended to be read by themselves or the author would have taken advantage, if writing at the present time, of the more popular series in individual units. In this bibliography, series for which the classification as sequences is dubious have special notes on the relation between the books.

If the author of any one of the types of popular novels mentioned above had enough notion of sequence form to give his connected volumes a series title — other than omnibus — and separate individual titles, he gets in under the wire. The Févals, père and fils, practically have a corner, a very commodious one, on the adventure sequence that has all the superficial earmarks of the real thing. Both of them were too persistent and prolific to be ignored, as one might ignore a single literary sport. The historical sequences of Dumas are included because they approximate sequence form and present a problem of establishing correct sequence order, but they emphasize romantic adventure and in that respect differ from later historical sequences.

Once the distinguishing features of the genre are as clearly defined as its manifold and often ambiguous forms permit, tracking down sequences is like hunting the Snark, with its annoying trick of proving to be a Boojum. But the difficulty of identifying sequences and often of establishing the correct order of works within series is sufficient indication of the practical usefulness of a reference bibliography of sequence novels. Existing bibliographies of fiction, none of which consistently recognize sequences as a distinct genre, have other serious limitations. Most of them are not complete and up to date. American and English guides to fiction do not distinguish between sequels and sequences and may give scanty information. Bibliographies of foreign novels are limited, are often difficult to use, and are no more reliable than those in English in classifying novels and indicating relations between volumes. Bibliographies of fiction are merely a starting point, useful for clues, but even within their limits needing confirmation and supplementary information.

Since this bibliography is intended as an index, not as a critical guide, inclusion of a sequence indicates that it was apparently intended as a unified series, not that it successfully achieves sequence form. The inclusion of minor works seemed advisable because data about these works are less accessible than are those about major sequences. Moreover, the development of the genre depends upon attempts as well as successes. Omissions are inevitable because of the practical difficulty of locating clues to minor works in so large a

INTRODUCTION TO THE SEQUENCE NOVEL 7

field as the modern novel. Those minor sequences which are listed are no doubt like the visible part of an iceberg, a sign of a vaster bulk still concealed.

The purpose of this bibliography, however, is not the purely utilitarian one of listing convenient information. The development of the sequence novel from its major initial impetus in the works of Balzac and Zola to its remarkable growth in the twentieth century, which in theory has no time for long-winded fiction, is a notable literary phenomenon, the more significant because of its simultaneous appearance in the major literatures and its sporadic occurrence in minor literatures which are little known outside their own countries.

Although the twentieth century is more important than the nineteenth in the production of sequence novels, the development of the genre began in the nineteenth, and no survey would be complete without Balzac and Zola. It seemed advisable, therefore, to include other nineteenth-century examples to complete the history and to show whether Balzac and Zola were the only major influences. The comparative rarity of nineteenth-century examples, with the exception of the works of a few unduly prolific writers, made it possible to include them without greatly lengthening the bibliography. For the twentieth century, entries have been brought up to the close of 1948 as far as is possible. Foreign bibliographies are not always complete after 1939 or 1940. The Columbia Dictionary of Modern European Literature, 1947, was extremely helpful in covering the war and postwar years. In preparing this volume for publication in 1949-50, a few obvious data were added, chiefly to complete or add to sequences already included.

Geographically, those countries are represented for which bibliographical material is accessible and usable, considering the limitations of the University of Minnesota and the University of Chicago libraries, which were relatively slight, and of the investigator, which were much greater. The lists for foreign countries are undoubtedly incomplete. The necessity of depending on literary history and criticism for initial clues and the impossibility of scanning all the relevant works ever written in the field made omissions inevitable. Furthermore, since critics do not consistently recognize sequence form, some omissions must be laid at their door. And, naturally, minor works are omitted from most critical and historical surveys and consequently were not detected. The foreign sections of the bibliography are therefore more selective than the English. Entries have been verified from the most authoritative bibliographies and catalogs available. Material on Slavic literature is the most difficult to obtain; where good literary histories are not available in non-Slavic languages, bibliographical data to supplement titles sometimes could not be secured, even with the generous aid of specialists in the field. The existence of major sequences in Polish and Russian is significant, and the chief examples in those languages are included, though the field has been only partially covered. The few sequences verified in the minor Slavic languages are grouped together, with subdivisions for the various countries.

For the other major European countries, literary histories are more numerous and more complete, and those in the language of the country are more readable. For eastern Europe, national catalogs are usually satisfactory. France, Germany, and the Scandinavian countries are prolific producers of sequences and of criticism. The major sequences of those countries and of Spain and Italy are included and as many minor works as could be traced and verified. The lack of discrimination by critics between sequels and sequences and the ambiguity of such terms as cycles, trilogies, and the like may have led to the inclusion of works that on examination, according to the criteria given above, would be excluded. Many works that sounded like sequences proved not to be and were discarded. Because of the huge bulk of works in all languages and the deficiencies of even the Library of Congress, examination of each work was impossible.

Sequences in English are both less carefully and more carefully selected than those in foreign languages. They are less carefully selected because current book reviews and the convenient Book Review Digest provide more comprehensive information than that available on foreign works. They are more carefully selected because the books themselves are accessible and a large proportion of even minor works were examined, many being tried and found wanting. Had I relied on British and American critics, I should have listed more series. No doubt I have fallen into the pitfalls dug by foreign critics, but at least the pitfalls were bigger, since books of criticism ignore the small fry that get into our current reviews. Conversely, I have included some British and American sequences that, on the basis of external evidence, would have been omitted; internal evidence has greater weight than any other single kind, and reading sometimes reveals unmistakable sequence structure where other evidence is inconclusive.

8 INTRODUCTION TO THE SEQUENCE NOVEL

To sum up the principles of selection that have been applied: For foreign works the criteria set forth above have been used, with much dependence on external evidence. Definite statements by critics have been accepted as evidence when supported by bibliographical data. For example, a critic may call a work a trilogy and a national trade catalog may use the same term or refer to the books as sequels. Publication data, such as later publication of the sequence in one volume under a series title, often supplement critical classifications Since indubitable sequences are sometimes listed by the Library of Congress or in national catalogs as sequels or continuations, if one source gives a basis for listing the work as a sequence and other sources verify the relation, the combined evidence has been accepted. An author's statement or clearly related titles have been taken at their face value, with due attention to dates and other bibliographical data.

For English and American works, emphasis has been given to themes and structure when other evidence is inconclusive. Many works commonly referred to as series, both foreign and British or American, have been omitted because they have only a casual connection. Occasionally a series well known by some such definite term as trilogy is included because of the popular designation. Louis Bromfield's trilogy, for example, does not sustain real sequence form beyond the second novel, but it is too well known to omit without splitting hairs. As examples of sequence form, British and American sequences and those by major foreign novelists are most reliable. Inconsistencies and omissions may occur most frequently among minor works.

To keep the bibliography within practical limits and to facilitate its use, data have been selected and entries arranged according to the following principles. The date given is the earliest that could be verified in an authoritative source. Generally it is the date of the first edition, though no fine distinctions have been drawn between copyright date and date of first edition. If the date is clearly that of other than the first edition, the number of the edition is given. For British novels, the date of British publication is regularly given, the place of publication thus serving to distinguish between British and American works. If works are published in both countries, they generally appear at about the same time in England and America. There is no attempt to list later editions or parallel British and American editions. Changes of title, however, are noted, because the same book may have completely different titles in Great Britain and America.

Changes of title of foreign works and differences in titles of translations are similarly noted. English translations are listed under the first American edition unless the British edition is appreciably earlier; usually translations published in both countries appear within the same year. Translations of foreign works into languages other than English and of works from English into other languages are not given. The listing of translations is as complete as possible but includes only publication in the United States or England. Translators so frequently ignore sequence relations that many sequences are translated only in part. The fact of translation does not indicate the importance of the work; some minor works are translated and many major ones are not.

The titles of foreign sequences, except proper names, are translated when the title of a translation varies from the original or when there is no translation. Often the titles show relationship between volumes or suggest themes. Titles of translations may be so altered that they are not helpful, especially when the whole sequence is not translated. Since some works in English on foreign literature translate titles without giving the original title, or vice versa, translation of titles is intended to facilitate identification of related works.

Incomplete sequences have been included, with special notes, because it is often difficult to discover whether a projected series has been completed. Some series announced in advance as trilogies and the like were never finished. Sequences sometimes appear incomplete because titles given in advance were changed on publication. A number of sequences are still in progress. Notes distinguish between the various kinds of incomplete sequences. The false starts and unfinished experiments have a certain historical interest in the development of the genre. And the sequences in progress are evidence of the continued vitality of the genre.

This bibliography is presented as an introduction to the sequence novel and not as the last word. Without the services of a crew of experts in the literatures represented, it would be impossible to produce a definitive bibliography. Although librarians and my colleagues at the University of Minnesota have been most helpful, one cannot foist one's brainchild on others for more than critical inspection. The bibliography is presented with a plea to users to inform the compiler of errors and omissions. The first map of any territory needs much emendation before it is perfect.

Key to Bibliography

LANGUAGE
Novels are listed under the language in which they were written. If such listing does not indicate the author's nationality, a note follows the author's name.

Place of publication distinguishes between British and American authors, and between Spanish, Portuguese, and Latin American authors. If places of publication do not furnish clear evidence of an author's nationality, a nationality note is given.

Works written in English are listed first. Other languages are arranged in groups (Romance, Teutonic, and so on), with subdivisions.

AUTHORS' NAMES
Entries are listed under the author's real name unless the pseudonym is much better known. In doubtful cases, the practice of the Library of Congress is followed.
Pseudonyms are indicated by quotation marks.
Cross-references from the pseudonyms or from the real names are used as needed.

Maiden names, Christian names not generally used, and the like are put in parentheses.

TITLES
Underscoring is used for: (1) sequence titles, (2) titles of individual novels, (3) alternative titles or subtitles.
Explanatory additions to titles are not underscored.

Quotation marks are used for: (1) titles of convenience for sequences, which were not actually used in publication, (2) titles announced for works in preparation but not written, or written and published under another title, (3) short pieces included with novels in a sequence, (4) titles of unpublished manuscripts.

Variant titles are underscored and follow the facts of publication.

Dates in parentheses after titles are dates of action in the novel.

Translations of titles of foreign works not translated or translated under an altered title, except obvious titles and proper names as titles, are put in parentheses after the original title.

PUBLICATION DATA
Complete data for some early novels and some foreign novels were not available.

The translator's name is given in full after the title for the first citation; successive references to the same translator abbreviate Christian names.
The language is not given in the translation entry, since works are grouped by language; however, irregularities, such as translation from some language other than the original or translation from manuscript, are noted.

Place of publication is that of the main office of the company if there are several branches in the same country. If the work is published by the same company in different countries, both places are given.

KEY TO BIBLIOGRAPHY

Place of publication distinguishes between British and American authors; if two places of publication are given for one book, that in the author's country is given first. A nationality note follows the author's name if place does not clearly indicate nationality.

Dates are the earliest that could be verified, both for publication of separate works and for publication of the sequence.

The publisher is listed only with the series entry if the publisher is the same for all parts of the sequence. Otherwise the publisher is given for each novel. See further explanation below.

MAIN SEQUENCE ENTRIES

The main entry for a sequence published under a series title is that of the edition in the fewest volumes. Parts of a sequence are listed, with indention, under the sequence entry.

If the facts of publication do not follow the series title, the sequence appeared only in the separate parts, as listed.

If the publisher is given without the number of volumes and a date, the sequence was issued only in separate volumes by that publisher. The publisher's name is not given after titles of individual novels if it is given after the series title.

Omission of the date after the title of a single novel indicates that the novel was first published in the edition given as the main entry.

SEQUENCES WITHOUT SERIES TITLES

If there is no series title, neither one used in publication nor a title of convenience, the parts are listed in logical order, with sequence relation indicated only by the grouping of titles.

Parts of sequences without a series title are not numbered except in translation.

ARRANGEMENT AND NUMBERING OF PARTS OF SEQUENCES

Parts of a sequence under a sequence title are indented and numbered. Subdivisions of parts of a sequence are indented further. Blue guide lines indicate these indentions.

Parts are listed in logical order if that can be determined; otherwise they are given in the order of publication.

Arabic numbers are used for: (1) parts of a sequence under a series title, (2) parts of a series in translation, matching the numbered parts of the original. Arabic numbers in parentheses are used for translations of parts of a series when the originals are not numbered.

Roman numerals are used for: (1) volume numbers when the volume is further divided into parts with Arabic numerals, (2) parts which contain more than one volume and are further divided.

SPACING

Spacing separates: (1) sequences by the same author, (2) sequences and continuations outside the series, (3) originals and translations, (4) different translations of the same sequence.

NOTES

Notes are differentiated according to source as notes from Library of Congress cards, author's notes, or compiler's notes. The latter are comments by the author of this bibliography.

All notes, unless otherwise indicated, refer to the entry directly preceding with the same indentation.

Unfinished sequences are noted. Authors' notes for unfinished sequences still in progress are given when possible, with prospective titles.

Sequels to and continuations of sequences are given, with notes on the relationship.

The relation between sequences is noted.

If a sequence includes one or two nonfiction works or volumes of short stories or novelle, these are listed, with a special note.

For long sequences including a number of works of nonfiction, only the novels are listed, with a note on the omission.

British and American

Place of publication distinguishes between British and American authors.

Aldrich, Mrs. Bess (Streeter), 1881-
  Lantern in her hand. New York: Appleton-Century, 1928.
  White bird flying. New York: Appleton-Century, 1931.
Allen, Hervey, 1889-1949
  Anthony Adverse. 3 vols., limited ed.; 1 vol., regular ed. New York: Farrar & Rinehart, 1933.
  Compiler's note: Written as a trilogy.

  "The disinherited." See note under 1.
    I. "Sylvania."
      1. The forest and the fort. New York: Farrar & Rinehart, 1943.
      Library of Congress card: "Part I of a projected historical novel which will be published in 2 volumes under the titles: I Sylvania, II Richfield Springs, and finally in a single volume under the title: The disinherited."
      2. Bedford Village. New York: Farrar & Rinehart, 1944.
      3. Toward the morning. New York: Rinehart, 1948.
      Compiler's note: The title announced in preparation, "The city in the dawn," was apparently to be used for a later volume.
    II. "Richfield Springs."
      Compiler's note: This was to have included 4-6, which were not written.
Allen, James Lane, 1849-1925
  "The day we earn."
  Compiler's note: The thematic structure planned for the trilogy anticipates one type of sequence structure.
    1. The bride of the mistletoe. New York: Macmillan, 1909.
    Compiler's note: The preface says that this is not a novel, but it would be so considered according to the present elastic meaning of the term.
    2. The doctor's Christmas Eve. New York: Macmillan, 1911.
    3. "The Christmas tree: an interpretation."
    Compiler's note: Announced in 1 but not written. Another projected title was "The pledge of the evergreen"; planned as nonfiction.
Aminoff, Constance Leonie Caroline (Borgstrom), Friherrinna, 1870-
  "Torchlight series of Napoleonic romances." New York: Dutton.
    1. Revolution. 1922.
    2. Love. 1922.
    3. Ambition. 1923.
    4. Success. 1924.
    5. Victory. 1925.
    6. Triumph. 1926.
    7. Glory. 1927.
    8. Arrogance. 1928.
    9. Storm. 1930.
    10. Retreat. 1938.
    11. "Defeat."
    12. "The end."
Anonymous
  Paul, the Jew. London: Hodder & Stoughton, 1927.
  Paul, the Christian. London: Hodder & Stoughton, 1931.
Atherton, Mrs. Gertrude Franklin (Horn), 1857-1948
  American wives and English husbands. New York: Dodd, Mead, 1898. Revised edition, 1919, has the title Transplanted.
  The Californians. New York, London: John Lane, 1898.
Austin, Frederick Britten, 1885-1941
  Road to glory: a biographical novel of Napoleon. London: Butterworth, 1935.
  Forty centuries look down: a biography of Napoleon. London: Butterworth, 1936.

Bacheller, Irving, 1859-1950
  "Lincoln trilogy."
    1. A boy for the ages. New York: Farrar & Rinehart, 1937.
    2. A man for the ages. Indianapolis: Bobbs-Merrill, 1919.
    3. Father Abraham. Indianapolis: Bobbs-Merrill, 1925.
Baker, James, 1847-1920
  The gleaming dawn. London: Chapman & Hall, 1894.
  The Cardinal's page. London: Chapman & Hall, 1898.
Bancroft, Francis
  "South African trilogy." London: Hutchinson.
    1. The veldt dwellers. 1912.
    2. Thane Brandon. 1913.
    3. Dalliance and strife. 1914.
"Baptist, R. Hernekin"
  Four handsome negresses; the record of a voyage. London: Jonathan Cape, 1931.
  Wild deer. London: Faber & Faber, 1933.
Barke, James, 1905-
  Immortal memory.
  Compiler's note: A tetralogy in progress on the life of Robert Burns.
    1. The wind that shakes the barley. London: Collins, 1946.
    2. The song in the green thorn tree. New York: Macmillan, 1948.
    3. "The wonder of all the gay world."
    4. "The crest of the broken wave."
Barrie, Sir James Matthew, 1860-1947
  Sentimental Tommy; a story of his boyhood. London: Cassell, 1896.
  Tommy and Grizel. London: Cassell, 1900.
Beaconsfield, Earl of, see Disraeli, Benjamin.
Beebe, Elswyth Thane, see Thane, Elswyth.
Bell, Adrian, 1901-
  "Trilogy." 1 vol., no title. London: Cobden-Sanderson, 1936. Later edition, 1941, has the title Omnibus.
    1. Corduroy. 1930.
    2. Silver Ley. 1931. U.S. edition, 1 vol., includes Corduroy.
    3. The cherry tree. 1932.
Bellamann, Henry, 1882-1945
  King's Row. New York: Simon & Schuster, 1940.
  Parris Mitchell of King's Row. Completed by Katherine Bellamann. New York: Simon & Schuster, 1948.
  Compiler's note: An unfinished trilogy.
Bennett, Arnold, 1867-1931
  The Clayhanger family. 1 vol. London: Methuen, 1925.
    1. Clayhanger. 1910.
    2. Hilda Lessways. 1911.
    3. These twain. 1916.

  The roll call. London: Hutchinson, 1919.
  Compiler's note: A sequel to These twain.
Benson, Blackwood Ketchem, 1845-   British
  Who goes there? The story of a spy in the Civil War. New York: Macmillan, 1900.
  A friend with the countersign. New York: Macmillan, 1901.
Benson, E. F., 1863-1940
  The Vintage. London: Methuen, 1898.
  The Capsina. London: Methuen, 1899.

  Colin. London: Hutchinson.
    Colin I. 1923.   Colin II. 1925.
Benson, Robert Hugh, 1871-1914
  The sentimentalists. London: Putnam's, 1906.
  The conventionalists. London: Hutchinson, 1908.

Bentley, Phyllis Eleanor, 1894-
  Take courage. (1625-72.) London: Gollancz, 1940. U.S. title: The power and the glory.
  Manhold. (1720-1805.) London: Gollancz, 1941.
  Inheritance. (1812-1931.) London: Gollancz, 1932.
  Carr. (1857-1927.) London: Benn, 1929.
  Sleep in peace. (1894-1936.) London: Gollancz, 1938.
  A modern tragedy. (1929-32.) London: Gollancz, 1934.
Beresford, John Davys, 1873-1947
  "Jacob Stahl trilogy." London: Sidgwick & Jackson.
    1. The early history of Jacob Stahl. 1911.
    2. A candidate for truth. 1912.
    3. The invisible event. 1915.

  Three generations. London: Collins.
    1. The old people. 1931.
    2. The middle generation. 1932.
    3. The young people. 1933.
Björkman, Edwin August, 1866-
  The soul of a child. New York: Knopf, 1922.
  The gates of life. New York: Knopf, 1923.
"Blake," see Strachey, Evelyn John St. Loe.
Blaker, Richard, 1893-1940
  Here lies a most beautiful lady. London: Heinemann, 1935.
  But beauty vanishes. London: Heinemann, 1936.
Boileau, Ethel (Young), Lady, 1882?-1942
  Turnip-tops. London: Hutchinson, 1932. U.S. title: A gay family.
  Ballade in G minor. London: Hutchinson, 1938.
Borrow, George Henry, 1803-81
  Lavengro; the scholar-the gipsy-the priest. 3 vols. London: John Murray, 1851.
  The Romany rye. 2 vols. London: John Murray, 1857.
"Bowen, Marjorie," pseud. of Mrs. Gabrielle Margaret Vere (Campbell) Long, 1888-   Other pseuds.: "Robert Paye," "George Preedy," "Joseph Shearing." Sequences published only under "Marjorie Bowen"
  William of Orange. London: Methuen.
    1. I will maintain. (1672-77.) 1910.
    2. Defender of the faith. (1672-79.) 1911.
    3. God and the king. (1688-1702.) 1911.

  William the Silent. London: Methuen.
    1. Prince and heretic. 1914.
    2. William by the grace of God. 1916.

  The golden roof. London: Hodder & Stoughton, 1928.
  The triumphant beast. London: John Lane, 1934.
  Trumpets at Rome. London: Hutchinson, 1936.

  God and the wedding dress. London: Hutchinson, 1938.
  Mr. Tyler's saints. London: Hutchinson, 1939.
  The circle in the water. London: Hutchinson, 1939.
Boyd, James, 1888-
  Roll river. 2 vols. in 1. New York: Scribner's, 1935.
    1. The dark shore. Published serially in Scribner's Magazine.
    2. Roll river.
Brereton, Frederick Sadleir, Lt. Col., 1872-
  "European War, 1914-18." London: Blackie.
    Western Front:
      1. With French at the front; a story of the great European war down to the battle of the Aisne. 1914.

2. Under French's command; a story of the Western Front from Neuve Chapelle to Loos. 1915.
3. With Joffre at Verdun. 1916.
4. Under Haig in Flanders; a story of Vimy, Messines, and Ypres. 1917.
5. Under Foch's command; a tale of the Americans in France. 1918.
6. With the Allies to the Rhine; a story of the finish of the war. 1919.

Eastern Front:
7. At grips with the Turk; a story of the Dardanelles campaign. 1915.
8. On the road to Bagdad. 1916.
9. From the Nile to the Tigris; a story of campaigning from western Egypt to Mesapotamia. 1917.
10. The armoured-car scouts; a tale of the campaign in the Caucasus. 1917.
11. With Allenby in Palestine; a story of the latest crusade. 1919.

Bridges, Roy, 1885-
"Australian trilogy." London: Hutchinson.
1. And all that beauty. 1929.
2. Negrohead. 1930.
3. Trinity. 1931.

Briffault, Robert, 1876-
Europa, the days of ignorance. London: R. Hale, 1935.
Europa in Limbo. London: R. Hale, 1937.

Brinig, Myron, 1900-
The Singermanns. New York: Farrar & Rinehart.
1. Singermann. 1929.
2. This man is my brother. 1932. British title: Sons of Singermann.

Bristow, Gwen, 1903-
Louisiana trilogy. 3 vols. New York: Crowell, 1941.
1. Deep summer. 1937.
2. The handsome road. 1938.
3. This side of glory. 1940.

Bromfield, Louis, 1896-
The Louis Bromfield trilogy. 1 vol. New York: Blue Ribbon Books, 1935.
1. The green bay tree. New York: Stokes, 1924.
2. Possession. New York: Stokes, 1925.
3. Early autumn. New York: Stokes, 1926.

A good woman. New York: Stokes, 1927.
Compiler's note: Related to the trilogy.
Author's note: "Taken together the four might be considered as a single volume with the . . . title 'Escape.'"

Brophy, John, 1899-
Greenglory. London: Collins, 1940.
Green ladies. London: Collins, 1940.

Broster, Dorothy Kathleen
"Trilogy." Issued in boxed set, 3 vols. London: Heinemann, 1930.
1. The flight of the heron. 1925.
2. The gleam in the North. 1927.
3. The dark mile. 1929.

Brown, Rollo Walter, 1880-
Emergence.
1. The fire-makers; a novel of environment. New York: Coward-McCann, 1931.
2. Toward romance. New York: Coward-McCann, 1932.
3. The hillikin. New York: Coward-McCann, 1935.
4. As of the gods. New York: Appleton-Century, 1937.

Brun, Vincenz, 1897-
Alcibiades, beloved of gods and men. London: Putnam's, 1935.
Alcibiades, forsaken by gods and men. London: Putnam's, 1936.

Buck, Mrs. Pearl (Sydenstricker), 1892-
House of earth. 1 vol. New York: Reynal & Hitchcock, 1935.

BRITISH AND AMERICAN

    1. The good earth. New York: John Day, 1931.
    2. Sons. New York: John Day, 1932.
    3. A house divided. 1935.

  Dragon seed. New York: John Day, 1942.
  The promise. New York: John Day, 1943.
Bullett, Gerald William, 1893-
  The Pandervils, Egg and Nicky. 1 vol. London: Heinemann, 1930.
    1. The history of Egg Pandervil. 1928.
    2. Nicky, son of Egg. 1929.
Bulwer-Lytton, Edward George Earle Lytton, 1st Baron Lytton, 1803-73
  The Eleusinia. London: 1838.
    1. Ernest Maltravers. 3 vols. London: Saunders & Otley, 1837.
    2. Alice, or The mysteries.

"The Caxton novels." Novels of Sir Edward Bulwer-Lytton. Library ed. 9 vols. Boston:
  Little, Brown, 1892. 1st ed., Edinburgh, London: Blackwood.
  Vols. 1-2. The Caxtons. 1849.
  Vols. 3-6. My novel. 1853.
  Vols. 7-9. What will he do with it? 1859.
"Burke, Fielding," see Dargan, Mrs. Olive (Tilford).
Cabell, James Branch, 1879-
  Biography of the life of Manuel.
Compiler's note: Titles are those listed in The witch-woman, omitting some volumes of short stories and nonfiction. Numbers are those of volumes in the Storisende Edition. New York: McBride, 1927-30.
    1. Beyond life. New York: McBride, 1919.
    Compiler's note: Prologue to the series. Nonfiction.
    2. Figures of earth; a comedy of appearances. New York: McBride, 1921.
    3. The silver stallion; a comedy of redemption. New York: McBride, 1926.
  The witch-woman. New York: Farrar, Straus, 1948.
    Contents (trilogy of short novels): "The music from behind the moon," 1926; "The way of Ecben," 1929; "The white robe," 1929.
    4. Domnei; a comedy of woman-worship. New York: McBride, 1920. 1st ed., 1913, has the title The Soul of Melicent.
    6. Jurgen; a comedy of justice. New York: McBride, 1919.
    Compiler's note: Jurgen, Figures of earth, and The silver stallion form a trilogy.
    8. The high place; a comedy of disenchantment. New York: McBride, 1923.
    10. Something about Eve; a comedy of fig-leaves. New York: McBride, 1927.
    12. The cords of vanity. New York: Doubleday, 1909.
    14. The rivet in grandfather's neck; a comedy of limitations. New York: McBride, 1915.
    15. The eagle's shadow; a comedy of purse-strings. New York: McBride, 1923. 1st ed., 1904.
    16. The cream of the jest; a comedy of evasions. Bound with The lineage of Lichfield.
  New York: McBride, 1921. 1st. ed., 1917.
    Compiler's note: The lineage of Lichfield gives the genealogy of Dom Manuel.
    17. Straws and prayerbooks; dizaine des diversions. New York: McBride, 1924.
    Compiler's note: Epilogue to the series. Nonfiction.
    18. Townsend of Lichfield; dizaine des adieux.
    Compiler's note: End of the biography. Nonfiction.

The nightmare has triplets.
  Smirt; an urbane nightmare. New York: McBride, 1934.
  Smith; a sylvan interlude. New York: McBride, 1935.
  Smire; an acceptance in the third person. Garden City, New York: Doubleday, Doran, 1937.

Heirs and assigns. New York: Farrar & Rinehart.
  1. Hamlet had an uncle; a comedy of honor. 1940.

2. The king was in his counting house; a comedy of commonsense. 1938.
3. The first gentleman of America; a comedy of conquest. 1942.

It happened in Florida. New York: Farrar & Rinehart; Farrar, Straus.
1. The St. John's. With A. J. Hanna. 1943.
Compiler's note: In Rivers of America series. Nonfiction.
2. There were two pirates; a comedy of division. 1946.
3. The devil's own dear son. 1949. Title announced in advance: "I go to my father."

Caldwell, (Janet) Taylor, 1900-   Full name: Janet Taylor (Caldwell) Reback
Dynasty of death. New York: Scribner's, 1938.
The eagles gather. New York: Scribner's, 1940.
The final hour. New York: Scribner's, 1944.

Cannan, Gilbert, 1884-
"The Lawrie saga."
1. Little brother. London: Heinemann, 1912.
2. Round the corner. London: Secker, 1914.
3. Three pretty men. London: Methuen, 1916. U.S. title: Three sons and a mother.
4. The stucco house. London: Unwin, 1918.
5. Time and eternity; a tale of three exiles. London: Chapman & Hall, 1919.
6. Annette and Bennett. London: Hutchinson, 1922.

"Novels of the new time."
1. Pugs and peacocks. London: Hutchinson, 1921.
2. Sembal. London: Hutchinson, 1922.
3. The house of prophecy. London: Butterworth, 1924.
4. "The soaring bird."
Compiler's note: Announced in preparation but not published.

Cary, Joyce, 1888-
Herself surprised. London: Michael Joseph, 1941.
To be a pilgrim. London: Michael Joseph, 1942.
The horse's mouth. London: Michael Joseph, 1944.

Chambers, Robert William, 1865-1933
Lorraine. New York, London: Harper, 1897.
Ashes of empire. New York: Stokes, 1898.
The red republic; a romance of the Commune. New York, London: Putnam's, 1902.

Cardigan. New York, London: Harper, 1901.
The maid-at-arms. New York, London: Harper, 1902.
The reckoning. New York: Appleton, 1905.

"Chapman, Maristan," pseud. of John Stanton Higham Chapman, 1891- , and Mrs. Mary (Ilsley) Chapman, 1895-
The happy mountain. New York: Viking Press, 1928.
Homeplace. New York: Viking Press, 1929.
The weather tree. New York: Viking Press, 1932.
Glen Hazard. New York: Knopf, 1933.

Charles, Mrs. Elizabeth (Rundle), 1828-96
The Draytons and the Davenants; a story of the civil wars. New York: Dodd, 1867.
On both sides of the sea; a story of the Commonwealth and the Restoration. New York: Dodd, Mead, 1867.

Christie, Robert Stuart
"The book of Sarah." 2 vols. London: Unwin, 1935.
1. Young experience.   2. Gay application.
Compiler's note: A third volume was planned but apparently was not published.

"Clayton, John," see Webb, H. B. L.

Cloete, Stuart, 1897-
Watch for the dawn. (1815.) London: Collins, 1939.
The turning wheels. (1837.) London: Collins, 1937.
The hill of doves. (1880.) Boston: Houghton, Mifflin, 1941.

"The neck of the tortoise." (1900.)
Compiler's note: Announced in preparation.
Cochran, Louis, 1899-
   Son of Haman. Caldwell, Idaho: Caxton Printers, 1937.
   Boss man. Caldwell, Idaho: Caxton Printers, 1939.
   Compiler's note: An unfinished trilogy.
"Connell F. Norreys," see O'Riordan, Conal O'Connell.
Cooke, John Esten, 1830-86
   "Surry of Eagle's Nest." Ed. from the mss. of Col. Surry by John Esten Cooke.
      1. Surry of Eagle's Nest, or Memoirs of a staff-officer serving in Virginia. New York: Bunce & Huntington, 1866.
      2. Hilt to hilt, or Days and nights on the Shenandoah in the autumn of 1864. New York: Dillingham, 1869.
      3. Mohun, or The last days of Lee and his paladins; final memoirs of a staff-officer serving in Virginia. New York: Dillingham, 1869.
Cooper, James Fenimore, 1798-1851
   Homeward bound, or The chase; a tale of the sea. Philadelphia: Carey, Lea, & Blanchard, 1838.
   Home as found. Philadelphia: Carey, Lea, & Blanchard, 1838.

   "The Littlepage manuscripts." New York: Burgess & Stringer.
      1. Satanstoe. 2 vols. 1845.
      2. The chainbearer. 2 vols. 1845.
      3. The redskins, or Indian and Injin. 2 vols. 1846.
Corbett, Elizabeth Frances, 1887-
   "Novels of Mount Royal." New York: Appleton-Century.
   Compiler's note: No recurrent characters, but studies of different classes in one community. Mount Royal; chronicles of an American town contains short stories.
      1. The Langworthy family. 1937.
      2. Light of other days. 1938.
      3. The far-down. 1939.

   Faye's folly. New York: Appleton-Century, 1941.
   Early summer. New York: Appleton-Century, 1942.
"Corelli, Marie," pseud. of Minnie Mackay, 1855-1924
   A romance of two worlds. 2 vols. London: Bentley, 1886.
   Vendetta; a life lost sight of. 3 vols. London: Bentley, 1886-87.
   Ardath; the story of a dead self. 3 vols. London: Bentley, 1889.
   The soul of Lilith. London: Bentley, 1892.
   Barabbas; a dream of the world's tragedy. London: Methuen, 1893.
   The master-Christian; a question of the time. London: Methuen, 1900.
   Author's note: "All linked together by the one theory."
Corey, Paul, 1903-
   Three miles square. Indianapolis: Bobbs-Merrill, 1939.
   The road returns. Indianapolis: Bobbs-Merrill, 1940.
   County seat. Indianapolis: Bobbs-Merrill, 1941.
Cournos, John, 1881-
   The mask. London: Methuen, 1919.
   The wall. London: Methuen, 1921.
   Babel. London: Heinemann, 1923.
Crabb, Alfred Leland, 1864-
   "Saga of Nashville." Indianapolis: Bobbs-Merrill.
      1. Lodging at the Saint Cloud; a tale of occupied Nashville. 1946.
      2. Dinner at Belmont; a novel of captured Nashville. 1942.
      3. Supper at the Maxwell House; a novel of recaptured Nashville. 1943.
      4. Breakfast at the Hermitage; a novel of Nashville rebuilding. 1945.

Craigie, Mrs. Pearl Mary Teresa (Richards), 1867-1906. Pseud., "John Oliver Hobbes"
   The school for saints. London: Unwin, 1896.
   Robert Orange. London: Unwin, 1900.
Crawford, Francis Marion, 1854-1909
   Saracinesca. New York: Macmillan, 1887.
   Sant' Ilario. New York: Macmillan, 1889.
   Don Orsino. New York: Macmillan, 1892.
   Corleone. 2 vols. New York: Macmillan, 1896.

   Katherine Lauderdale. 2 vols. New York, London: Macmillan, 1894.
   The Ralstons. 2 vols. New York, London: Macmillan, 1895.

   The singer's trilogy. New York, London: Macmillan.
     1. Fair Margaret, a portrait. 1905. British title: Soprano.
     2. The primadonna. 1908.
     3. The diva's ruby. 1908.
Cripps, Arthur Shearly, 1869-
   A martyr's servant. London: Duckworth, 1915.
   A martyr's heir. London: Duckworth, 1916.
Dargan, Mrs. Olive (Tilford). Pseud., "Fielding Burke"
   Call home the heart. London, New York: Longmans, Green, 1932.
   A stone came rolling. Toronto, New York: Longmans, Green, 1935.
Dell, Floyd, 1884-
   Moon-calf. New York: Knopf, 1920.
   The briary bush. New York: Knopf, 1921.

   Souvenir. New York: Knopf, 1929.
   Compiler's note: A sequel to the above sequence.
Derleth, August William, 1909-
   Sac Prairie saga. New York: Scribner's.
   Author's note: "A projected life story of Sac Prairie, Wisconsin, from the early 1800's to 1950 or thereabouts, planned to include fifty books of all kinds, each book to be a perfect unit in itself, and yet each contributing in background to the history of Sac Prairie and of the Mid West generally."
   Compiler's note: Nonfiction, short stories, and poetry are omitted.
     1. Bright journey. (1812-43.) 1940.
     2. Wind over Wisconsin. (1830s.) 1938.
     3. Restless is the river. (1839-50.) 1939.
     4. Shadow of night. (1840s.) 1943.
     5. Still is the summer night. (1880s.) 1937.
     6. Sweet Genevieve. (1916-18.) 1942.
     7. Evening in spring. (1920s.) 1941.
     8. The shield of the valiant. (1940s.) 1945.
Disraeli, Benjamin, 1st Earl of Beaconsfield, 1804-81
   Coningsby, or The new generation. 3 vols. London: Colburn, 1844.
   Sybil, or The two nations. 3 vols. London: Colburn, 1845.
   Tancred, or The new crusade. London: Routledge, 1847.
Diver, Mrs. (Katherine Helen) Maud (Marshall), 1867-1945
   Men of the frontier force. 1 vol. London: George Newnes, 1930.
     1. Captain Desmond, V. C. Edinburgh, London: Blackwood, 1907.
     2. The great amulet. Edinburgh, London: Blackwood, 1908.
     3. Desmond's daughter. Edinburgh, London: Blackwood, 1916.

   Far to seek. Edinburgh, London: Blackwood, 1921.
   Lilámani; a study in possibilities. Edinburgh, London: Blackwood, 1911. U.S. title: Awakening.
   The singer passes. Edinburgh, London: Blackwood, 1934.

BRITISH AND AMERICAN

The dream prevails. London: John Murray, 1938.
Compiler's note: These four novels continue the story of the Desmonds from Men of the frontier force.

The hero of Herat. London: Constable, 1912.
The judgment of the sword. London: Constable, 1913.

Strange roads. London: Constable, 1918.
Strong hours. London: Constable, 1919.

The Challoners.
    1. The Challoners. London: John Murray, 1923.
    2. But yesterday. London: John Murray, 1927.
    3. Wild bird. London: John Murray, 1929.
    4. Ships of youth. Edinburgh, London: Blackwood, 1931.

Dixon, Thomas, 1864-1946
  "Trilogy of reconstruction." New York: Doubleday, Page.
    1. The leopard's spots; a romance of the white man's burden. 1902.
    2. The clansman. 1905.
    3. The traitor; a story of the fall of the invisible empire. 1907.

Dos Passos, John, 1896-
  U.S.A. 1 vol. New York: Harcourt, Brace, 1937.
    1. The 42nd parallel. New York: Harper, 1930.
    2. Nineteen nineteen. 1932.
    3. The big money. 1936.

Dowdey, Clifford, 1904-
  Gamble's Hundred. Boston: Little, Brown, 1939.
  Bugles blow no more. Boston: Little, Brown, 1937.
  Sing for a penny. Boston: Little, Brown, 1941.

Downing, John Hyatt, 1888-
  Sioux City. New York: Putnam's, 1940.
  Anthony Trant. New York: Putnam's, 1941.

Dreiser, Theodore (Herman Albert), 1871-1945
  "Trilogy of desire."
    1. The financier. New York, London: Harper, 1912.
    2. The Titan. New York, London: John Lane, 1914.
    3. The stoic. New York: Doubleday, 1947.

Drummond, Hamilton, 1857-1935
  For the religion; the records of Blaise de Bernuald. London: Smith & Elder, 1898.
  A man of his age. London: Ward & Lock, 1900.
  A king's pawn. Edinburgh, London: Blackwood, 1900.

Dudley, Owen Francis, 1882-
  Problems of human happiness. London, New York: Longmans, Green.
    1. Will men be like gods? 1924.
    Compiler's note: Nonfiction.
    2. The shadow of the earth. 1926.
    3. The masterful monk. 1929.
    4. Pageant of life. 1932.
    5. The coming of the monster. 1936.
    6. The Tremaynes and the masterful monk. 1940.
    7. Michael, a tale of the masterful monk. 1948.

Duke, Winifred
  "Harold Fieldend." London: Jarrolds.
    1. Bastard verdict. 1932.
    2. The dark hill. 1932.
    3. The sown wind. 1932.
    4. Finale. 1933.
    5. These are they. 1933.
    6. Magpie's hoard. 1934.

Prince Charles Edward and the forty-five. London: R. Hale, 1938.
Out of the north. London: Jarrolds, 1939.

Dunkerley, William Arthur, see "Oxenham, John."
Eddison, Eric Rucker, 1882-
  The worm Ouroboros. New York: Boni, 1926.
  Compiler's note: The prelude to the following two novels.
  A fish-dinner in Memison. New York: Dutton, 1941.
  Mistress of mistresses. New York: Dutton, 1935.
Eggleston, George Cary, 1839-1911
  "A trilogy of romances." Boston: Lothrop.
    1. Dorothy South; a love story of Virginia just before the war. 1902.
    2. The master of Warlock; a Virginia war story. 1903.
    3. Evelyn Byrd. 1904.

  A captain in the ranks; a romance of affairs. New York: A. S. Barnes, 1904.
  Compiler's note: A supplement to the trilogy.
Eldridge, Paul, see Viereck, George Sylvester.
"Falstaff, Jake," see Fetzer, Herman.
Farrell, James Thomas, 1904-
  Studs Lonigan. 1 vol. New York: Vanguard Press, 1935.
    1. Young Lonigan. 1932.
    2. The young manhood of Studs Lonigan. 1934.
    3. Judgment Day. 1935.

  "Danny O'Neill tetralogy." New York: Vanguard Press.
    1. A world I never made. 1936.   3. Father and son. 1940.
    2. No star is lost. 1938.   4. My days of anger. 1943.

  Bernard Clare. New York: Vanguard Press, 1946.
  Compiler's note: The hero's name is changed to Bernard Carr in the second novel.
  The road between. New York: Vanguard Press, 1949.

  Author's note: "As far as my books are concerned, they are part of an extended series of works, novels, novelettes, plays, sketches, stories and character sketches which are envisioned as one project, loosely integrated, but withal, integrated and connected. . . . This series, when completed, should run from twenty-five to fifty volumes."
  Compiler's note: Characters from the sequence novels recur in other works.
Faulkner, William, 1897-
  "Jefferson cycle."
    1. Sartoris. New York: Harcourt, Brace, 1929.
    2. The sound and the fury. New York: Smith & Haas, 1929.
    3. As I lay dying. New York: Smith & Haas, 1930.
    4. Sanctuary. New York: Smith & Haas, 1931.
    Compiler's note: Rewritten as part of the cycle before publication.
    5. Light in August. New York: Smith & Haas, 1932.
    6. Absalom, Absalom. New York: Random House, 1936.
    7. The hamlet. New York: Random House, 1940.
"Fedorovna, Nina," see Riasanovsky, Antonina Fedorovna.
Fergusson, Harvey, 1890-
  Followers of the sun; a trilogy of the Santa Fe trail. 3 vols. in 1. New York: Knopf, 1936.
    1. Wolf song. 1927.
    2. In those days. 1929.
    3. The blood of the conquerors. 1921.
Fetzer, Herman, 1899-1935. Pseud., "Jake Falstaff"
  Jacoby's Corners. Boston: Houghton, Mifflin, 1940.
  The big snow; Christmas at Jacoby's Corners. Boston: Houghton, Mifflin, 1941.
  Come back to Wayne County. Boston: Houghton, Mifflin, 1942.
Fisher, Vardis Alvero, 1895-
  "Vridar Hunter tetralogy." New York: Doubleday, Doran.
    1. In tragic life. Caldwell, Idaho: Caxton Printers, 1932. British title: I see no sin.

2. Passions spin the plot. 1934.
3. We are betrayed. 1935.
4. No villain need be. 1936.

The testament of man. New York: Vanguard Press.
1. Darkness and the deep. 1943.
2. Golden rooms. 1944.
3. Intimations of Eve. 1946.
4. Adam and the serpent. 1947.
5. The divine passion. 1948.
Compiler's note: The sequence may still be in progress.

Fletcher, (Mrs.) Inglis (Clark), 1888-
"Carolina series." Indianapolis: Bobbs-Merrill.
1. Raleigh's men. 1940.
2. Men of Albemarle. 1942.
3. Lusty wind for Carolina. 1944.
4. Toil of the brave. 1946.

Ford, Ford Madox, 1873-1939. Originally Ford Madox Hueffer
The fifth queen and how she came to court. London: Alston Rivers, 1906.
Privy seal; his last venture. London: Alston Rivers, 1907.
The fifth queen crowned. London: Eveleigh Nash, 1908.

Some do not. London: Duckworth, 1924.
No more parades. London: Duckworth, 1925.
A man could stand up. London: Duckworth, 1926.

The last post. London: Duckworth, 1928.
Compiler's note: A pendant to the above trilogy.

The rash act. London: Jonathan Cape, 1933.
Henry for Hugh. Philadelphia: Lippincott, 1934.

Forester, Cecil Scott, 1899-
Captain Hornblower, R. N. 1 vol. London: Michael Joseph, 1938.
1. The happy return. 1937. U.S. title: Beat to quarters.
2. Ship of the line. 1938.
3. Flying colours. 1938.

Commodore Hornblower. Boston: Little, Brown, 1945. British title: The Commodore.
Lord Hornblower. Boston: Little, Brown, 1946.

Frank, Waldo David, 1889-
The death and birth of David Markand; an American story. New York: Scribner's, 1934.
The bridegroom cometh. New York: Doubleday, Doran, 1938.
Author's note: "An articulation which I hope to be able to proceed with in subsequent novels, independent, but allied like panels of a great mural."

Freeman, Harold Webber, 1899-
Fathers of their people. London: Chatto & Windus, 1932.
Pond Hall's progress. London: Chatto & Windus, 1933.

Furman, Lucy
Quare women; a story of the Kentucky mountains. Boston: Atlantic Monthly Press, 1923.
Glass windows; a story of the quare women. Boston: Little, Brown, 1925.

Galsworthy, John, 1867-1933
The Forsyte saga. 1 vol. London: Heinemann, 1922.
1. The man of property. 1906.
"Indian summer of a Forsyte." First published in Five Tales. London: Heinemann, 1918.
2. In chancery. 1920.
"Awakening." 1920.
3. To let. 1921.

A modern comedy. 1 vol. London: Heinemann, 1929.
1. The white monkey. 1924.

"A silent wooing." Published with "Passersby" in Two Forsyte interludes. London: Heinemann, 1928.
  2. The silver spoon. 1926.
"Passersby."
  3. Swan song. 1928.

The end of the chapter. London: Heinemann, 1935; New York: Scribner's, 1934.
  1. Maid in waiting. 1931.
  2. Flowering wilderness. 1932.
  3. Over the river. 1933. U.S. title: One more river.

Compiler's note: The three trilogies are related by recurrent characters. In addition to the Forsyte novels, there are several volumes containing short stories about the Forsytes. Worshipful society, which contains three novels, is not a sequence.

Garstin, Crosbie, 1887-1930
  The owl's house. London: Heinemann, 1925.
  High noon. London: Heinemann, 1924.
  West wind. London: Heinemann, 1926.

"Gibbon, Lewis Grassic," see Mitchell, James Leslie.

Graves, Charles (Patrick Ranke), 1899-
  The thin blue line. London: Hutchinson, 1941.
  The avengers. London, New York: Hutchinson, 1942.
  Seven pilots. London, New York: Hutchinson, 1943.

Graves, Robert, 1895-
  "Claudius." Issued in boxed set, 2 vols. London: Arthur Barker, 1934.
    1. I, Claudius; from the autobiography of Tiberius Claudius.
    2. Claudius, the god, and his wife Messalina.

Sergeant Lamb of the Ninth. London: Methuen, 1940. U.S. title: Sergeant Lamb's America.
Proceed, Sergeant Lamb. London: Methuen, 1941.

Greenwood, Robert. British
  Mr. Bunting in peace and war. 1 vol. Indianapolis: Bobbs-Merrill, 1941.
    1. Mr. Bunting. London: Dent, 1940.
    2. Mr. Bunting at war. London: Dent, 1941.

Greenwood, Walter, 1903-
  Love on the dole; a tale of the two cities. London: Jonathan Cape, 1933.
  His Worship the Mayor. London: Jonathan Cape, 1934. U.S. title: The time is ripe.

Gregg, Hilda Carolina, 1868-1935. Pseud., "Sydney Carlyon Grier"
  The path to honour. Edinburgh, London: Blackwood, 1909.
  The keeper of the gate. Edinburgh, London: Blackwood, 1911.

The strong hand. Edinburgh, London: Blackwood, 1920.
Out of prison. Edinburgh, London: Blackwood, 1922.

"Grier, Sydney Carlyon," see Gregg, Hilda Caroline.

Haggard, Sir Henry Rider, 1856-1925
  She. London: Longmans, 1887.
  Ayesha; the return of She. New York: Doubleday, Page, 1905.
  Wisdom's daughter. Garden City, New York: Doubleday, Page, 1923.

"Quatermain trilogy."
  1. Marie. London: Cassell, 1912.
  2. Child of storm. London: Cassell, 1913.
  3. Finished. London: Ward & Lock, 1917.

Compiler's note: Although other novels are connected by recurrent characters, the two trilogies are the only distinct sequences.

Hall, James Norman, see Nordhoff, Charles.

Hamilton, Patrick, 1904-
  20,000 streets under the sky. 1 vol. London: Constable, 1935.

1. The midnight bell. 1929.
2. The siege of pleasure. 1932.
3. The plains of cement. 1934.

Hanley, James, 1901-
  The Furys. London: Chatto & Windus, 1935.
  The secret journey. London: Chatto & Windus, 1936.
  Our time is gone. London: John Lane, 1940.

Harris, Bernice (Kelly)
  Purslane. Chapel Hill: University of North Caroline Press, 1939.
  Portulaca. New York: Doubleday, Doran, 1941.

Hartley, Leslie Poles, 1895-
  "Eustace Cherrington trilogy." London: Putnam's.
    1. Shrimp and the anemone. 1944. U.S. title: The west window.
    2. Sixth heaven. 1946.
    3. Eustace and Hilda. 1947.

Hatch, Richard Warren, 1898-
  The Bradfords.
    1. Into the wind. New York: Macmillan, 1929.
    2. Leave the salt earth. New York: Covici-Friede, 1933.

Hayes, Frederick William, 1848-1918
  A Kent squire; being a record of certain adventures of Ambrose Gwynett, Esquire of Thornhaugh. London: Hutchinson, 1900.
  Gwynett of Thornhaugh. London: Hutchinson, 1900.
  The shadow of a throne. London: Hutchinson, 1904.

Henham, Ernest George, 1870-   Pseud., "John Trevena"
  Furze the cruel. London: Alston Rivers, 1907.
  Heather. London: Alston Rivers, 1908.
  Granite. London: Alston Rivers, 1909.

Herbst, Josephine, 1897-
  Pity is not enough. New York: Harcourt, Brace, 1933.
  The executioner waits. New York: Harcourt, Brace, 1934.
  Rope of gold. New York: Harcourt, Brace, 1939.

Hewlett, Maurice Henry, 1861-1923
  Halfway House; a comedy of degrees. London: Chapman & Hall, 1908.
  Open country; a comedy with a sting. London: Macmillan, 1909.
  Rest Harrow; a comedy of resolution. London: Macmillan, 1910.

Hobart, Mrs. Alice Tisdale (Nourse), 1882-
  River supreme. Indianapolis: Bobbs-Merrill, 1933. First published as Pidgin cargo. New York: Century, 1929.
  Oil for the lamps of China. Indianapolis: Bobbs-Merrill, 1933.
  Yang and Yin. Indianapolis: Bobbs-Merrill, 1936.

  Their own country. Indianapolis: Bobbs-Merrill, 1940.
  Compiler's note: A sequel to Oil for the lamps of China.

"Hobbes, John Oliver," see Craigie, Mrs. Pearl Mary Teresa (Richards).

Hodges, Arthur, 1864-
  "The Blake family." London: Hurst & Blackett.
    1. The man of substance. 1931.
    2. The glittering hour. 1933.

Hodson, James Lansdale, 1891-
  Harvest in the North. London: Gollancz, 1934.
  God's in His heaven. London: Gollancz, 1935.

Hooke, Nina Warner, 1907-
  Striplings. London: Faber & Faber, 1933.
  Close of play. London: Putnam's, 1936.
  Own wilderness. London: Putnam's, 1938.

Horgan, Paul, 1903-
  Main line west. New York: Harper, 1936.

A lamp on the plains. New York: Harper, 1937.
Compiler's note: An unfinished trilogy.
Hoult, Norah, 1901-
   Holy Ireland. London: Heinemann.
     1. Holy Ireland. 1935.   2. Coming from the fair. 1937.

   Smilin' on the vine. London: Heinemann, 1941.
   Augusta steps out. London: Heinemann, 1942.
"Hudson, Stephen." Pseud. of Sidney Schiff
   A true story. 1 vol. London: Constable, 1930.
   Compiler's note: A rewritten version of the following four novels.
     1. Prince Hempseed. London: Secker, 1923.
     2. Elinor Colhouse. London: Secker, 1919.
     3. Richard Kurt. London: Secker, 1921.
     4. Myrtle. London: Secker, 1925. Abridged in the 1 vol. edition.
   Compiler's note: The series as originally planned and as announced in 2 and 3 was to begin with Elinor Colhouse; the third novel was to be "The rock," but it was not published under that title.

   Tony. London: Constable, 1924.
   Richard, Myrtle, and I. London: Constable, 1926.
   Compiler's note: Both of these novels are related to the sequence.
Hueffer, Ford Madox, see Ford, Ford Madox.
Hummel, George Frederick, 1882-
   Heritage. Philadelphia: Stokes, 1935.
   Tradition. New York: Coward-McCann, 1936.
Idell, Albert Edward, 1901-   Pseud., "Phillips Rogers"
   Centennial summer. New York: Holt, 1943.
   Bridge to Brooklyn. New York: Holt, 1944.
   The great blizzard. New York: Holt, 1948.
Irwin, Margaret E. F. (Mrs. John Robert Monsell)
   Royal flush; the story of Minette. London: Chatto & Windus, 1932.
   The proud servant; the story of Montrose. London: Chatto & Windus, 1934.
   The bride; the story of Louise and Montrose. London: Chatto & Windus, 1939.
   Stranger prince; the story of Rupert of the Rhine. London: Chatto & Windus, 1937.

   Young Bess. London: Chatto & Windus, 1944.
   Elizabeth, the captive princess. London: Chatto & Windus, 1948.
Jacob, Naomi Ellington, 1889-
   "Gollantz family." London: Hutchinson.
     1. The founder of the house. 1936.
     2. That wild lie. 1930.
     3. Young Emmanuel. 1932.
     4. Four generations. 1934.
     5. Private Gollantz. 1943.
Jameson, (Margaret) Storm, 1897-   (Mrs. Guy Chapman)
   The triumph of time. 1 vol. London: Heinemann, 1932.
     1. The lovely ship. 1927.
     2. The voyage home. 1930.
     3. A richer dust. 1931.

   That was yesterday. London: Heinemann, 1932.
   Farewell night, welcome day. London: Cassell, 1939. U.S. title: The captain's wife.
   The journal of Mary Hervey Russell. London, New York: Macmillan, 1945.
   Compiler's note: These three novels are related to the sequences but are not a separate sequence. That was yesterday links the sequences.

   The mirror in darkness. London: Cassell.
     1. Company parade. 1934.

2. *Love in winter*. 1935.
3. *None turn back*. 1936.
Compiler's note: The novels announce a plan to include five novels in the sequence.
Johnston, Mary, 1870-1936
  The long roll. Boston: Houghton, Mifflin, 1911.
  Cease firing. Boston: Houghton, Mifflin, 1912.
Keable, Robert, 1880-
  Simon called Peter. London: Constable, 1921.
  Recompense. London: Constable, 1924.
Kelland, Clarence Budington, 1861-
  Hard money. New York, London: Harper, 1930.
  Gold. New York, London: Harper, 1931.
  Jealous house. New York, London: Harper, 1934.
Kelly, Mrs. Eleanor (Mercein), 1880-
  Basquerie. New York: Harper, 1927.
  The book of Bette, recording further adventures of the family Urruty among the Spains and elsewhere. New York: Harper, 1929.
  Nacio: his affairs. New York: Harper, 1931.
Kennedy, Margaret, 1896-
  The constant nymph. London: Heinemann, 1925.
  Fool of the family. London: Heinemann, 1930.
"Knight, Brigid," see Sinclair, Kathleen Henrietta (Nash-Webber).
Larsson, Gösta, 1898-
  Our daily bread. New York: Vanguard Press, 1934.
  Fatherland, farewell! New York: Harcourt, Brace, 1938.
Compiler's note: Apparently an unfinished trilogy.
Lawrence, David Herbert, 1885-1930
  The rainbow. New York: Huebsch, 1916.
  Women in love. New York: Privately printed, 1920.
Lewis, Clive Staples, 1898-
  Out of the silent planet. London: John Lane, 1938.
  Perelandra. London: John Lane, 1943.
  That hideous strength. London: John Lane, 1945.
Lewis, Wyndham, 1886-
  The Childermass, I. London: Chatto & Windus, 1926.
Compiler's note: A continuation, announced for the spring of 1929, was not published.
Lindsay, Jack, 1900-
  Rome for sale. London: Mathews & Marrot, 1934.
  Caesar is dead. London: Nicholson & Watson, 1934.
  Last days of Cleopatra. London: Nicholson & Watson, 1935.
Long, Mrs. Gabrielle Margaret Vere (Campbell), see "Bowen, Marjorie."
Lorimer, Norma Octavia, 1864-
  There was a king in Egypt. New York: Brentano's, 1918.
  The shadow of Egypt. London: Hutchinson, 1923.
Lytton, Lord, see Bulwer-Lytton, Edward George.
McCormick, Renée (De Fontarce), 1899-   (Mrs. Leander J. McCormick)
  Little coquette. Trans. from the French by Leander J. McCormick. Boston: Houghton, Mifflin, 1944.
  Rustle of petticoats. Trans. by L. J. McCormick. Boston: Houghton, Mifflin, 1946.
McCrone, Guy
  "The Moorhouse family."
  Author's note: "I am intending to make this a series touching upon the Scottish way of life, and dealing with the same family up to the present time. It will be a kind of social record."
    Wax fruit. 1 vol. London: Constable, 1947. U.S. title: *Red plush; the story of the Moorhouse family*.
    1. *Antimacassar city*. 1940.
    2. *The Philistines*.

3. *The Puritans.*
 Aunt Bel. New York: Farrar, Straus, 1949.

MacDonald, George, 1824-1905
 Annals of a quiet neighborhood. London: Strahan, 1868.
 The seaboard parish. 3 vols. London: Tinsley, 1868.
 The vicar's daughter; an autobiographical story. 3 vols. London: Tinsley, 1872.

 Malcolm. 3 vols. London: H. S. King, 1874.
 The Marquis of Lossie. London: Hurst & Blackett, 1877.

MacGill, Patrick, 1890-
 Children of the Dead End; the autobiography of a navvy. London: Jenkins, 1914.
 The rat-pit. London: Jenkins, 1915.

MacKay, Minnie, see "Corelli, Marie."

McKee, Ruth Eleanor, 1903-
 The Lord's anointed. New York: Doubleday, Doran, 1934.
 After a hundred years. New York: Doubleday, Doran, 1935.

McKenna, Stephen, 1888-
 "Sonia."
  1. *Sonia: between two worlds.* London: Methuen, 1917.
  2. *Sonia married.* London: Hutchinson, 1919.
  3. *To-morrow and to-morrow.* London: Butterworth, 1924.

 The sensationalists. London: Hutchinson.
  1. *Lady Lilith.* 1920.
  2. *The education of Eric Lane.* 1921.
  3. *The secret victory.* 1921.
Compiler's note: "Sonia" and *The sensationalists* are related.

 The realists. London: Butterworth.
  1. *Saviours of society.* 1926.   2. *The Secretary of State.* 1927.   3. *Due reckoning.* 1927.

 Dermotts rampant. London: Chapman & Hall, 1931.
 The way of the phoenix. London: Chapman & Hall, 1932.

Mackenzie, Agnes Mure, 1891-
 Keith of Kinnellan. 1 vol. London: Constable, 1932; New York: Smith, 1930.
  1. *Lost Kinnellan.* London: Heinemann, 1927.   2. *The falling wind.*

Mackenzie, (Edward Montagu) Compton, 1882-
 Sinister street. 2 vols. London: Secker, 1913-14. U.S. titles: vol. 1, *Youth's encounter;* vol. 2, *Sinister street.*

 The life and adventures of Sylvia Scarlett. London, New York: Harper.
  1. *The early life and adventures of Sylvia Scarlett.* 1918.
  2. *Sylvia and Michael.* 1919.
  Author's note, *Sylvia and Michael:* "Book Three of *Sylvia Scarlett.*" (Books One and Two are not indicated.)
Compiler's note: The two sequences together complete the story of Sylvia and Michael, the hero of *Sinister street.*

 Guy and Pauline. London: Secker, 1915. U.S. title: *Plashers Mead.*
Compiler's note: Related to the Sylvia-Michael story and to the following trilogy.

 The altar steps. London, New York: Cassell, 1922.
 The parson's progress. London, New York: Cassell, 1923.
 The heavenly ladder. London, New York: Cassell, 1924.

 Poor relations. London: Secker, 1919.
 Rich relatives. London, New York: Harper, 1921.

 The four winds of love.
  1. *The east wind of love.* London: Rich & Cowan, 1937.

2. The south wind of love. London: Rich & Cowan, 1937.
3. The west wind of love. London: Chatto & Windus, 1940.
West to north. London: Chatto & Windus, 1940.
4. The north wind of love. 2 vols. London: Chatto & Windus, 1944-45. U.S. title, vol. 2: Again to the north.

Maclean, Catherine Macdonald
Seven for Cordelia. London, Edinburgh: Chambers, 1941.
Three for Cordelia. Toronto: Collins, 1943. U.S. title: The Tharrus three.
Farewell to Tharrus. New York: Macmillan, 1944.

MacLeod, LeRoy, 1893-
The years of peace. New York, London: Century, 1932.
The crowded hill. New York: Reynal & Hitchcock, 1934.

Marshall, Archibald, 1866-1934
The squire's daughter. London: Methuen, 1909.
The eldest son. London: Methuen, 1911.
The honour of the Clintons. London: Stanley Paul, 1913.
Rank and riches. London: Stanley Paul, 1915. U.S. title: The old order changeth.

Joan and Nancy. New York: Dodd, Mead, 1925.
Publisher's note: "Made up of episodes from the Clinton series."
Compiler's note: Two volumes of short stories deal in part with the Clintons.

Abington Abbey. New York: Dodd, Mead, 1917.
The Graftons. New York: Dodd, Mead, 1918.

"Anthony Dare." London: Collins.
1. Anthony Dare. 1924.
2. The education of Anthony Dare. 1924.
3. Anthony Dare's progress. 1925.

Masefield, John, 1878-
Dead Ned. Live and Kicking Ned. 1 vol. New York: Macmillan, 1941.
1. Dead Ned; the autobiography of a corpse. London: Heinemann, 1938.
2-3. Live and kicking Ned. 1 vol. London: Heinemann, 1939.
2. Live Ned.   3. Kicking Ned.

Basilissa; a tale of the Empress Theodora. London: Heinemann, 1940.
Conquer; a tale of the Nika rebellion in Byzantium. London: Heinemann, 1941.

Mason, (Francis) Van Wyck, 1897-
"Tetralogy of the American Revolution." Philadelphia: Lippincott.
1. Three harbours. (1774-75.) 1938.
2. Stars on the sea. (1776-77.) 1940.
3. Rivers of glory. (1776-79.) 1942.
4. Eagle in the sky. (1780-81.) 1948.

Maurice, Michael
Not in our stars. London: Unwin, 1923.
But in ourselves. London: Hutchinson, 1928.

Maxwell, William Babington, 1866-1938
Men and women. London: Hutchinson.
1. Tudor Green. 1935.
2. The emotional journey. 1936.
3. Everslade. 1938.
Compiler's note: Announced in preparation as "Our little lives."

Meredith, George, 1828-1909
Emilia in England. 3 vols. London: Chapman & Hall, 1864. Reissued as Sandra Belloni.
Vittoria. 3 vols. London: Chapman & Hall, 1866.

Metcalfe, Thomas Washington, 1884-
Santa Ana trilogy.
1. One night in Santa Ana. London: Cassell, 1931.

  2. The life and adventures of Aloysius O'Callaghan. London: Heinemann, 1932.
  3. Fare you well, my shining city. London: Faber & Faber, 1933.
Miln, Mrs. Louise (Jordan), 1864-1933
 Mr. and Mrs. Sên. London: Hodder & Stoughton, 1923.
 Ruben and Ivy Sên. London: Hodder & Stoughton, 1925.
Mitchell, James Leslie, 1901-35. Pseud., "Lewis Grassic Gibbon"
 A Scots quair. London: Jarrolds.
  1. Sunset gun. 1932.
  2. Cloud Howe. 1933.
  3. Grey granite. 1934.
Monkhouse, Allan Noble, 1858-1936. British
 My daughter Helen. 1 vol. New York: Harcourt, Brace, 1924.
  1. My daughter Helen. London: Jonathan Cape, 1922.
  2. Marmaduke. London: Jonathan Cape, 1924.
Monsell, Mrs. John Robert, see Irwin, Margaret E. F.
Moore, Frank Frankfort, 1855-1931
 Castle Omeragh. London: Constable, 1903.
 Captain Latymer. London: Cassell, 1907.

 The Jessamy bride. London: Hutchinson, 1904.
 Fanny's first novel. London: Hutchinson, 1913. Also published as Discovering Evelina.

 "Raymond Monk." London: Hutchinson.
  1. The rise of Raymond. 1916.
  2. The fall of Raymond. 1917.
Moore, George, 1852-1933
 Evelyn Innes. London: Unwin, 1898.
 Sister Teresa. London: Unwin, 1901. 2d ed., rewritten, 1909.
Morley, Iris, 1910-
 Cry treason. London: Davies, 1940.
 We stood for freedom. London: Davies, 1941.
 The mighty years. London: Davies, 1943.
Morrow, Mrs. Honoré (McCue) Willsie, 1880-1940
 The great Captain. 1 vol. New York: Morrow, 1935.
  1. Forever free. 1927.
  2. With malice toward none. 1928.
  3. The last full measure. 1930.
Mottram, Ralph Hale, 1883-
 The Spanish Farm trilogy. 1 vol. London: Chatto & Windus, 1927.
  1. The Spanish Farm. 1924.
  2. Sixty-four, ninety-four! 1925.
  3. The crime at Vanderlynden's. 1926.
Compiler's note: There are three connecting pieces: "D'Archeville," "The winner," "The stranger."

 Ten years ago. London: Chatto & Windus, 1928. U.S. title: Armistice and other memories.
Compiler's note: A pendant to the trilogy; short stories.

 Europa's beast. London: Chatto & Windus, 1930. U.S. title: A rich man's daughter.
Compiler's note: A sequel to the trilogy.

 Our Mr. Dormer. London: Chatto & Windus, 1927.
 Castle Island. London: Chatto & Windus, 1931.
Murasaki shikibu, 978?- Japanese
 The tale of Genji. Trans. by Arthur Waley. 2 vols. Boston: Houghton, Mifflin, 1935. 1-4,
  1 vol., Literary Guild, 1935.
  Vol. I:
  1. The tale of Genji. 1925.

2. The sacred tree. 1926.
   3. The wreath of cloud. 1927.
   Vol. II:
   4. Blue trousers. 1928.
   5. The lady of the boat. 1932.
   6. The lady of the boat, Part II: The bridge of dreams. 1933.
Myers, Leopold Hamilton, 1881-1944
  The near and the far. 1 vol. London: Jonathan Cape, 1940.
   1. The root and the flower. 1 vol., 1935.
     The near and the far. 1929.
     Prince Jali. 1931.
     Rajah Amar.
   2. The Pool of Vishnu. 1940.
Nepean, Evelyn Maud (Reid). (Mrs. Evan Nepean)
  Lanterns of horn. (1670-74.) London: John Lane, 1923.
  Ivory and apes. (1674-85.) London: Bale & Danielson, 1921.
  My two kings. (1674-86.) London: Melrose, 1917.
Nordhoff, Charles, 1887-1947, and James Norman Hall, 1887-
  The Bounty trilogy. 1 vol. Boston: Little, Brown, 1936.
   1. Mutiny on the Bounty. 1932. British title: Mutiny!
   2. Men against the sea. 1934.
   3. Pitcairn's Island. 1934.
Norris, Frank, 1870-1902
  The epic of the wheat. New York: Doubleday, Page.
   1. The octopus; a story of California. 1901.
   2. The pit; a story of Chicago. 1903.
   3. "The wolf."
  Compiler's note: Planned but not written.
Ogilvie, Elizabeth, 1918?-
  High tide at noon. New York: Crowell, 1944.
  Storm tide. New York: Crowell, 1945.
  The ebbing tide. New York: Crowell, 1947.
O'Grady, Standish James, 1846-1928
  The coming of Cuculain; a romance of the heroic age of Ireland. Dublin: Talbot Press,
    1919.
  In the gates of the North. Dublin: Talbot Press, 1919.
  The triumph and passing of Cuculain. Dublin: Talbot Press, 1919.
O'Hara, Mary," see Sture-Vasa, Mrs. Mary.
Oldmeadow, Ernest James, 1867-
  Coggin. London: Richards, 1919.
  The hare. London: Richards, 1920.
  Wild fang. London: Richards, 1922.
Oliphant, Mrs. Margaret Oliphant (Wilson), 1828-97
  Passages in the life of Mistress Margaret Maitland. London: Ward & Lock, 1849.
  Lilliesleaf; being a concluding series of passages in the life of Mrs. Margaret Maitland
    of Sunnyside. Written by herself. London: Hurst & Blackett, 1856.

  Chronicles of Carlingford.
   1. Salem Chapel. 2 vols. Edinburgh, London: Blackwood, 1863.
   2. The rector and the doctor's family. Edinburgh, London: Blackwood, 1863.
   3. The perpetual curate. 3 vols. Edinburgh, London: Blackwood, 1864.
   4. Miss Marjoribanks. Edinburgh, London: Blackwood, 1866.
   5. Phoebe junior; a last chronicle of Carlingford. London: Hurst & Blackett, 1876.
Oliver, George, see "Onions, Oliver."
Ollivant, Alfred, 1874-
  A romance of Sussex. London: Allen & Unwin.
   1. Two men. 1919.   2. One woman. 1921.

"Onions, Oliver," pseud. of George Oliver, 1873-
  Whom God hath sundered. 1 vol. London: Secker, 1925.
  Compiler's note: A revision of the trilogy, with the third novel interpolated in the first two.
     1. In accordance with the evidence. 1912.
     2. The debit account. 1913.
     3. The story of Louie. 1913.

  Gray youth; the story of a very modern courtship and a very modern marriage. 1 vol. New York: Doran, 1914.
     1. The two kisses; a tale of a very modern courtship. London: Methuen, 1913.
     2. A crooked mile. London: Methuen, 1914.
O'Riordan, Conal (Holmes) O'Connell, 1874- Pseud., "F. Norreys Connell"
  Adam of Dublin; a romance of today. London: Collins, 1920.
  Adam and Caroline. London: Collins, 1921.
  In London; the story of Adam and marriage. London: Collins, 1922.
  Married life. London: Collins, 1924.

  Yet do not grieve. 1 vol. New York: Scribner's, 1928.
     1. Soldier born; a story of youth. London: Collins, 1927.
     2. Soldier of Waterloo; a story of manhood. London: Collins, 1928.
  3. Soldier's wife. Bristol: Arrowsmith, 1935.
  4. Soldier's end. Bristol: Arrowsmith, 1938.

  Judith Quinn; a novel for women. Bristol: Arrowsmith, 1939.
  Judith's love. Bristol: Arrowsmith, 1940.
  Compiler's note: The Quinn family, major characters in the second and third series, are minor characters in the first series.
"Oxenham, John," pseud. of William Arthur Dunkerly
  Jesus of Nazareth. 3 vols. London, New York: Longmans, Green, 1932.
     1. The hidden years. 1925.
     2. Anno Domini. 1932. U.S. title: The Master's golden year.
     3. The splendour of the dawn. 1930.

  God's candle. London, New York: Longmans, Green, 1929.
  Compiler's note: Linked at the end with The splendour of the dawn.
Pakington, Hon. Humphrey Arthur, 1888-
  The Warmstrys of Romanfield. 1 vol. London: Chatto & Windus, 1933.
     1. Four in family. 1931.
     2. The roving eye. 1932.
     3. In company with Crispin. London: Chatto & Windus, 1934. U.S. title: The eligible bachelor.
Pargeter, Edith, 1913-
  The eighth champion of Christendom. London: Heinemann.
     1. The eighth champion of Christendom; lame crusade. 1945.
     2. Reluctant Odyssey. 1946.
     3. Warfare accomplished. 1947.
Payne, Pierre Stephen Robert, 1911-
  Love and peace. London, Toronto: Heinemann, 1945. U.S. title: Torrents of spring.
  Library of Congress card: "The first of a series of novels describing the life of a Chinese family from 1908 to the present day."
Pearce, Charles E.
  Love besieged; a romance of the defence of Lucknow. London: Stanley Paul, 1911.
  Sad revenge; a romance of Cawnpore. London: Stanley Paul, 1911.
  A star of the East; a romance of Delhi. London: Stanley Paul, 1912.
Pease, Howard
  Magnus Sinclair. (1649-51.) London: Constable, 1904.

Of Mistress Eve. (1653-63.) London: Constable, 1906.
The burning cresset; a story of the "Last rising of the North." (1715.) London: Constable, 1908.

Penton, Brian
　Landtakers; the story of an epoch. Sydney: Endeavor, 1934.
　Giant's stride. London: Cassell, 1936.
　Inheritors. Sydney: Angus, 1936.

Phillpotts, Eden, 1862-
　Dartmoor novels and tales. Widecombe Edition (limited ed.), 20 vols. London: Macmillan, 1931.
　　1. Widecombe Fair. 1913.
　　2. The thief of virtue. 1910.
　　3. The three brothers. 1909.
　　4. The river. 1902.
　　5. Brunel's tower. 1914.
　　6. Demeter's daughter. 1911.
　　7. The mother. 1908. U.S. title: The mother of the man.
　　8. Children of the mist. 1898.
　　9. The forest. 1912. Original title: The forest on the hill.
　　10. The virgin in judgment. 1907. Abridged reprint: A fight to the finish. 1911.
　　11. Miser's money. 1920.
　　12. The secret woman. 1905.
　　13. Orphan Dinah. 1920.
　　14. The portreeve. 1906.
　　15. Sons of the morning. 1900.
　　16. The beacon. 1911.
　　17. The whirlwind. 1907.
　　18. Children of men. 1923.
　　19. The fun of the fair. 1909.
　　　Compiler's note: Short stories.
　　20. Brother man. 1928.
　　　Compiler's note: Short stories.

　The book of Avis. 1 vol. London: Hutchinson, 1936.
　　1. Bred in the bone. 1932.
　　2. Witch's cauldron. 1933.
　　3. A shadow passes. 1933.

Piper, Warrene
　The son of John Winteringham. Boston: Houghton, Mifflin, 1930. British title: New lives.
　The sun in his own house. Boston: Houghton, Mifflin, 1931. British title: Full flower.

Pool, Maria Louise, 1841-98
　Roweny in Boston. New York: Harper, 1892.
　Mrs. Keats Bradford. New York: Harper, 1892.

　The two Salomes. New York: Harper, 1893.
　Out of step. New York: Harper, 1894.

Porter, Rose, 1845-1906
　Summer driftwood for the winter fire. New York: Randolph, 1870.
　The winter fire. New York: Randolph, 1874.

Portman, Lionel
　Hugh Rendal; a public school story. London: Alston Rivers, 1905.
　The progress of Hugh Rendal. London: Heinemann, 1907.

Pound, Arthur, 1884-
　Once a wilderness. New York: Reynal & Hitchcock, 1934.
　Second growth. New York: Reynal & Hitchcock, 1935.

Prouty, Mrs. Olive (Higgins), 1882-
　White fawn. Boston: Houghton, Mifflin, 1931.
　Lisa Vale. Boston: Houghton, Mifflin, 1938.
　Now, voyager. Boston: Houghton, Mifflin, 1941.

Pugh, Edwin William, 1874-
   The eyes of a child. London: Chapman & Hall, 1917.
   The secret years. London: C. Palmer, 1923.
Quick, Herbert, 1861-1925
   Vandemark's folly. Indianapolis: Bobbs-Merrill, 1922.
   The Hawkeye. Indianapolis: Bobbs-Merrill, 1923.
   The invisible woman. Indianapolis: Bobbs-Merrill, 1924.
Raymond, Ernest, 1888-
   Daphne Bruno. London, New York: Cassell.
      1. Daphne Bruno. 1925.
      2. The fulfilment of Daphne Bruno. 1926.

   Once in England. 1 vol. London: Cassell, 1932.
      1. The family that was. 1930.
      2. The jesting army. 1930.
      3. Mary Leith. 1931.
Riasanovsky, Antonina Fedorovna, 1895-   Pseud., "Nina Fedorovna"
   The family. Boston: Little, Brown, 1940.
   The children. Boston: Little, Brown, 1942.
Richardson, Dorothy M., 1882-
   Pilgrimage. 4 vols. London: Dent, 1938. 1st ed., 1-10. London: Duckworth.
      Vol. I:
      1. Pointed roofs. 1915.
      2. Backwater. 1916.
      3. Honeycomb. 1917.
      Vol. II:
      4. The tunnel. 1919.   5. Interim. 1919.
      Vol. III:
      6. Deadlock. 1921.
      7. Revolving lights. 1923.
      8. The trap. 1925.
      Vol. IV:
      9. Oberland. 1927.   11. Clear horizon. Dent, 1935.
      10. Dawn's left hand. 1931. 12. Dimple Hill.
"Richardson, Henry Handel," pseud. of Mrs. Henrietta (Richardson) Robertson, 1880-1946
   The fortunes of Richard Mahony. 1 vol. London: Heinemann, 1930.
      1. Australia Felix. 1929. First published as The fortunes of Richard Mahony. 1917.
      2. The way home. 1929. 1st ed., 1925.
      3. Ultima Thule. 1929.
   Compiler's note: Characters from the trilogy recur in short stories.
Richter, Conrad (Michael), 1890-
   "Ohio frontier series." New York: Knopf.
      1. The trees. 1940.
      2. The fields. 1946.
      3. The town. 1950.
Ripperger, (Mrs.) Henrietta (Sperry), 1889-
   112 Elm Street. New York: Putnam's, 1946.
   The Bretons of Elm Street. New York: Putnam's, 1946.
   Library of Congress card: Both novels are "based on a series published in Redbook under the title 'U.S. today.'"
Roberts, Sir Charles George Douglas, 1860-1944
   The forge in the forest. London: John Lane, 1897.
   A sister to Evangeline. London: John Lane, 1898.
Roberts, Kenneth, 1885-
   "Chronicles of Arundel." Garden City, New York: Doubleday, Doran.
      1. Arundel; a chronicle of the province of Maine and of the secret expedition led by Benedict Arnold against Quebec. 1930.

    2. Rabble in arms; a chronicle of Arundel and the Burgoyne invasion. 1933.
    3. The Lively Lady; a chronicle of Arundel, of privateering, and of the circular prison on Dartmoor. 1931.
    4. Captain Caution; a chronicle of Arundel. 1934.

Robertson, Mrs. Henrietta (Richardson), see "Richardson, Henry Handel."

Robinson, Frederick William, 1830-1901
  Female life in prison. By a prison matron. 2 vols. 2d ed. London: Hurst & Blackett, 1862.
  Memoirs of Jane Cameron, female convict. 2 vols. London: Hurst & Blackett, 1864.
  Prison characters drawn from life. By a prison matron. 2 vols. London: Hurst & Blackett, 1866.

"Rogers, Phillips," see Idell, Albert Edward.

"Rutherford, Mark," see White, William Hale.

Sale, Elizabeth
  Recitation from memory. New York: Dodd, Mead, 1943.
  My mother bids me bind my hair. New York: Dodd, Mead, 1944.

Sassoon, Siegfried, 1886-
  The memoirs of George Sherston. 1 vol. London: Faber & Faber, 1937.
    1. Memoirs of a fox-hunting man. 1928.
    2. Memoirs of an infantry officer. 1930.
    3. Sherston's progress. 1936.

Sawyer, Edith A., 1869-
  The way of Umê. New York: W. E. Rutledge, 1928.
  The abiding of Umê. New York: J. L. Pratt, 1932.

Scanlan, Nelle Margaret
  New Zealand trilogy. London: Jarrolds.
    1. Pencarrow. 1932.
    2. Tides of youth. 1933.
    3. Winds of heaven. 1934.

Schiff, Sidney, see "Hudson, Stephen."

Schumacher, Henry
  The fair enchantress. London: Hutchinson, 1912.
  Nelson's last love. London: Hutchinson, 1913.

Scott, Sir Walter, Bart., 1771-1832
  The monastery. 3 vols. 1820.
  The abbott. 3 vols. 1820.

Selby, John, 1897-
  Elegant journey. New York: Farrar & Rinehart, 1944.
  Island in the corn. New York: Farrar & Rinehart, 1941.
  Starbuck. New York: Farrar & Rinehart, 1943.

Seymour, Beatrice Kean (Stapleton)
  Three wives. London: Chapman & Hall, 1927.
  Youth rides out. London: Chapman & Hall, 1928.

  Maids and mistresses. London: Heinemann, 1932.
  Interlude for Sally. London: Heinemann, 1934.
  Summer of life. London: Heinemann, 1936.

Sheppard, Alfred Tresidder, 1871-
  The rise of Ledgar Dunstan. London: Duckworth, 1916.
  The quest of Ledgar Dunstan. London: Duckworth, 1917.

Sidgwick, Ethel, 1877-
  Promise. London, Toronto: Sidgwick & Jackson, 1910.
  Succession; a comedy of generations. London, Toronto: Sidgwick & Jackson, 1913.

  A lady of leisure. London: Sidgwick & Jackson, 1914.
  Duke Jones. London: Sidgwick & Jackson, 1914.
  The accolade. London: Sidgwick & Jackson, 1915.

Simms, William Gilmore, 1806-70
  The partisan. 2 vols. New York: Harper, 1835.

Mellichampe; a legend of the Santee. 2 vols. New York: Harper, 1836.
The kinsman, or The black riders of Congaree. 2 vols. Philadelphia: Lea and Blanchard, 1841. Reissued as The scout.
Katherine Walton, or The rebel of Dorchester; an historical romance of the Revolution in Carolina. Philadelphia: Hart, 1851.

The sword and the distaff, or "Fair, fat, and forty"; a story of the South at the close of the Revolution. Philadelphia: Lippincott, Grambo, 1853. Reissued as Woodcraft.
The forayers, or The raid of the dog-days. New York: Redfield, 1855.
Eutaw. New York: Redfield, 1856.
Compiler's note: The two series are related by subject and characters.

Sinclair, Harold, 1907-
  American years. New York: Doubleday, Doran, 1938.
  The years of growth. (1861-93.) New York: Doubleday, Doran, 1940.
  Years of illusion. (1900-14). New York: Doubleday, Doran, 1941.

Sinclair, Kathleen Henrietta (Nash-Webber), 1905- Pseud., "Brigid Knight"
  Walking the whirlwind. London: Cassell, 1940.
  The piping on the wind. London: Cassell, 1940.

Sinclair, Upton Beall, 1878-
  The metropolis. New York: Moffatt & Yard, 1908.
  The money-changers. New York: Dodge, 1908.

  Sylvia. Philadelphia: Winston, 1913.
  Sylvia's marriage. Philadelphia: Winston, 1914.

  "Lanny Budd novels," or "World's end series." New York: Viking Press.
    1. World's end. 1940.   6. Dragon harvest. 1945.
    2. Between two worlds. 1941. 7. A world to win. 1946.
    3. Dragon's teeth. 1942.   8. Presidential mission. 1947.
    4. Wide is the gate. 1943.   9. One clear call. 1948.
    5. Presidential agent. 1944. 10. O shepherd, speak! 1949.

Skidmore, Hubert, 1911-46
  I will lift up mine eyes. New York: Doubleday, Doran, 1936.
  Heaven came so near. New York: Doubleday, Doran, 1938.

Smith, Chard Powers, 1894-
  Artillery of time. New York: Scribner's, 1939.
  Ladies' day. New York: Scribner's, 1941.

Spring, Howard, 1889-
  Hard facts. London: Collins, 1944.
  Dunkerley's. London, New York: Harper, 1947.
  Compiler's note: A trilogy in progress.

Stacpoole, Henry De Vere, 1865-
  The blue lagoon. London: Unwin, 1908.
  The garden of God. London: Hutchinson, 1923.
  The gates of morning. London: Hutchinson, 1925.

Stern, Gladys Bronwyn, 1890-
  The Rakonitz chronicles. 1 vol. London: Chapman & Hall, 1932.
    1. Tents of Israel. 1924. U.S. title: The matriarch.
    2. A deputy was king. 1926.
    3. Mosaic. 1930.

  The matriarch chronicles. 1 vol. New York: Knopf, 1936.
    The above trilogy.
    4. Shining and free. London: Heinemann, 1935.

  The young matriarch. London: Cassell, 1942.
  Compiler's note: A continuation of the sequence.

Stevenson, Dorothy E., 1892-
  Mrs. Tim; leaves from the diary of an officer's wife. 1 vol. London: Collins, 1941. U.S.
    title: Mrs. Tim of the regiment.
    1. Mrs. Tim of the regiment. London: Jonathan Cape, 1932.
    2. Golden days. London: Jenkins, 1934.
  Mrs. Tim carries on; leaves from the diary of an officer's wife in the year 1940. London:
    Collins, 1941.
  Mrs. Tim gets a job. New York, Toronto: Rinehart, 1947.
Stevenson, Robert Louis, 1850-94
  David Balfour. London: Cassell.
    1. Kidnapped; being memoirs of the adventures of David Balfour in the year 1751. 1886.
    2. Catriona; memoirs of the further adventures of David Balfour at home and abroad.
      1893. U.S. title: David Balfour.
Strachey, Evelyn John St. Loe, 1901-   Pseud., "Blake"
  Readiness at dawn. London: Gollancz, 1941.
  We rendezvous at ten. London: Gollancz, 1942.
Stribling, Thomas Sigismund, 1881-
  The forge. Garden City, New York: Doubleday, Doran, 1931.
  The store. Garden City, New York: Doubleday, Doran, 1932.
  The unfinished cathedral. New York: Doubleday, Doran, 1934.
Stringer, Arthur John Arbuthnot, 1874-
  Prairie omnibus. 1 vol. New York: Grosset & Dunlap, 1945.
    1. The prairie wife. Indianapolis: Bobbs-Merrill, 1915.
    2. The prairie mother. Indianapolis: Bobbs-Merrill, 1920.
    3. The prairie child. Indianapolis: Bobbs-Merrill, 1922.
Sture-Vasa, Mrs. Mary (Alsop), 1885-   Pseud., "Mary O'Hara"
  My friend Flicka. Philadelphia: Lippincott, 1941.
  Thunderhead. Philadelphia: Lippincott, 1943.
  Green grass of Wyoming. Philadelphia: Lippincott, 1946.
Sutton, Marvin
  Children of Ruth. London: Cranley & Day, 1934.
  This promised land. London: Cranley & Day, 1934.
Swanson, Neil Harmon, 1896-
  The Judas tree. New York: Putnam's, 1933.
  Compiler's note: Companion novel to The unconquered.
  The silent drum. New York: Farrar & Rinehart, 1940.
  The unconquered. New York: Doubleday, 1947.
  Compiler's note: These are the first three volumes of a long sequence. Prospective titles
  listed in The unconquered: "The temporary gentleman" (to be next in the series), "The
  rock in the sun," "The vandals," "The stubborn flesh," "The calico tree," "The precious
  hour," "The broadhorn."
  Author's note: "When the project is finished the thirty volumes will form one continuous
  story beginning with the settlement of Maryland, Delaware, and Pennsylvania, and following
  the advance of the 'middle border' through the Ohio country to the Mississippi. The novels
  will deal primarily with the same families, their descendants and neighbors."
Tarkington, (Newton) Booth, 1869-1946
  Growth. 1 vol. Garden City, New York: Doubleday, Page, 1927.
    1. The magnificent Ambersons. 1918.
    2. The turmoil. New York, London: Harper, 1915.
    3. National Avenue.
Taylor, Colonel (Philip) Meadows, 1808-76
  Tara; a Mahratta tale. (1657.) 3 vols. Edinburgh, London: Blackwood, 1863.
  Ralph Darnell. (1757.) 3 vols. Edinburgh, London: Blackwood, 1865.
  Seeta. (1857.) 3 vols. London: H. S. King, 1872.
Thane, Elswyth, 1900-   (Mrs. Elswyth Thane Beebe)
  The Williamsburg pentalogy. New York: Duell, Sloan, & Pearce.
    1. Dawn's early light. 1943.
    2. Yankee stranger. 1944.

  3. *Ever after*. 1945.
  4. *Light heart*. 1947.
  5. *Kissing kin*. 1948.
Thompson, Edward John, 1886-
 Introducing the Arnisons. Toronto: Macmillan, 1935.
 John Arnison. Toronto: Macmillan, 1939.
Thompson, Flora
 Lark Rise to Candleford. 1 vol. London: Oxford University Press, 1945.
  1. *Lark Rise*. 1942.
  2. *Over to Candleford*. 1942.
  3. *Candleford Green*. 1943.
Thompson, James Myers, 1906-
 Heed the thunder. New York: Greenberg, 1946.
 Compiler's note: The first volume of a tentative trilogy.
Thurston, Ernest Temple, 1879-1933
 The antagonists. London: Chapman & Hall, 1912.
 Richard Furlong. London: Chapman & Hall, 1913.
 The achievement. London: Chapman & Hall, 1914. Reissued as *The achievement of Richard Furlong*. 1915.
"Trevena, John," see Henham, Ernest George.
Trollope, Anthony, 1815-82
 The Barsetshire novels. London: Bell. U.S. title: *The chronicles of Barsetshire*.
  1. *The warden*. London: Longmans, Green, 1855.
  2. *Barchester towers*. 3 vols. London: Longmans, Green, 1857.
  3. *Doctor Thorne*. 3 vols. London: Chapman & Hall, 1858.
  4. *Framley Parsonage*. 3 vols. London: Smith & Elder, 1861.
  5-6. *The small house at Allington*. 2 vols. London: Smith & Elder, 1864.
  7-8. *Last chronicle of Barset*. 2 vols. London: Smith & Elder, 1867.

 Parliamentary novels.
  1. *Can you forgive her?* 2 vols. London: Chapman & Hall, 1864.
  2. *Phineas Finn, the Irish member*. 2 vols. London: Virtue, 1869.
  3. *The Eustace diamonds*. 3 vols. London: Chapman & Hall, 1873.
  4. *Phineas redux*. 2 vols. London: Chapman & Hall, 1874.
  5. *Prime minister*. 4 vols. London: Chapman & Hall, 1876.
  6. *The Duke's children*. 3 vols. London: Chapman & Hall, 1880.
Tucker, Augusta, 1904-
 The man Miss Susie loved. New York, London: Harper, 1942.
 Miss Susie Slagle's. New York, London: Harper, 1939.
Viereck, George Sylvester, 1884- , and Paul Eldridge, 1888-
 My first two thousand years; the autobiography of the Wandering Jew. New York: Macaulay, 1929.
 Salomé, the Wandering Jewess; my first two thousand years of love. New York: Liveright, 1930.
 The invincible Adam. New York: Liveright, 1932.
Voynich, Mrs. Ethel Lillian (Boole), 1864-
 Put off thy shoes. New York: Macmillan, 1945.
 The gadfly. New York: Holt, 1897.
 An interrupted friendship. New York: Dimondstein, 1928. 1st ed., 1910.
 Compiler's note: The two stories connecting the first and second novels were not written; a note at the end of the first novel supplies the connection.
Waldman, Emerson, 1912-
 The land is large. New York: Farrar & Rinehart, 1938.
 Broad is the way. New York: Farrar & Rinehart, 1939.
Walmsley, Leo, 1892-
 Three fevers. London: Jonathan Cape, 1932.
 The phantom lobster. London: Jonathan Cape, 1933.
 Sally Lunn. London: Collins, 1937.

BRITISH AND AMERICAN

Walpole, Sir Hugh, 1884-1941
  The rising city.
    1. The Duchess of Wrexe; her decline and death, a romantic commentary. London: Secker, 1914.
    2. The green mirror; a quiet story. London: Macmillan, 1917.
    3. The captives. London: Macmillan, 1920.

"The Herries series." London: Macmillan.
    1. The bright pavilions. 1940.
    2. Katherine Christian. 1944.
    Herries; a chronicle in four parts. 1 vol. 1933. Title of later editions and U.S. editions: The Herries chronicle.
    3. Rogue Herries. 1930   5. The fortress. 1932.
    4. Judith Paris. 1931.   6. Vanessa. 1933.

Warner, Charles Dudley, 1829-1900
  A little journey in the world. New York: Harper, 1889.
  The golden house. New York: Harper, 1895.
  That fortune. New York: Harper, 1899.

Waters, Frank, 1902-
  The wild earth's nobility. New York: Liveright, 1935.
  Below grass roots. New York: Liveright, 1937.
  The dust within the rock. New York: Liveright, 1940.

Watson, Edmund Henry Lacon, 1865-
  "The Strange family." London: Hodder & Stoughton.
    1. The Strange family. 1926.
    2. Rudolf Strange. 1927.
    3. The last of the Stranges. 1928.

Webb, H. B. L. Pseud., "John Clayton"
  Gold of Toulouse. London: Heinemann, 1932.
  Dew in April. London: Heinemann, 1934.
  Anger of the North. London: Heinemann, 1936.

White, Stewart Edward, 1873-1946
  The blazed trail. New York: McClure, Phillips, 1902.
  The riverman. New York: McClure, 1908.
  The rules of the game. New York: Doubleday, Page, 1910.

  The story of California. 1 vol. Garden City, New York: Doubleday, Page, 1927.
    1. Gold. 1913.   2. The gray dawn. 1915.   3. The rose dawn. 1920.

  The saga of Andy Burnett. 1 vol. New York: Doubleday, 1947.
    1. The long rifle. 1932.   3. Folded hills. 1934.
    2. Ranchero. 1933.   4. Stampede. 1942.

White, Terence Hanbury, 1906-
  The sword in the stone. London: Collins, 1938.
  The witch in the wood. London: Collins, 1940.
  The ill-made knight. London: Collins, 1941.

White, William Hale, 1831-1913. Pseud., "Mark Rutherford"
  The autobiography of Mark Rutherford, dissenting minister. London: Trübner, 1881.
  Mark Rutherford's deliverance. London: Trübner, 1885.

Williams, Ben Ames, 1889-
  Come spring. Boston: Houghton, Mifflin, 1940.
  Thread of scarlet. Boston: Houghton, Mifflin, 1939.
  Strange woman. Boston: Houghton, Mifflin, 1941.
  Time of peace. Boston: Houghton, Mifflin, 1942.

Williams, William Carlos, 1883-
  White mule. Norfolk, Conn.: New Directions.
    1. White mule. 1937.   2. In the money. 1940.

Williamson, Henry, 1897-
  The flax of dream; a novel in four books. 1 vol. London: Faber & Faber, 1936.

1. The beautiful years; a tale of childhood. London: Collins, 1921.
2. Dandelion days. London: Collins, 1922.
3. The dream of fair women; a tale of youth after the great war. London: Collins, 1924. Rewritten version, 1931.
4. The pathway. London: Jonathan Cape, 1928.

The star-born. London: Faber & Faber, 1933.
Author's note: "Written from notes and rough manuscripts belonging to William Maddison," hero of The flax of dream.
Williamson, Thames Rose, 1894-
The American panorama. Boston: Small, Maynard.
1. The man who cannot die. 1926.
2. Gipsy down the lane. 1926.
Compiler's note: An unfinished sequence.

Hunky. New York: Coward-McCann, 1929.
In Krusack's house. New York: Harcourt, Brace, 1931.
Winther, Sophus Keith, 1895-
Take all to Nebraska. New York: Macmillan, 1936.
Mortgage your heart. New York: Macmillan, 1937.
This passion never dies. New York: Macmillan, 1938.
Wolfe, Thomas (Clayton), 1900-38
Look homeward, angel; a story of the buried life. New York: Scribner's, 1929.
Of time and the river; a legend of man's hunger in his youth. New York: Scribner's, 1935.

The web and the rock. New York, London: Harper, 1939.
You can't go home again. New York, London: Harper, 1940.
Compiler's note: Although the two pairs of novels have different heroes, the four novels form virtually one thinly disguised autobiographical sequence, with unifying themes. Some characters recur in short stories.
Wren, Percival Christopher, 1885-1941. British
The Foreign Legion omnibus. New York: Grosset & Dunlap, 1936.
1. Beau Geste. London: John Murray, 1924.
2. Beau Sabreur. London: John Murray, 1926.
3. Beau Ideal. London: John Murray, 1928.

Good Gestes. London: John Murray, 1929.
Spanish Main. London: John Murray, 1935. U.S. title: The desert heritage.
Compiler's note: The last two novels are sequels to the trilogy.
Young, Emily Hilda, 1880-
Jenny Wren. London: Jonathan Cape, 1932.
The curate's wife. London: Jonathan Cape, 1934.
Young, Francis (Eric) Brett, 1884-
They seek a country. London: Heinemann, 1937.
The city of gold. London: Heinemann, 1939.
Zangwill, Israel, 1864-1926
The Celibates' Club. 1 vol. London, New York: Macmillan, 1905.
1. The Bachelors' Club. 1891.
2. The Old Maids' Club. New York: Tait, 1892.

Romance Languages

FRENCH

Adam, Paul, 1862-1920
  L'époque. (The epoch.)
    1. Chair molle. (Soft flesh.) 1885.
    2. Le thé chez Miranda. (Tea at Miranda's.) With Jean Moréas. Paris: Tresse & Stock, 1886.
    3. Les demoiselles Goubert. With Jean Moréas. Paris: Tresse & Stock, 1886.
    4. La glèbe. Paris: Tresse & Stock, 1887.
    5. Robes rouges. (Red robes.) Paris: Kolb, 1891.
    6. Les coeurs utiles. (Useful hearts.) Paris: Kolb, 1892.
    7. Le vice filial. Paris: Kolb, 1892.
    8. Le conte futur. (The future story.) Paris: Librairie de l'art indépendant, 1893.
    9. La parade amoureuse. (The amorous parade.) Paris: Ollendorff, 1894.
    Compiler's note: Tales.
    10. Les coeurs nouveaux. (New hearts.) Paris: Ollendorff, 1896.
    11. La force du mal. (The power of evil.) Paris: A. Colin, 1896.
    12. L'année de Clarisse. (Clarissa's year.) Paris: Ollendorff, 1897.
    13. Clarisse et l'homme heureux. (Clarissa and the happy man.) Paris: Ollendorff, 1907.
    Compiler's note: Tales.
    14. Le troupeau de Clarisse. (Clarissa's set.) Paris: Ollendorff, 1908.
    Compiler's note: Tales.
    15. Les tentatives passionnées. (Impassioned endeavors.) Paris: Ollendorff, 1897.
    Compiler's note: Tales.
    16. Le serpent noir. (The black serpent.) Paris: Ollendorff, 1905.
    17. Combats. Paris: Ollendorff, 1905.
    18. Les lions. Paris: Ollendorff, 1906.
    19. Le rail du Sauveur. (The Savior's railway.) Paris: Librairie des Annales, 1908.
    20. La ville inconnue. (The unknown city.) Paris: Ollendorff, 1907.
    21. Stéphanie. Paris: Fasquelle, 1913.

  Le temps et la vie; histoire d'un idéal à travers les siècles. (The times and life; history of an ideal through the centuries.)
    1. Soi. (Oneself.) Paris: Tresse & Stock, 1886.
    Les volontés merveilleuses. (Marvelous desires.)
      2. Être. (Existence.) Paris: Stock, 1888. Reissued as Les feux du Sabbat. (Sabbath fires.)
      3. L'essence du soleil. (The sun's essence.) Paris: Tresse & Stock, 1890. Reissued as Les puissances de l'amour. (Powers of love.)
      4. En décor. (In a frame.) Paris: A. Savine, 1890. Reissued as Jeunesse et amour de Manuel Héricourt. (Youth and love of M. H.)
      5. Princesses byzantines. Paris: A. Colin, 1893.
        Contents: "La très pieuse Irène," "Anne Comnène."
    6. Les images sentimentales. Paris: Ollendorff, 1893.
    7. La mystère des foules. (The mystery of crowds.) 2 vols. Paris: Ollendorff, 1895.
    8. La bataille d'Uhde. (The battle of Uhde.) Paris: Ollendorff, 1897.
    9. Basile et Sophia. Paris: Ollendorff, 1900.
    10. Irène et les eunuques. (Irene and the eunuchs.) Paris: Ollendorff, 1907.
    "Tetralogy."
      11. La force. (Power.) 2 vols. Paris: Ollendorff, 1899.
      12. L'enfant d'Austerlitz. (The child of Austerlitz.) Paris: Ollendorff, 1902.
      13. La ruse. (1827-28.) Paris: Ollendorff, 1903.

    14. Au soleil de juillet. (1829-30.) (In the July sun.) Paris: Ollendorff, 1903.
    15. Le trust. Paris: Fayard, 1910.
    16. Le lion d'Arras. Paris: Flammarion, 1920.
    17. Le culte d'Icare. (The cult of Icarus.) Paris: Flammarion, 1924.
Compiler's note: Series lists are inconsistent, some novels being assigned at different times to each of the sequences. The lists above follow in general those in Camille Mauclair's Paul Adam (Paris: 1921). The order is that of publication, except that closely related books within a series are listed together, e.g., the Clarisse group.

Aicard, Jean François Victor, 1848-1921
  Maurin des Maures. Paris: Flammarion, 1908.
  L'illustre Maurin. Paris: Flammarion, 1908.
  Le rire de Maurin des Maures. (The laugh of Maurin of the Moors.) Paris: Flammarion, 1923.

  (1) The diverting adventures of Maurin. Trans. by Alfred Allinson. New York, London: John Lane, 1909.
  (2) Maurin, the illustrious. Trans. by A. Allinson. New York, London: John Lane, 1910.

  Un bandit à la française, Gaspard de Besse; raconté aux poilus de France par Jean d'Auriol. (A bandit after the French fashion, Gaspard de Besse; told to the poilus of France by Jean d'Auriol.) Paris: Flammarion, 1919.
  Le fameux chevalier Gaspard de Besse; ses dernières aventures. (The last adventures of the famous chevalier, Gaspard de Besse.) Paris: Flammarion, 1919.

Aragon, Louis, 1897-
  Le monde réel.
    1. Les cloches de Bâle. Paris: Denoël & Steele, 1934.
    2. Les beaux quartiers. Paris: Denoël & Steele, 1936.
    3. Les voyageurs de l'impériale. (Passengers on the upper deck.) Paris: Nouvelle Revue française, 1941; Gallimard, 1947, complete ed.
    4. Aurélien. 2 vols. Paris: Nouvelle Revue française, 1945

  The real world.
    1. The bells of Basel. Trans. by Haakon M. Chevalier. New York: Harcourt, Brace, 1936.
    2. Residential quarter. Trans. by H. M. Chevalier. New York: Harcourt, Brace, 1938.
    3. The century was young. Trans. by Hannah Josephson. New York: Duell, Sloan, & Pearce, 1941. World first edition.
    4. Aurélien. 2 vols. Trans. by Eithne Wilkins. New York: Duell, Sloan, & Pearce, 1947.

Arnaud, Robert, 1873- Pseud., "Robert Randau"
  Rabbin; roman des moeurs judéo-marocaines. (Rabbi; a novel of Judeo-Moroccan customs.) With Sadia Lévy. Paris: Havard, 1896.
  Les colons; roman de la patrie algérienne. (The colonists; a novel of the Algerian fatherland.) Paris: Sansot, 1907.
  Les explorateurs; roman de la grande brousse. (The explorers; a novel of the great wilderness.) Paris: Sansot, 1909.
  Les algérianistes; roman de la patrie algérienne. (The Algerianists.) Paris: Sansot, 1911.

Audoux, Marie, 1863-1937
  Marie-Claire. Paris: Fasquelle, 1910.
  L'atelier de Marie-Claire. Paris: Fasquelle, 1920.

  (1) Marie-Claire. Trans. by John M. Raphael. London: Hodder & Stoughton, 1911.
  (2) Marie-Claire's workshop. Trans. by F. S. Flint. New York: Seltzer, 1920.

Aveline, Claude, 1901-
  La vie de Philippe Denis. (The life of Philippe Denis.) 2 vols. Paris: Emile-Paul, 1930.
    1. Madame Maillart.
    2. La fin de Madame Maillart. (The end of Madame Maillart.)

  1-2. Madame Maillart. Trans. by Hamish Miles. New York: Dutton, 1933.

Balzac, Honoré de, 1799-1850
  La comédie humaine. 1829-47.

FRENCH

Compiler's note: A complete classified list of the series is given in Le Vte. de Spoelberch de Lovenjoul, Histoire des oeuvres de Balzac (Paris: Calmann Lévy, 1888); and Katherine Prescott Wormely, Memoir of Honoré de Balzac (Boston: Roberts, 1892).

The human comedy.
Compiler's note: A complete list of translations, classified according to Balzac, with notes and original titles, is given in Ernest Baker and James Packman, A guide to the best fiction, English and American (London: Routledge, 1932).

Barrès, Maurice, 1862-1923
  La culte du moi. (The cult of the ego.)
    1. Sous l'oeil des barbares. (Under barbarian eyes.) Paris: Lemerre, 1888.
    2. Un homme libre. (A free man.) Paris: Perrin, 1889.
    3. Le jardin de Bérénice. (Bérénice's garden.) Paris: Perrin, 1891.
  La culte du moi; examen de trois idéologies. (Examination of three ideologies.) Paris: Perrin, 1892.
  Compiler's note: Nonfiction, based on the above trilogy.

  Le roman de l'énergie nationale. (The novel of national energy.)
    1. Les déracinés. (The uprooted.) Paris: Fasquelle, 1897.
    2. L'appel du soldat. (Roll-call for the soldier.) Paris: Fasquelle, 1900.
    3. Leurs figures. (Their faces.) Paris: Juven, 1902.

  Les bastions de l'Est. (Bastions of the East.)
  Columbia Dictionary of Modern European Literature: "a logical sequence to the novel of national energy."
    1. Au service de l'Allemagne. (In the service of Germany.) Paris: Fayard, 1905.
    2. Colette Baudoche; histoire d'une jeune fille de Metz. Paris: Juven, 1909.
    3. Le génie du Rhin. (The genius of the Rhine.) Paris: Plon-Nourrit, 1921.

    2. Colette Baudoche; the story of a young girl of Metz. Trans. by Frances Wilson Huard. New York: Doran, 1918.

Behaine, René, 1880-
  Histoire d'une société. (History of a society.)
    1. Histoire d'une société: Alfred Varambaud, Céline Armelle, Michel Varambaud. Paris: Fasquelle, 1906. Reissued as Les nouveaux venus. (The new comers.) Paris: Grasset, 1928.
    2. Les survivants. Paris: Grasset, 1914.
    3. Si jeunesse savait. (If youth but knew.) Paris: Grasset, 1919.
    4. La conquête de la vie. Paris: Grasset, 1924.
    5. L'enchantement du feu. (The spell of fire.) Paris: Grasset, 1926.
    6. Avec les yeux de l'esprit. (With the eyes of the spirit.) Paris: Grasset, 1928.
    7. Au prix même du bonheur. (At the price even of happiness.) Paris: Grasset, 1930.
    8. Dans la foule horrible des hommes. (In the horrible mass of men.) Paris: Grasset, 1932.
    9. La solitude et le silence. Paris: Grasset, 1933.
    10. Les signes dans le ciel. (Signs in the sky.) Paris: Grasset, 1935.
    11. O peuple infortuné. (O, ill-fated people.) Paris: Grasset, 1936.
    12. La jour de gloire. (The day of glory.) Paris: Mercure de France, 1939.

    2. The survivors. Trans. by Edward Crankshaw. London: Allen & Unwin, 1938.
    4. The conquest of life. Trans. by E. Crankshaw. London: Allen & Unwin, 1939.

Bernanos, Georges, 1888-
  1. Sous le soleil de Satan. Paris: Plon-Nourrit, 1926.
  2. L'imposture. Paris: Plon, 1927.
  Compiler's note: Omitted from the series in translation.
  3. La joie. Paris: Plon, 1929.
  4. Journal d'un curé de campagne. Paris: Plon, 1936.

  "Trilogy of the spiritual life."
    1. The star of Satan. Trans. by Pamela Morris. New York: Macmillan, 1940.

2. _Joy._ Trans. by Louise Varèse. New York: Pantheon Press, 1946.
3. _The diary of a country priest._ Trans. by Pamela Morris. New York: Macmillan, 1937.

Bertrand, Louis, 1866-1941
  Le cycle africain. (The African cycle.)
    1. _Pépète et Balthasar._ Paris: Ollendorff, 1920. First ed.: _Pépète le bien-aimé._ (Pépète the well-beloved.) 1904.
    2. _Le sang des races._ (The blood of races.) Revised ed., Paris: Ollendorff, 1920. First ed., 1899.
    3. _Le jardin de la mort._ (The garden of death.) New ed., Paris: Ollendorff, 1921. First ed., 1905.
    4. _Les villes d'or; Algérie et Tunisie romaines._ (The cities of gold; Roman Algeria and Tunisia.) Paris: Fayard, 1921.
  Compiler's note: Nonfiction.

  Une destinée. (A destiny.)
    1. _Jean Perbal._ Paris: Fayard, 1925.
    2. _La nouvelle éducation sentimentale._ (The new sentimental education.) Paris: Plon, 1928.
    3. _Hippolyte porte-couronnes._ (Hippolyte, crown bearer.) 2d ed. Paris: Fayard, 1932.
    4. _Sur les routes du sud._ (On the southern roads.) Paris: Fayard, 1936.
    5. _Mes années d'apprentissage._ (My years of apprenticeship.) Paris: Fayard, 1938.

"Binet-Valmer, Gustave," pseud. of Jean Auguste Gustave Binet, 1875-
  L'homme et les hommes. (Man and men.) Paris: Flammarion.
    1. _L'enfant qui meurt._ (The child who dies.) 2 vols. 1921.
    2. _Les jours sans gloire._ (Days without glory.) 1922.
    3. _Le désordre (Disorder._) 1923.

Bloch, Jean-Richard, 1884-
  L'aigle et Ganymède. (The eagle and Ganymede.)
    1. _Sybilla._ Paris: Gallimard, 1932.
    2. "_Clotilde._"
  Compiler's note: Announced in preparation but not published.

Bourget, Paul Charles Joseph, 1852-1935
  Le roman des quatre. (The novel of the four.) Paris: Plon-Nourrit.
    1. _Le roman des quatre._ With Gerard d'Houville, Henri Duvernois, Pierre Benoit. 1923.
    2. _Micheline et l'amour._ (Micheline and love.) 1926.

Bourillon, Pierre, _see_ "Hamp, Pierre."
Boutelleau, Jacques, _see_ "Chardonne, Jacques."
"Boylesve, René," pseud. of René Tardiveau, 1867-1926
  La becquée. (Spoon-feeding.) Paris: Revue Blanche, 1901.
  L'enfant à la balustrade. (The child at the balustrade.) Paris: Calmann-Lévy, 1903.

  (1-2) _Young vigilance._ Trans. by H. V. Marrot. 1 vol. London: Elkin Mathews & Marrot, 1929.

  La jeune fille bien élevée. (The well-brought-up young girl.) Paris: Fayard, 1909.
  Madeleine, jeune femme. (Madeleine, young woman.) Paris: Calmann-Lévy, 1912.

  (2) _A gentlewoman of France._ Trans. by Aphra Wilson. New York: Brentano's, 1916.

Chamson, André, 1900-
  Roux le bandit. Paris: Grasset, 1925.
  Les hommes de la route. (Men of the road.) Paris: Grasset, 1927.
  Le crime des justes. Paris: Grasset, 1928.

  (1) _Roux the bandit._ Trans. by Van Wyck Brooks. New York: Scribner's, 1929.
  (2) _The road._ Trans. by V. W. Brooks. New York: Scribner's, 1929.
  (3) _The crime of the just._ Trans. by V. W. Brooks. New York: Scribner's, 1930.

"Chardonne, Jacques," pseud. of Jacques Boutelleau, 1884-
  Les destinées sentimentales. (Sentimental destinies.) Paris: Grasset.
    1. _La femme de Jean Barnery._ (The wife of Jean Barnery.) 1934.

FRENCH

    2. <u>Pauline</u>. 1934.
    3. <u>Porcelaine de Limoges</u>. 1936.
Colette, Sidonie Gabrielle, 1873-   Pseud., "Willy," used with Henry Gauthier-Villars. Full
  name: Mme. Sidonie Gabrielle Claudine (Colette) de Jouvenel
  "Claudine."
    1. <u>Claudine à l'école</u>. By "Willy." Paris: Ollendorff, 1900.
    2. <u>Claudine à Paris</u>. By "Willy." Paris: Ollendorff, 1901.
    3. <u>Claudine en ménage</u>. (Claudine keeping house.) Paris: Ollendorff, 1902.
    4. <u>Claudine s'en va</u>. (Claudine leaves.) Paris: Ollendorff, 1903.
    5. <u>La maison de Claudine</u>. (Claudine's house.) Paris: Ferenczi, 1922.

    1. <u>Claudine at school</u>. New York: Boni, 1930.
    2. <u>Young lady of Paris</u>. Trans. by James Whitall. New York: Boni, 1931. British title:
       <u>Claudine in Paris</u>.
    3. <u>The indulgent husband</u>. Trans. by Frederick A. Blossom. New York: Farrar & Rinehart,
       1935.
    4. <u>The innocent wife</u>. Trans. by F. A. Blossom. New York: Farrar & Rinehart, 1934.

<u>L'ingenue libertine</u>. 1 vol: Paris: Ollendorff, 1909.
    1. <u>Minne</u>. 1904.
    2. <u>Les égarements de Minne</u>. (Minne's mistakes.) 1905.

    1. <u>The gentle libertine</u>. Trans. by Rosemary Carr Benét. New York: Farrar & Rinehart,
       1931.

<u>La vagabonde</u>. Paris: Ollendorff, 1910.
<u>L'entrave</u>. (The fetter.) Paris: Flammarion, 1919.

(1) <u>Renée la vagabonde</u>. Trans. by Charlotte Remfry-Kidd. Garden City, New York: Doubleday,
Doran, 1931.
(2) <u>Recaptured</u>. Trans. by Violet Gerard Garvin. London: Gollancz, 1931.

<u>Chéri</u>. Paris: Fayard, 1920.
<u>La fin de Chéri</u>. Paris: Flammarion, 1926.

(1) <u>Chéri</u>. Trans. by Janet Flanner. New York: Boni, 1929.
(2) <u>The last of Chéri</u>. Trans. by Viola Gerard Garvin. New York: Putnam's, 1932.
Degée, Olivier, 1890-1944. Pseud., "Jean Tousseul"
<u>Jean Clarambaux</u>.
    1. <u>Le village gris</u>. Paris: Rieder, 1927.
    2. <u>Le retour</u>. Paris: Rieder, 1930.
    3. <u>L'éclaircie</u>. Paris: Rieder, 1931.
    4. <u>La rafale</u>. Brussels: Editions de Belgique, 1933.
    5. <u>Le testament</u>. Brussels: Editions de Belgique, 1936.

<u>Jean Clarambaux</u>. Trans. by Elisabeth Abbott. 1 vol. Philadelphia: Lippincott, 1939.
    1. <u>The gray village</u>.   3. <u>Clearing</u>.
    2. <u>The return</u>.   4. <u>The storm</u>.
                   5. <u>The testament</u>.
Duchêne, Ferdinand, 1868-
<u>Les Barbaresques</u>. (The people of Barbary.) Paris: Albin Michel.
    1. <u>Au pas lent des caravanes</u>. (At the slow pace of the caravans.) 1922.
    2. <u>Thamil'la</u>. 1923.
    3. <u>Le roman du meddah, de Fez la cruelle à Tlemcen la fleuri</u>. (The novel of the meddah,
       from Fez the cruel to Tlemcen the flowery.) 1924.
    4. <u>Au pied des monts éternels</u>. (At the foot of the eternal mountains.) 1925.
    5. <u>Kamir, roman d'une femme arabe</u>. (Novel of an Arab woman.) 1926.
    6. <u>La Rek'ba, histoire d'une vendetta kabyle</u>. (Story of a Kabyle vendetta.) 1927.

ROMANCE LANGUAGES

    7. Le berger d'Akfadou, roman kabyle. (The shepherd of Akfadou.) 1928.
    8. L'aventure de Sidi-Flouss. (The adventure of Sidi-Flouss.) 1929.

    2. Thamilla (The turtle dove); a story of the mountains of Algeria. Trans. by Isabelle May and Emily D. Newton. New York: Revell, 1927.
Dudevant, Amandine Aurore Lucie (Dupin), baronne, see "Sand, George."
Duhamel, Georges, 1884-   Pseud., "Denis Thévenin"
  Vie et aventures de Salavin. (Life and adventures of Salavin.) Paris: Mercure de France.
    1. Confession de minuit. (Midnight confession.) 1920.
    2. Deux hommes. (Two men.) 1924.
    Compiler's note: Omitted in translation.
    3. Journal de Salavin. 1927.
    4. Le club des Lyonnais. 1929.
    5. Tel qu'en lui-même. (Such a one as in himself.) 1932. Translated under the title End of illusion.

Salavin. Trans. by Gladys Billings. 1 vol. New York: Putnam's, 1936.

Chronique des Pasquier. Paris: Mercure de France.
    1. Le notaire du Havre. 1933.
    2. Le jardin des bêtes sauvages. 1934.
    3. Vue de la Terre promise. 1934.
    4. La nuit de la Saint-Jean. 1935.
    5. Le désert de Bièvres. 1937.
    6. Les maîtres. 1938.
    7. Cécile parmi nous. (Cécile among us.) 1938.
    8. Le combat contre les ombres. 1939.
    9. La passion de Joseph Pasquier. 1941. Printed in Canada.
    10. Suzanne et les jeunes hommes. (Suzanne and the young men.) 1941.

The Pasquier chronicles. Trans. by Beatrice de Holthoir. 1 vol. New York: Holt, 1938. 1-3 published in 3 vols., London: Dent, 1936.
    1. News from Havre.
    2. Caged beasts. British title: Young Pasquier.
    3. In sight of the Promised Land.
    4. St. John's Eve.
    5. The house in the desert.
Cécile Pasquier. Trans. by B. de Holthoir. 1 vol. New York: Holt, 1940. British title: Cécile among the Pasquiers.
    6. Pastors and masters.
    7. Cécile.
    8. The fight against the shadows.
    9-10. Suzanne and Joseph Pasquier. Trans. by B. de Holthoir. 1 vol. London: Dent, 1946.

    1. Papa Pasquier. Trans. by Samuel Putnam. New York: Harper, 1934.
    2-3. The fortunes of the Pasquiers. Trans. by S. Putnam. 2 vols. New York: Harper, 1934.
Dumas, Alexandre, père, 1802-70.
  Le chevalier d'Harmental. With Auguste Maquet. 4 vols. Paris: Dumont, 1843.
  Une fille du régent. Paris: Cadot, 1845.
  Compiler's note: Attributed by Quérard to Couailhac.

(1) Chevalier d'Harmental. London: Clarke, 1856. Other translations have the titles The conspirators; Love and conspiracy; The orange plume, or The bride of the Bastille.
(2) The regent's daughter. Trans. by Charles H. Town. New York: Harper, 1845.

"The D'Artagnan romances." With Auguste Maquet.
    1. Les trois mousquetaires. 8 vols. Paris: Beaudry, 1844.

2. Vingt ans après. 10 vols. Paris: Beaudry, 1845.
   3. Le vicomte de Bragelonne, ou Dix ans plus tard. (Ten years later.) 26 vols. Paris: Lévy, 1848-50.

   1. The three musketeers. London: Routledge, 1857. Some translations have the title The three guardsmen.
   2. Twenty years after. London: Routledge, 1856. One translation has the title Milady's son.
   3. Vicomte de Bragelonne. 2 vols. London: Routledge, 1857. Also published in translation in three parts:
      Bragelonne, son of Athos. Trans. by Thomas Williams. New York: Dean, 1848.
      The iron mask. Trans. by T. Williams. Philadelphia: Peterson, 1850.
      Louise de La Vallière. Trans. by T. Williams. Philadelphia: Peterson, 1851.
      Later translations have the titles, in order, Louise de La Vallière; the Man in the iron mask; The son of Porthos, or The death of Aramis.

La guerre des femmes. (Women's war.) With Auguste Maquet. 8 vols. Paris: De Potter, 1845-46.
   Vols. 1-2. Nanon de Lartigues.   Vols. 5-6. La vicomtesse de Cambes.
   Vols. 3-4. Madame de Condé.   Vols. 7-8. L'abbaye de Peyssac.

   1-2. Nanon, or Women's war. New York: Munro, 1877.

"The Valois romances."
   1. La reine Margot. 6 vols. Paris: Garnier, 1845.
   2. La dame de Monsoreau. 8 vols. Paris: Pétion, 1846.
   3. Les quarante-cinq. 10 vols. Paris: Cadot, 1848.

   1. Marguerite de Valois. London: Bogue, 1846. Other translations have the title Margaret of Navarre.
   2. Chicot the jester. London: 1857. U.S. translations have the titles The lady of Monsoreau and Diana of Meridor, or The lady of Monsoreau.
   3. Forty-five guardsmen. London: Clarke, 1861.

"Romances of the reign of Henry IV."
   1. Les deux Diana. 10 vols. Paris: Cadot, 1846-47.
   Compiler's note: Attributed by Parran to Paul Meurice.
   2. Le page du duc de Savoie. 8 vols. Paris: Cadot, 1855.

"Romances of the reign of Henry IV."
   1. The two Dianas. London: Clarke, 1862.
   2. The page of the Duke of Savoy. London: Clarke, 1861.

"The Marie Antoinette romances." With Auguste Maquet. Paris: Cadot.
   1. Mémoires d'un médecin. 19 vols. 1846-48.
   2. Le collier de la reine. 9 vols. 1849-50.
   3. Ange Pitou. 8 vols. 1852.
   4. La comtesse de Charny. 19 vols. 1852-55.
   5. Le chevalier de Maison-Rouge. 6 vols. 1846.

"The Marie Antoinette romances."
   1. Memoirs of a physician. 2 vols. London: Clarke, 1854. Also published in translation in two parts: Joseph Balsamo and Memoirs of a physician.
   2. The queen's necklace. 2 vols. London: Clarke, 1861.
   3. Taking the Bastille. 2 vols. London: Clarke, 1860. Another translation has the title Six years later.
   4. The Countess of Charny. London: Clarke, 1861.

5. Andrée de Taverney, or The downfall of the French monarchy. 2 vols. Trans. by Henry L. Williams, Jr. Philadelphia: Peterson, 1862. Reprinted in 1892 as The mesmerist's victim, or Andrée de Taverney. Other translations have the titles: Chevalier and Reign of terror.

Le trou d'enfer. (The mouth of hell.) 4 vols. Paris: Cadot, 1850-51.
Dieu dispose. (God disposes.) 6 vols. Paris: Cadot, 1852.

Les Mohicans de Paris. With Paul Bocage. Paris: Cadot.
   1. Les Mohicans de Paris. 19 vols. 1854-55.
   2. Salvator. 14 vols. 1855-59.

   1. The Mohicans of Paris. Philadelphia: Peterson, 1859.
   2. Salvator. Trans. by Mary Neal Sherwood. New York: Munro, 1882. An incomplete translation has the title The horrors of Paris.

Mémoires d'une aveugle. (Memoirs of a blind woman.)
   1. Madame du Deffand. 8 vols. Paris: Cadot, 1856-57.
   2. La confessions de la marquise. 2 vols. Paris: Lévy, 1862.

"The Napoleon romances."
   1. Les Blancs et les Bleus. 3 vols. Paris: Lévy, 1867-68.
   2. Les compagnons de Jehu. 7 vols. Paris: Cadot, 1857-58.
   3. Les louves de Machecoul. 10 vols. Paris: Cadot, 1859.

"The Napoleon romances." Boston: Little, Brown, 1894.
   1. The Whites and the Blues. 2 vols.
   2. The companions of Jehu. 2 vols.
   3. The she-wolves of Machecoul. 2 vols. Another translation has the title: The last vendée.

Mémoires de mademoiselle de Luynes. Paris: Lévy.
   1. La dame de volupté. (The lady of pleasure.) 2 vols. 1863.
   2. Les deux reines. (The two queens.) 2 vols. 1864.

La San-Félice. 9 vols. Paris: Lévy, 1865. Vols. 5-9 were reissued, 1888-95, as Emma Lyonna.
Souvenirs d'une favorite. 4 vols. Paris: Lévy, 1865.

(1) The lovely Lady Hamilton, or The beauty and the glory. Trans. by H. L. Williams. London: 1903.
(1) The Neapolitan lovers. Trans. by R. S. Garnett. London: Stanley Paul, 1916. An abridged version has the title Love and liberty.

Création et rédemption. Paris: Lévy, 1872.
   1. Le docteur mystérieux. 2 vols.
   2. La fille du marquis. (The daughter of the marquis.) 2 vols.

Le prince des voleurs. 2 vols. Paris: Lévy, 1872.
Robin Hood, le proscrit. 2 vols. Paris: Lévy, 1873.

(1) The prince of thieves. Trans. by Alfred Allinson. London: Methuen, 1904.
(2) Robin Hood, the outlaw. Trans. by A. Allinson. London: Methuen, 1904.

Erckmann, Emile, 1829-99, and Alexandre Chatrian, 1826-90
   Histoire d'un conscrit de 1813. Paris: Librairie internationale, 1864.
   Waterloo. Paris: Librairie internationale, 1865.

   (1-2) The history of a conscript of 1813 and Waterloo. Trans. by Russell David Gilman. 1 vol. New York: Dutton, 1909. "Everyman's Library," 2 vols. New York: Scribner's, 1869.

   Histoire d'un paysan. 4 vols. Paris: Hetzel, 1868-70.

    1. Les états généraux. (1789.)
    2. La patrie en danger. (1792.)
    3. L'an I de la République. (1793.)
    4. Le citoyen Bonaparte. (1794-1815.)

The story of a peasant. 2 vols. London: Ward & Lock, 1871. 4 vols., 1870-78.
    1. The States-General.
    2. The country in danger.
    3. Year One of the Republic.
    4. Citizen Bonaparte.

Farigoule, Louis, see "Romains, Jules."

Féval, Paul Henri Corentin, 1817-87

La quittance de minuit. (The midnight discharge.) 2 vols. Paris: Dentu, 1846.
    1. L'heritière. (The heiress.)
    2. La galerie du géant. (The giant's gallery.)

Les bandits. 2 vols. Paris: Permain, 1847. Reissued as Les bandits de Londres.
    1. Les aventures d'un émigré. (The adventures of an émigré.)
    2. Le tour de bâton. (The trick.)

Les belles de la nuit, ou Les anges de la famille. (The gay women, or The angels of the family.) 8 vols. Paris: Dentu, 1850. 2 vols., 1866. Reissued as L'oncle Louis. 2 vols. Paris: Palmé, 1886.
    1. L'aventurier. (The adventurer.)
    2. Les filles de Penhoël. (The girls of Penhoël.)

Le jeu de la mort. (The game of death.) Paris: Permain, 1850.

La tontine infernale. Paris: Dentu, 1892.

Le château de velours. (The velvet castle.) 2 vols. Paris: Permain, 1852.
    1. Le mal d'enfer. (The evil of hell.)
    2. Le comte Barbe-bleue. (Count Bluebeard.)

Les mémoires d'une pièce de cinq francs. (The memoirs of a five-franc piece.) With E. Chavelet. Lyons: De Potter.
    1. Roch Farelli. 2 vols. 1854. Chavelet.
    2. Madame Pistache. 2 vols. 1854. Féval.
    3. Le roi de la barrière. (The king of the gate.) 4 vols. 1855. Chavelet.

Le paradis des femmes. (The paradise of women.) 7 vols. Paris: Chappe, 1854-57.
    1. Les limbes. (Limbo.)
    2. Paris.
    3. Le docteur Sulpice.

Madame Gil Blas. 22 vols. Paris: Cadot.
    1. Madame Gil Blas. 4 vols. 1857.
    2. La princesse Maxime. 5 vols. 1858.
    3. Mes amours. (My loves.) 6 vols. 1858.
    4. Mes vingt ans. (My twentieth year.) 7 vols. 1858.

Jean-Diable. 3 vols. Paris: Dentu. 2d ed., 2 vols., 1863.
    1. Une nuit à Londres. (A night in London.)

2. Le chateau de Belcamp.
   3. Le procès criminel. (The criminal trial.)

Le roi des gueux. (The king of the beggars.) Paris: De Potter, 1860.
   1. Le roi des gueux. 6 vols.
   2. La maison de Pilate. (Pilate's house.)

Le roman de minuit. (The novel of midnight.)
   1. Le roman de minuit. Paris: Dubuisson, 1862.
   2. La cosaque. (The Cossack woman.) Paris: Dentu, 1866.

Souvenirs d'un page de M. de Vendôme. (Memories of a page of M. de Vendôme.)
   1. Madame Eliane. Paris.
   2. Le mari embaumé. (The embalmed husband.) 2 vols. Paris: Hachette, 1866.

La cavalière. (The equestrienne.) 2 vols. Paris: Dentu, 1866.
   1. Le rival de Cartouche.
   2. La treizième femme. (The thirteenth woman.)

L'avaleur de sabres. (The sabre swallower.) Paris: Dentu, 1868.
Mademoiselle Saphir. Paris: Dentu, 1868.

Les habits noirs. (The black habits.) Paris: Dentu.
   1. Les habits noirs. 2 vols. 1863.
   2. Coeur d'acier. (Heart of steel.) 2 vols. 1865.

Le secret des habits noirs. 4 vols. Paris: Dentu, 1869-70.
   1. L'arme invisible. (The invisible weapon.)
   2. Maman Léo.
   3. La rue de Jérusalem. (Jerusalem street.)
   4. Les demoiselles de Champmas. (The young ladies of Champmas.)

Le quai de la Ferraille. 2 vols. Paris: Dentu, 1869.
   1. Mariotte la basquaise. (Mariotte the Basque.)
   2. Messieurs de l'aventure. (Gentlemen adventurers.)

Le cavalier Fortune. 2 vols. Paris: Dentu, 1869-71.
   1. Chizac le riche.   2. Le duc de Richelieu.

Le tache rouge. (The red stain.) Paris: Dentu, 1871.
   1. Maman Marquis.   2. Le numéro 72,349.

Les compagnons du trésor. (The associates of the treasure.) 2 vols. Paris: Dentu, 1872.
   1. L'aventure de Vincent Carpentier. (Vincent Carpentier's adventure.)
   2. L'histoire d'Irène. (The story of Irene.)

Le dernier vivant. (The last living person.) 2 vols. Paris: Dentu, 1873.
   1. Les ciseaux d'accusé. (The scissors of the accused.)
   2. Le défenseur de sa femme. (The defender of his wife.)

Les cinq. (The five.) 2 vols. Paris: Dentu, 1875.
   1. Laura-Maria.   2. Princesse Charlotte.

La bande cadet. 2 vols. Paris: Dentu, 1875.
   1. Une évasion et un contrat.
   2. Clement-le-Manchot.

Les étapes d'une conversion. (The stages of a conversion.) 4 vols. Paris: Palmé, 1877-81.
   1. La mort d'un père. (The death of a father.)

FRENCH

    2. Pierre Blot: second récit de Jean. (Jean's second narration.)
    3. La première communion. (First communion.)
    4. La coup de grâce; dernière étape. (The death-blow; last stage.)

Les compagnons du silence. (The companions of silence.) Paris: Palmé, 1880.
Le prince Coriolani. Paris: Palmé, 1880.

Le capitaine Fantôme. Paris: Dentu, 1890-91.
    1. Les grenadiers écossais. (The Scotch grenadiers.) 1862.
    2. Les filles de Cabanil. (The girls of Cabanil.) 1862.
    3. Talavera-de-la-reine. 1891.

Féval, Paul, fils, 1860-
  Les amours du docteur. (The doctor's loves.) 2 vols. Paris: Guyot, n.d.
    1. Tuteur infâme. (Infamous guardian.)
    2. La Vierge-Mère. (The Virgin Mother.)

  Histoires d'outretombe. (Stories from beyond the tomb.) 3 vols. Paris: Guyot, n.d.
    1. Une soirée chez la marquise. (An evening at the marquise's.)
    2. Le Judas breton. (The Breton Judas.)
    3. Le bouquet du moribund. (The bouquet of the dying.)

  Les bandits de Londres. 3 vols. Paris: Guyot, n.d.
    1. L'oeil de diamant. (The diamond eye.)
    2. La belle Indienne. (The beautiful Indian.)
    3. Trois policiers. (Three policemen.)

  Le fils de Lagardère. (The son of Lagardère.) Paris: Geoffroy, 1893.
  Compiler's note: Continuation of Le Bossu, by Paul Feval, père.
    1. Le sergent Belle-Epée. With Le duc de Nevers published under above series title.
      2 vols. Paris: Ollendorff, 1893.
    2. La folie d'Aurore. (Aurora's madness.)
    3. L'instrument de M. de Peyrolles.
    4. Le duc de Nevers.
    5. Le Parc-aux-Cerfs.
    6. Les aventuriers. (The adventurers.)

  Les jumeaux de Nevers; fin du Bossu. (The Nevers twins; end of the Hunchback.) Paris: Ollendorff, 1895.
    1. Le Parc-aux-Cerfs. See 5, above.
    2. Mme. du Barry.

  Le Bossu. (The Hunchback.) 3 vols. Paris: Ollendorff, 1922.
  Les chevauchées de Lagardère. (The raids of Lagardère.) Paris: Juven, 1909.
  Cocardasse et passepoil. (Cockade and epaulette.) Paris: Juven, 1909.

  Coeur d'amour. (Heart of love.)
    1. Le mignon du roi. (The king's darling.)
    2. La trinité diabolique. Paris: Ollendorff, 1923.
    3. L'homme au visage voilé. (The man with the veiled face.)
    4. L'éborgnade. Paris: Albin Michel, 1925.

  D'Artagnan contre Cyrano de Bergerac. (D'Artagnan versus Cyrano.) With M. Lassez. 4 vols. Paris: Baudinière, 1925.
    1. Le chevalier mystère.
    2. Martyre de reine.
    3. Le secret de la Bastille.
    4. L'heritage de Buckingham.

  The years between; adventures of D'Artagnan and Cyrano de Bergerac. London, New York: Longmans, Green.
    1. The mysterious cavalier. Trans. by Cleveland B. Chase. 1928.

2. Martyr to the Queen. Trans. by C. B. Chase. 1928.
3. The secret of the Bastille. Trans. by John W. Chase. 1929.
4. The heir of Buckingham. Trans. by J. W. Chase, 1929.

D'Artagnan et Cyrano reconciliés. Paris: Baudinière.
1. Secret d'état. (State secret.) 1928.
2. L'évasion du Masque de fer. (The escape of the Iron Mask.) 1928.
3. Les noces de Cyrano. (Cyrano's wedding.) 1929.

The further adventures of D'Artagnan and Cyrano. Trans. by Cleveland B. Chase. London, New York: Longmans, Green.
1. Comrades at arms. 1930.   2. Salute to Cyrano. 1931.

Les exploits de Cyrano. 2 vols. Paris: Baudinière, 1932.
1. Le démon de bravoure. (The demon of courage.)
2. Pour sauver Roxane. (To save Roxane.)

Mademoiselle de Lagardère. Paris: Baudinière.
1. Contre Robespierre. (Against Robespierre.) 1929.
2. L'héroïne de thermidor. 1930.

Félifax. Paris: Baudinière.
1. L'homme tigre. (The tiger man.) 1929.
2. Londres en folie. (London goes mad.) 1930.

La guerre des étoiles. (The war of the stars.) 2 vols. Paris: Baudinière, 1930.
1. Les fiancés de Trianon.
2. Soldats de l'amour. (Soldiers of love.)

La petite-fille du "Bossu." (The granddaughter of the Hunchback.) 2 vols. Paris: Baudinière, 1931.
1. L'estafette de Waterloo. (The express messenger of Waterloo.)
2. L'aigle enchaîné. (The eagle in chains.)

"France, Anatole," pseud. of Jacques Anatole Thibault, 1844-1924
Histoire contemporaine. Paris: Calmann-Lévy.
1. L'orme du mail. 1897.
2. Le mannequin d'osier. 1897.
3. L'anneau d'améthyste. 1899.
4. Monsieur Bergeret à Paris. 1901.

Chronicles of our own times. London, New York: John Lane.
1. The elm-tree on the mail. Trans. by M. P. Willcocks. 1910.
2. The wicker-work woman. Trans. by M. P. Willcocks. 1910.
3. The amethyst ring. Trans. by B. Drillien. 1919.
4. Monsieur Bergeret in Paris. Trans. by B. Drillien. 1921.

Le livre de mon ami. Paris: Calmann-Lévy, 1885.
Pierre Nozière. Paris: Lemerre, 1899.
Le petit Pierre. Paris: Calmann-Lévy, 1918.
La vie en fleur. Paris: Calmann-Lévy, 1922.

(1) My friend's book. Trans by J. Lewis May. London, New York: John Lane, 1913.
(2) Pierre Nozière. Trans. by J. L. May. London, New York: John Lane, 1916.
(3) Little Pierre. Trans. by J. L. May. London, New York: John Lane, 1920.
(4) The bloom of life. Trans. by J. L. May. London: John Lane; New York: Dodd, Mead, 1923.

"Francis, Robert," pseud. of Jean Godmé
L'histoire d'une famille sous la troisième République. (The history of a family under the Third Republic.)

FRENCH

   1. La grange aux trois belles. (The farm of the three belles.) Paris: Rédier, 1933.
La chute de la maison de verre. (The fall of the glass house.)
    2. La maison de verre. Paris: Rédier, 1934.
    3. Le bateau-refuge. (The boat refuge.) Paris: Gallimard, 1934.
   4. Les mariés de Paris. (Married people of Paris.) Paris: Gallimard, 1935.
   5. Le gardien d'épaves. (The guardian of waifs.) Paris: Gallimard, 1937.

   1. The wolf at the door. Trans. by Françoise Delisle. Boston: Houghton, Mifflin, 1935.
Genevoix, Maurice, 1890-
  Un homme et sa vie. (A man and his life.) Paris: Flammarion.
   1. Marcheloup. 1934.
   2. Tête baisée. (Bowed head.) 1935.
   3. Bernard. 1938.
Giono, Jean, 1895-
  "Trilogy of earth." Paris: Grasset.
   1. Colline. (The hill.) 1929.
   2. Un de Baumugnes. (The man from Baumugnes.) 1929.
   3. Regain. 1930.

  "Trilogy of earth."
   1. Hill of destiny. Trans. by Jacques Le Clercq. New York: Brentano's, 1929.
   2. Lovers are never losers. Trans. by J. Le Clercq. New York: Brentano's, 1931.
   3. Harvest. Trans. by Henri Fluchère and Geoffrey Myers. New York: Viking Press, 1939.

Le chant du monde. Paris: Gallimard, 1934.
Batailles dans la montagne. (Battles in the mountains.) Paris: Gallimard, 1937.
Que ma joie demeure. Paris: Grasset, 1935.

(1) The song of the world. Trans. by Henri Fluchère and Geoffrey Myers. New York: Viking Press, 1937.
(3) Joy of man's desiring. Trans. by Katherine Clarke. New York: Viking Press, 1940.
Godmé, Jean, see "Francis, Robert."
Gras, Félix, 1845-1901
  Li Rouge dou miejour; roman istouri. Avignon: Roumanaille, 1896. Written in Provençal.
   Data not available on other two volumes, translated in (2) and (3) below.
  Les rouges du midi. 3 vols. Paris: Rouff, 1898.

(1) Reds of the Midi; an episode of the French Revolution. Trans. from the Provençal by C. A. Janvier. New York: Appleton-Century, 1896.
(2) The terror; a romance of the French Revolution. Trans. from the Provençal by C. A. Janvier. New York: Appleton-Century, 1898.
(3) The white terror; a romance of the French Revolution and after. Trans. from the Provençal by C. A. Janvier. New York: Appleton-Century, 1899.
"Hamp, Pierre," pseud. of Pierre Bourillon, 1876-
  La peine des hommes. (The labor of man.)
Compiler's note: Numbered in order of publication. Lorenz gives no series numbers for most volumes, and numbers given in other sources are inconsistent. Lorenz, Catalogue général de la librairie française, lists 1 and 3 as 3 and 4, but gives no earlier works with the series title.
   1. Marée fraîche. (Fresh sea-fish.) Paris: Union pour la vérité, 1908.
   2. Le vin de Champagne. (Champagne wine.) Paris: Union pour la vérité, 1909. Bound with Marée fraîche, 1 vol. Paris: Nouvelle Revue française, 1913.
   3. Le rail. (The iron rail.) 2d ed. Paris: N. R. f., 1912.
   4. L'enquête. (The inquest.) Paris: N. R. f., 1914.
   5. Le travail invincible. (The insurmountable task.) Paris: N. R. f., 1918.
Compiler's note: Nonfiction.
   6. Les métiers blessés. (Injured trades.) Paris: N. R. f., 1919.
Compiler's note: Nonfiction.

7. La victoire mécanicienne. (Mechanical victory.) Paris: N. R. f., 1920.
   Compiler's note: Novel.
   Compiler's note: 5, 6, and 7 form a war trilogy.
8. Les chercheurs d'or. (Gold seekers.) Paris: N. R. f., 1920.
9. Le cantique des cantiques. (The song of songs.) Paris: N. R. f., 1922.
10. Un nouvel honneur. (A new honor.) Paris: N. R. f., 1922.
    Compiler's note: Nonfiction.
11. Le lin. (Linen.) Paris: N. R. f., 1924.
12. Une nouvelle fortune. (A new fortune.) Paris: N. R. f., 1926.
    Compiler's note: Nonfiction.
13. Mes métiers. (My occupations.) Paris: N. R. F., 1930.
14. La laine. (Wool.) Paris: Flammarion, 1931.
15. Mektoub. Paris: Flammarion, 1932.
16. Mineurs et métiers de fer. (Miners and iron trades.) 1932.
17. Dieu est le plus grand. (God is the greatest.) Paris: Flammarion, 1932.
18. La mort de l'or. (The death of gold.) Paris: Flammarion, 1933.
19. Glück auf! (Good luck.) Paris: Gallimard, 1934.
20. Il faut que vous naissiez de nouveau. (You must be born again.) Paris: Gallimard, 1935.

13. Kitchen prelude. Trans. by Dorothy Bolton. New York: Dutton, 1933.
"Harry, Myriam," see Perrault-Harry, Mme. Myriam.
Hermant, Abel, 1862-
Scènes de la vie des cours et des ambassades. (Scenes from court and embassy life.) Paris: Ollendorff.
   1. La carrière. (The career.) 1894.
   2. Le sceptre. 1896.
   3. Le char de l'état. (The chariot of state.) 1900.

Mémoires pour servir à l'histoire de la société. (Memoirs to be used for the history of society.)
   1. Confession d'un enfant d'hier. (Confession of a child of yesterday.) Paris: Ollendorff, 1903.
   2. Confession d'un homme d'aujourd'hui. (Confession of a man of today.) Paris: Ollendorff, 1903.
   3. Souvenirs du vicomte de Courpière, par un témoin. (Memories of the Viscount de Courpière, by a witness.) Paris: Ollendorff, 1901.
   4. Monsieur de Courpière, marié. (M. de Courpière, married.) Paris: Flammarion, 1906.
   5. Les confidences d'une biche. (The confidences of a darling.) Paris: Lemerre, 1909.
   6. La biche relancée. (The darling started again.) Paris: Lemerre, 1911.
   7. Les grands bourgeois. (Bourgeois great.) Paris: Lemerre, 1906.
   8. La discorde. Paris: Lemerre, 1907.
   9. Les affranchis. (The emancipated.) Paris: Lemerre, 1908.
   10. Histoire d'un fils de roi. (Story of a king's son.) Paris: Fayard, 1911.
   11. Les renards. (The foxes.) Paris: Louis-Michaud, 1912.
   12. Chronique du cadet de Coutras. (Chronicle of the younger son of Coutras.) Paris: Juven, 1909.
   13. Coutras, soldat. (Coutras, soldier.) Paris: Juven, 1909.
   14. Coutras voyage. (Coutras travels.) Paris: Louis-Michaud, 1912.
   15. D'un guerre à l'autre guerre. (From one war to the other.) Paris: Lemerre.
      Vol. I. L'aube ardente. (The burning dawn.) 1919.
      Vol. II. La journée brève. (The short day.) 1920.
      Vol. III. Le crépuscule tragique. (The tragic twilight.) 1921.
   16. La flamme renversée. (The inverted flame.) Paris: Flammarion, 1929.
   17. Epilogue de la vie amoureuse. (Epilogue of the amorous life.) Paris: Flammarion, 1929.
   18. La dernière incarnation de monsieur de Courpière. (The last incarnation of M. de Courpière.) Paris: Flammarion, 1937.

Scènes de la vie cosmopolite. (Scenes of cosmopolitan life.) Paris: Lemerre.

1. Le joyeux garçon. (The happy boy.) 1913.
2. La petite femme. (The little wife.) 1914.
3. L'autre aventure du joyeux garçon. (The other adventure of the happy boy.) 1916.
Compiler's note: Three stories.
4. Le caravansérail. 1917.
5. Le rival inconnu. (The unknown rival.) 1918.

Le cycle de lord Chelsea. 4 vols. Paris: Nouvelle Revue française, 1923.
1. Le suborneur. (The briber.)
2. Le loyal serviteur. (The loyal servant.)
3. Dernier et premier amour.
4. Le procès du très honorable lord. (The lawsuit of the very honorable lord.)

3. First and last love. Trans. by Slater Brown. New York: Macaulay, 1930.

Houssaye, Arsène, 1815-96
Le chien perdu et la femme fusillée. (The lost dog and the woman shot to death.) 2 vols. Paris: Dentu, 1872.
1. Les épouvantements. (Terrors.)
2. Les abîmes. (The depths.)

Les grandes dames. (Great ladies.) 1st series. 4 vols. Paris: Dentu, 1868.
1. Monsieur Don Juan.
2. Madame Vénus.
3. Les pécheresses blondes. (Blond sinners.)
4. La maîtresse anonyme et une tragédie à Enis en 1868. (The anonymous mistress and a tragedy at Enis in 1868.)

Les grandes dames. 2d series: Les Parisiennes. 4 vols. Paris: Dentu, 1869.
1. Le jeu des femmes. (Women's sport.)
2. Mademoiselle Phryné.
3. Les femmes adultères. (Adulterous women.)
4. Les femmes déchues. (Fallen women.)

Les grandes dames. 3d series: Les courtisanes du monde. (Society courtesans.) 4 vols. Paris: Dentu, 1870.
1. La Messaline blanche. (White Messalina.)
2. Violette.
3. Les femmes desmasquées. (Women unmasked.)
4. Comment finissent les passions. (How passions end.)

Les milles et une nuits parisiennes. (The thousand and one Parisian nights.) 4 vols. Paris: Dentu, 1875.
1. Le marquis de Satanas.
2. Confessions de Caroline. (Caroline's confessions.)
3. Princesses au grain de beauté. (Princesses with a mole.)
4. La dame aux diamants. (The lady with the diamonds.)

L'éventail brisé. (The broken fan.) 2 vols. Paris: Dentu, 1879.
1. Régina.   2. Angèle.

"Huysmans, Joris Karl," pseud. of Charles Marie Georges Huysmans, 1848-1907
Là-bas. Paris: Tresse & Stock, 1891.
Compiler's note: Related to the tetralogy.

Down there. Trans. by Keene Wallis. New York: Boni, 1924.

En route. Paris: Tresse & Stock, 1895.
La cathédrale. Paris: Stock, 1898.

L'oblat. Paris: Stock, 1903.
Les foules de Lourdes. Paris: Stock, 1906.

(1) En route. Trans. by C. Kegan Paul. London: Kegan Paul, 1896.
(2) The cathedral. Trans. by Clara Bell. London: Paul, Trench, Trübner, 1898.
(3) The oblate. Trans. by Edward Perceval. London: Paul, Trench, Trübner, 1924.
(4) The crowds of Lourdes. Trans. by W. H. Mitchell. London: Burns, Oates, Washbourne, 1925.

Istrati, Panaït, 1884-1935
  Adrien Zograffi
    Les récits d'Adrien Zograffi. (The tales of Adrien Zograffi.) 4 vols. Paris: Rieder, 1924-29.
      1. Kyra Kyralina.
      2. Oncle Anghel.
      3. Les haïdoucs. 2 vols.
        I. Présentation des haïdoucs.
        II. Domnitza de Snagov.

      1. Kyra Kyralina. Trans. by James Whitall. New York: Knopf, 1926.
      2. Uncle Anghel. Trans. by Maude V. White. New York: Knopf, 1927.
      3. The bandits. Trans. by William A. Drake. New York: Knopf, 1929.

  Enfance d'Adrien Zograffi: Codine. (Childhood of Adrien Zograffi.) Paris: Rieder, 1926.
  Adolescence d'Adrien Zograffi: Mikhail. Paris: Rieder, 1927.
  Vie d'Adrien Zograffi. Paris: Rieder.
    1. La maison Thüringer. (The Thüringer house.) 1933.
    2. Le bureau de placement. (The registry office.) 1933.
    3. Méditerranée: lever du soleil. (Mediterranean: sunrise.) 1934.
    4. Méditerranée: coucher du soleil. (Sunset.) 1935.

Jouhandeau, Marcel, 1888-   Pseud., "Marcel Provence"
  Monsieur Godeau intime. (M. Godeau, intimate.) Paris: Gallimard, 1926.
  Monsieur Godeau marié. (M. Godeau married.) Paris: Gallimard, 1933.
  Chroniques maritales. (Marital chronicles.) Paris: Nouvelle Revue française, 1938.

  Chaminadour.
    1. Chaminadour I, Chaminadour, propos et anecdotes. (Talk and anecdotes.) Paris: Gallimard, 1934.
    2. Chaminadour II. Paris: Nouvelle Revue française, 1936.
    3. L'arbre de visages. Chaminadour III. (The tree of faces.) Paris: N. R. f., 1941.

Lacretelle, Jacques de, 1888-
  Silbermann. Paris: Nouvelle Revue française, 1922.
  Le retour de Silbermann. (The return of Silbermann.) Paris: N. R. F., 1930.

  (1) Silbermann. Trans. by Brian Lunn. New York: Boni & Liveright, 1923.

  Les Haut-Ponts. Paris: Gallimard.
    1. Sabine. 1932.
    2. Les fiançailles. (The betrothal.) 1933.
    3. Années d'espérance. (Years of hope.) 1935.
    4. La monnaie de plomb. (Lead money.) 1935.

Leblond, Marius, 1877-   , and Ary Leblond, 1880-
  Les martyrs de la République; romans contemporains. (Martyrs of the Republic; contemporary novels.) Paris: Ferenczi.
    1. La guerre des âmes. (The war of souls.) 1926.   3. La damnation. 1927.
    2. L'écartèlement. (The quartering.) 1927.   4. La grâce. (Pardon.) 1928.

Lemonnier, Camille, 1844-1913
  La légende de la vie. (The legend of life.)
    1. L'île vierge. (Virgin island.) Paris: Dentu, 1896.
    2. "Le liberateur."
  Compiler's note: Planned but not written.

FRENCH

   3. "L'aube des dieux." (The dawn of the gods.)
   Compiler's note: Planned but not written.

L'homme en amour. (Man in love.) Paris: Ollendorff, 1897.
Adam et Eve. Paris: Ollendorff, 1898.
Au coeur frais de la forêt. (In the cool heart of the forest.) Paris: Ollendorff, 1899.
Compiler's note: Planned as a trilogy but not completed in sequence form.

Lichtenberger, André, 1870-
  Mon petit Trott. Paris: Plon-Nourrit, 1898.
  La petite soeur de Trott. Paris: Plon-Nourrit, 1898.

  (1-2) Trott and his little sister. Trans. by Blanche and Irma Weill. New York: Viking Press, 1931.

Malraux, André, 1895-
  Les puissances du désert. (The powers of the desert.)
    1. La voie royale. (The royal highway.)
  Compiler's note: Apparently an unfinished sequence.

  La lutte avec l'ange. (The wrestling with the angel.)
    1. Les noyers de l'Altenburg. (The walnut trees of Altenburg.) Lausanne: Yverdon Editions du Haut-Pays, 1943.
  Compiler's note: Apparently an unfinished sequence.

Margueritte, Paul, 1860-1918, and Victor Margueritte, 1866-1942
  Une époque. (An epoch.) Paris: Plon-Nourrit.
    1. Le désastre. (Metz, 1870.) 1898.
    2. Les tronçons du glaive. (Défense nationale, 1870-71.) (Fragments of the sword.) 1901.
    3. Les braves gens. (Épisodes du 1870-71.) (Brave people.) 1901.
    4. La commune. (Paris-Versailles, 1871.) 1904.

    1. The disaster. Trans. by Frederic Lees. New York: Appleton, 1898.
    3. Strasbourg. Trans. by "S. G. Tallentyre." London: Smith & Elder, 1915.
  Compiler's note: An incomplete translation.
    4. The Commune. Trans. by F. Lees and R. B. Douglas. London: Chatto & Windus, 1904.

Martin du Gard, Roger, 1881-
  Les Thibault. Paris: Gallimard, Nouvelle Revue française.
    1. Le cahier gris. 1922.
    2. Le pénitencier. 1923.
    3. La belle saison. (The beautiful season.) 2 vols. 1923.
    4. La consultation. 1928.
    5. La sorellina. (The little sister.) 1928.
    6. La mort du père. (The father's death.) 1928.
    7. L'été 1914. 3 vols. 1936.
    8. Épilogue. 1940.

  The world of the Thibaults. Trans. by Stuart Gilbert. 2 vols. New York: Viking Press.
    Vol. I:
    1-6. The Thibaults. 1939. Without titles of separate parts.
    Vol. II:
    7-8. Summer 1914. 1941

  The Thibaults. Trans. by Madeleine Boyd. 2 vols. New York: Boni & Liveright, 1926.
    Vol. I:
    1. The gray notebook.
    2. The penitentiary.
    Vol. II:
    3. The springtime of life.

  The Thibaults. 2 vols. London: John Lane, 1933.
    Vol. I:
    1-2. Trans. by Stuart Haden Guest.

Vol. II:
3-4. Trans. by Stuart Gilbert.
  3. High summer.   4. The consultation.
Mauriac, François, 1885-
  Les Péloueyre. 1 vol. Paris: Calmann-Lévy, 1925.
    1. Le baiser au lepreux. (The kiss to the leper.) Paris: Grasset, 1922.
    2. Genitrix. Paris: Grasset, 1923.

  The family. Trans. by Lewis Galantière. 1 vol. New York: Covici-Friede, 1930.

  Thérèse Desqueyroux. Paris: Grasset, 1927.
  La fin de la nuit. Paris: Grasset, 1935.
  Author's note, translated by compiler: ". . . the portrait of a woman in her decline whom I have already depicted in the time of her criminal youth."

  Thérèse. Trans. by Gerard Hopkins. 1 vol. New York: Holt, 1947.
    (1) Thérèse Desqueyroux. Earlier translation by Eric Sutton. New York: Boni & Liveright, 1928.
    "Thérèse and the doctor."
    Compiler's note: Short story.
    "Thérèse at the hotel."
    Compiler's note: Short story.
    (2) The end of the night.
Montherlant, Henry de, 1893-
  La jeunesse d'Alban de Bricoule. (The youth of Alban de Bricoule.) Paris: Grasset.
    1. Les bestiares. Les taureaux. (The bulls.) 1926.
    2. "La ville dont le prince est un enfant." Le collège. (The city whose prince is a child.)
    Compiler's note: Announced in preparation but apparently not published.
    3. Le songe. La guerre. (The dream. The war.) 1922.

    1. The bullfighters. Trans. by Edwin Gile Rich. New York: MacVeagh, The Dial Press, 1927.

  Les jeunes filles. Paris: Grasset.
    1. Les jeunes filles. 1936.
    2. Pitié pour les femmes. 1936.
    3. Le démon du bien. 1937.
    4. Les lepreuses. 1939.

  "Young girls." New York: Knopf.
    Pity for women. 2 vols. in 1. 1938.
      1. Young girls. Trans. by Thomas McGreevy.
      2. Pity for women. Trans. by John Rodker.
    Costals and the hippogriff. Trans. by John Rodker. 2 vols. in 1. 1940. British title: The lepers.
      3. The demon of good.
      4. The lepers.
Ohnet, Georges, 1848-1918
  Les batailles de la vie. (The battles of life.) Paris: Ollendorff.
  Compiler's note: Numbered according to consistent series lists in separate novels.
    1. Serge Panine. 1881.
    2. Le maître de forges. 1882.
    3. La comtesse Sarah. 1883.
    4. Lise Fleuron. 1884.
    5. La grande marnière. 1885.
    6. Les dames de Croix-Mort. 1886.
    7. Volonté. 1888.

8. Le docteur Rameau. 1888.
9. Dernier amour. 1889.
10. Nemrod et Cie. 1892.
11. Dette de haine. 1891.
12. Le lendemain des amours. (Loves' morrow.) 1893.
13. Le droit de l'enfant. (The right of the child.) 1894.
14. La dame en gris. (The lady in gray.) 1895.
15. L'inutile richesse. (Useless wealth.) 1896.
16. Le curé de Favières. (The priest of Favières.) 1897.
17. Les vieilles rancunes. (Old grudges.) 1895.
18. Roi de Paris. (King of Paris.) 1898.
19. L'âme de Pierre. 1890.
20. Au fond du gouffre. (At the bottom of the abyss.) 1899.
21. Gens de la noce. (Wedding attendants.) 1900.
22. La ténébreuse. (The lady of darkness.) 1900.
23. Le brasseur d'affaires. (The business brewer.) 1901.
24. Le crépuscule. (Twilight.) 1902.
25. Marchand de poison. (Poison vendor.) 1903.
26. Le chemin de la gloire. (The road of glory.) 1904.
27. La marche de l'amour. (The course of love.) 1902.
28. La conquérante. (The conquering woman.) 1905.
29. La dixième muse. (The tenth muse.) 1906.
30. L'aventure de Raymond Dhautel. (The adventure of Raymond Dhautel.) 1910.
31. L'amour commande. (Love commands.) 1914.
32. Le revenant. (The ghost.) 1912.
33. L'étoile. (The star.) 1921.
34. Tout se paie. (Everything is paid for.) 1921.
35. La route rouge. (The red road.) 1908.
36. Noir et rose. (Black and rose.) 1867.
    Contents: "Le chant du cygne," "Le malheur de tante Ursule."
37. Coeurs en deuil. (Hearts in mourning.) 1907.
38. Un mariage américain. (An American marriage.) 1908.
39. La fille du député. (The deputy's daughter.) 1896.

The battles of life.
1. Serge Panine. Trans. by Ruth Russell. New York: G. Munro, 1883.
2. Claire and the forge-master. Trans. by F. C. Valentine. New York: M. L. Munro, 1884. Other translations have the titles The iron master, or Love and pride; The master of the forge.
4. The rival actresses. London: Vizetelly, 1889.
5. Antoinette, or The marl-pit mystery. Trans. by Remington Bramwell and "Al." St. Louis: Waverly, 1889.
7. Will. London: Vizetelly, 1888.
8. Dr. Rameau. Trans. by J. C. Curtin. New York: Rand, McNally, 1889. Also published with the title The double wrong, or A broken life.
9. A last love. Philadelphia: Lippincott, 1890.
10. Nimrod and Co. Trans. by Mary J. Serrano. New York: Cassell, 1892.
11. A debt of hatred. Trans. by E. P. Robins. New York: Cassell, 1891.
19. Pierre's soul. Trans. by Remington Bramwell. New York: Waverly, 1890. Other translations have the titles The soul of Pierre; What Pierre did with his soul; A weird gift.
36. Cloud and sunshine. Trans. by Mrs. Helen Scott. London: Vizetelly, 1887.
    Contents: "The song of the swan," "Aunt Ursula's gift."

Perrault-Harry, Mme. Myriam, 1875-   Pseud., "Myriam Harry"
  Siona. Paris: Fayard.
    1. Siona chez les Barbares. (Siona in Barbary.) 1918.
    2. Siona à Paris. 1919.
    3. Le tendre cantique de Siona. (Siona's tender song.) 1922.
    4. Siona à Berlin. 1927.

Pourrat, Henri, 1887-
  Les vaillances, farces, et gentillesses de Gaspard des montagnes. (The courage, tricks, and kind deeds of Gaspard of the mountains.) Paris: Albin Michel.
    1. Gaspard des montagnes. 1922.
    2. A la belle bergère, ou Quand Gaspard de guerre revint. (At the Belle Bergère, or When Gaspard returned from war.) 1925.
    3. Le pavillon des amourettes, ou Gaspard et les bourgeois d'Ambert. (The pavilion of love intrigues, or Gaspard and the bourgeois of Ambert.) 1930.
    4. Le tour du levant, ou Quand Gaspard mit fin à l'histoire. (The tour of the East, or When Gaspard put an end to the story.) 1931.
Prevost, Marcel, 1862-1941
  Les vierges fortes. (The vigorous virgins.) 2 vols. Paris: Lemerre, 1900.
    1. Frédérique.   2. Léa.

    1. Frédérique. Trans. by Ellen Marriage. New York: Crowell, 1902.
Proust, Marcel, 1871-1922
  A la recherche du temps perdu. (In quest of lost time.) 11 vols. Paris: Nouvelle Revue française.
    Vol. I:
    1. Du côté de chez Swann. Paris: Grasset, 1913.
    Vol. II:
    2. A l'ombre des jeunes filles en fleurs. (In the shadow of young girls in bloom.) 1919.
    Vol. III:
    3. Le côté de Guermantes, I. 1920.
    Vol. IV:
    Le côté de Guermantes, II. 1921.
    4. Sodome et Gomorrhe, I. 1921.
    Vol. V:
    Sodome et Gomorrhe, II. 1922.
    Vol. VI:
    5. La prisonnière. Sodome et Gomorrhe, III. 1923.
    Vols. VII-VIII:
    6. Albertine disparue. (Albertine vanished.) 2 vols. 1925.
    Vols. IX-X:
    7. Le temps retrouvé. 2 vols. 1927.

    Remembrance of things past. 1-6 trans. by C. K. Scott-Moncrieff; 7 trans. by Frederick A. Blossom. 4 vols. New York: Random House, 1934. 2 vols., 1941.
      Vol. I:
      1. Swann's way. New York: Holt, 1922.
      2. Within a budding grove. New York: Seltzer, 1924.
      Vol. II:
      3. The Guermantes way. New York: Seltzer, 1925.
      4. Cities of the plain, I. New York: Boni, 1927.
      Vol. III:
      Cities of the plain, II. New York: Boni, 1929.
      5. The captive. New York: Boni, 1929.
      Vol. IV:
      6. The sweet cheat gone. New York: Boni, 1930.
      7. The past recaptured. New York: Boni, 1932. Title of British translation: Time regained.
"Provence, Marcel," see Jouhandeau, Marcel.
Psichari, Ernest, 1883-1914
  L'appel des armes. (The call to arms.) Paris: Oudin, 1913.
  Le voyage du centurion. Paris: Conard, 1915.

    (2) A soldier's pilgrimage. Trans. by E. M. Walker and M. Harriet M. Capes. London: Melrose, 1917.
"Randau, Robert," see Arnaud, Robert.

FRENCH

Ratel, Simonne
  Isabelle Comtat. Paris: Plon.
    1. La maison des Bories. 1932.
    2. Le raisin vert. 1935.

    1. The house in the hills. Trans. by Eric Sutton. New York: Macmillan, 1934.
    2. The green grape. Trans. by Marie Sneyd and E. Sutton. New York: Macmillan, 1937.

Rod, (Louis) Edouard, 1857-1910
  La course à la mort. (The road to death.) Paris: Perrin, 1885.
  Le sens de la vie. (The sense of life.) Paris: Perrin, 1889.
  Les trois coeurs. (The three hearts.) Paris: Perrin, 1890.

  La vie privée de Michel Tessier. (The private life of Michel Tessier.) Paris: Perrin, 1893.
  La seconde vie de Michel Tessier. (The second life of Michel Tessier.) Paris: Perrin, 1894.

Rolland, Romain, 1866-1944
  Jean-Christophe. Paris: Ollendorff.
    I: 1-3. Jean-Christophe. 3 vols. 1905-6.
    II: 4-8. Jean-Christophe, II. 5 vols. 1906-9.
    III: 9-10. Jean-Christophe: la fin de la voyage. 2 vols. 1911-12.
Compiler's note: Later French editions were divided like the 3 vol. translation below. The 10 vol. edition shows individual novels most clearly.
Jean-Christophe. 10 vols. Paris: Albin Michel, 1923-29.
    1. L'aube.
    2. Le matin.
    3. L'adolescent.
    4. La révolte.
    5. La foire sur la place.
      (The fair in the market.)
    6. Antoinette.
    7. Dans la maison.
    8. Les amis. (The friends.)
    9. Le buisson ardent.
    10. La nouvelle journée.

  Jean-Christophe. Trans. by Gilbert Cannan. 1 vol. New York: Holt, 1927.
    Book I. Jean-Christophe. 1 vol. 1910.
      1. Dawn.
      2. Morning.
      3. Youth.
      4. Revolt.
    Book II. Jean-Christophe in Paris. 1 vol. 1911.
      5. The market place.
      6. Antoinette.
      7. The house.
    Book III. Journey's end. 1 vol. 1913.
      8. Love and friendship.
      9. The burning bush.
      10. The new dawn.

  L'âme enchantée. 4 vols. in 7. Paris: Ollendorff, 1922-23.
    1. Annette et Sylvie.
    2. L'été.
    3. Mère et fils. 2 vols.
    4. L'annonciatrice. (Forewarning.)
      I. La mort d'un monde.
      II. L'enfantement. 2 vols.

  The soul enchanted. New York: Holt.
    1. Annette and Sylvie. Trans. by Ben Ray Redman. 1925.
    2. Summer. Trans. by Eleanor Stimson and Van Wyck Brooks. 1925.
    3. Mother and son. Trans. by V. W. Brooks. 1927.
    4. I. Death of a world. Trans. by Amalia De Alberti. 1933. II. A world in birth. Trans. by A. De Alberti. 1934. British edition in 2 vols.: The combat and Via sacra.

"Romains, Jules," pseud. of Louis Farigoule, 1885-
  Psyché. Paris: Gallimard, Nouvelle Revue française.
    1. Lucienne. 1922.

2. Le dieu des corps. (The god of the body.) 1928.
  3. Quand le navire . . . (When the ship . . .) 1929.

The body's rapture. Trans. by John Rodker. 3 vols. in 1. New York: Liveright, 1937.
  1. Lucienne. Trans. by Waldo Frank. New York: Boni & Liveright, 1925.

Les hommes de bonne volonté. 1-18, Paris: Flammarion. 19-27, New York: Editions de la Maison française.
  1. Le 6 octobre. 1932.
  2. Crime de Quinette. 1932.
  3. Les amours enfantines. 1932.
  4. Eros de Paris. 1932.
  5. Les superbes. 1933.
  6. Les humbles. 1933.
  7. Recherche d'une église. (Quest for a church.)
  8. Province. 1934.
  9. Montée des périls. (Ascent of perils.) 1935.
  10. Les pouvoirs. 1935.
  11. Recours à l'abîme. (Turn to perdition.) 1936.
  12. Les créateurs. (Creators.) 1936.
  13. Mission à Rome. 1937.
  14. Le drapeau noir. 1937.
  15. Prélude à Verdun. 1938.
  16. Verdun. 1938.
  17. Vorge contre Quinette. 1939.
  18. La douceur de la vie. 1939.
  19. Cette grande lueur à l'est. 1941.
  20. Le monde est ton aventure. 1941.
  21. Journées dans la montagne. 1942.
  22. Les travaux et les joies. 1943.
  23. Naissance de la bande. 1944.
  24. Comparutions. 1944.
  25. Le tapis magique.
  26. Françoise.
  27. Le 7 octobre. 1946.

Men of good will. 1-3 trans. by Warre Bradley Welles; 4-27 trans. by Gerard Hopkins. 14 vols. New York: Knopf.
  Vol. I. Men of good will. 1933.
    1. The sixth of October.
    2. Quinette's crime.
  Vol. II. Passion's pilgrims. 1934.
    3. Childhood's loves.
    4. Eros in Paris.
  Vol. III. The proud and the meek. 1934.
    5. The proud.
    6. The meek.
  Vol. IV. The world from below. 1935.
    7. The lonely.
    8. Provincial interlude.
  Vol. V. The earth trembles. 1936.
    9. Flood warning.
    10. The powers that be.
  Vol. VI. The depths and the heights. 1937.
    11. To the gutter.
    12. To the stars.
  Vol. VII. Death of a world. 1938.
    13. Mission to Rome.
    14. The black flag.
  Vol. VIII. Verdun. 1939.
    15. The prelude.
    16. The battle.
  Vol. IX. Aftermath. 1941.
    17. Vorge against Quinette.
    18. The sweets of life.
  Vol. X. The new day. 1942.
    19. Promise of dawn.
    20. The world is your adventure.

FRENCH

    Vol. XI. Work and play. 1944.
      21. Mountain days.   22. Work and play.
    Vol. XII. The wind is rising. 1946.
      23. The gathering of the gangs.   24. Offered in evidence.
    Vol. XIII. Escape in passion. 1946.
      25. The magic carpet.   26. Françoise.
    Vol. XIV. 27. Seventh of October, 1946.

"Sand, George," pseud. of Amandine Aurore Lucie (Dupin), baronne Dudevant, 1804-76
  Consuelo. 8 vols. Paris: De Potter, 1842-43.
  La comtesse de Rudolstadt. 5 vols. Paris: De Potter, 1843-44.

  (1) Consuelo. Trans. by Francis G. Shaw. 2 vols. Boston: Ticknor, 1846.
  (2) The Countess of Rudolstadt. Trans. by F. G. Shaw. 2d ed. Boston: Ticknor, 1847.

Sartre, Jean-Paul, 1905-
  Les chemins de la liberté. Paris: Gallimard.
    1. L'âge de raison. 1945.
    2. Le sursis. 1945.
    3. "La dernière chance." (The last chance.) In serial form, 1949.
    4. Not yet written.

  The roads to freedom. New York: Knopf.
    1. The age of reason. Trans. by Eric Sutton. 1947.
    2. The reprieve. Trans. by E. Sutton. 1947.

Sue, Eugène (Joseph Marie), 1804-57
  Les mystères du peuple et les mystères du monde, ou Histoire d'une famille de prolétaires à travers les âges. 16 vols. Paris: Rue Notre-Dame-des-Victoires, 1849-57.
Compiler's note: Titles of separate volumes are not available, except in translation as given below.

  The mysteries of the people, or The history of a proletarian family across the ages. Trans. by Daniel De Leon; 2 and 18 trans. by Solon De Leon. New York: New York Labor News Co.
    1. The gold sickle, or Hena, the virgin of the Isle of Sen; a tale of Druid Gaul. 1904.
    2. The brass bell, or The chariot of death; a tale of Caesar's Gallic invasion. 1907.
    3. The iron collar, or Faustina and Syomara; a tale of slavery under the Romans. 1909.
    4. The silver cross, or The carpenter of Nazareth; a tale of Jerusalem. 1909.
    5. The casque's lark, or Victoria, the mother of camps; a tale of the Frankish invasion of Gaul. 1909.
    6. The poniard's hilt, or Karadeucq and Ronan; a tale of Bagauders and Vagres. 1907.
    7. The branding needle, or The monastery of Charolles; a tale of the first communal charter. 1908.
    8. The abbatial crosier, or Bonaik and Septimine; a tale of a medieval abbess. 1908.
    9. The Carlovignian coins, or The daughters of Charlemagne; a tale of the ninth century. 1908.
    10. The iron arrow head, or The buckler maiden; a tale of the Northman invasion. 1909.
    11. The infant's skull, or The end of the world; a tale of the millennium. 1904.
    12. The iron trevet, or Jocelyn the champion; a tale of the Jacquerie. 1906.
    13. The iron pincers, or Mylio and Karvel; a tale of the Albigensian crusades. 1909.
    14. The pilgrim's shell, or Fergan the quarryman; a tale from the feudal times. 1904.
    15. The executioner's knife, or Joan of Arc; a tale of the Inquisition. 1910.
    16. The pocket Bible, or Christian the printer; a tale of the sixteenth century. 1910.
    17. The blacksmith's hammer, or The peasant code; a tale of the Grand Monarch. 1910.
    18. The sword of honor, or The foundation of the French Republic; a tale of the French Revolution. 1910.
    19. The galley slave's ring, or The family of Lebrenn; a tale of the French revolution of 1848. 1911.

  Le diable médecin. (The devil doctor.) Paris: Chappe.
    1. Adèle de Verneuil, ou La femme séparée de corps et de biens. (The wife separated from person and property.) 2 vols. 1855.

2. Madame de Sénancourt; la Grande Dame. 1856.
3. Emilia Lambert; la lorette. (The gay woman.) 1856.
4. Clémence Hervé; la femme de lettres. (The woman of letters.) 1857.
5. Henriette Dumesnil, ou La belle-fille. (The daughter-in-law.) 1857.

Tardiveau, René, see "Boylesve, René."
"Thévenin, Denis," see Duhamel, Georges.
Thibault, Jacques Anatole, see "France, Anatole."
Vallès, Jules Louis Joseph, 1832-85
  Jacques Vingtras. 3 vols. Paris: Fasquelle, 1924-27.
    1. L'enfant. (The child.) Paris: Charpentier, 1879.
    2. Le bachelier. (Bachelor's degree.) Paris: Charpentier, 1881.
    3. L'insurgé. (1871.) (The insurgent.) Paris: Charpentier, 1886.
Werth, Léon, 1879-
  Clavel soldat. (Clavel the soldier.) Paris: Albin Michel, 1919.
  Clavel chez les majors. (Clavel at the majors'.) Paris: Albin Michel, 1919.
"Willy," see Colette, Sidonie Gabrielle.
Zola, Emile, 1840-1902
  Les Rougon-Macquart: histoire naturelle et sociale d'une famille sous le Second Empire. In Zola, Les oeuvres complètes. Paris: Bernouard, 1918. Based on the Fasquelle texts. 1-17 first published by Charpentier; 18-20 by Charpentier & Fasquelle.
    1. La fortune des Rougon. 1871.
    2. La curée. 1872.
    3. Le ventre de Paris. 1873.
    4. La conquête de Plassans. 1874.
    5. La faute de l'Abbé Mouret. 1875.
    6. Son Excellence, Eugène Rougon. 1876.
    Compiler's note: Sequel to 1.
    7. L'assommoir. 1877.
    8. Une page d'amour. 1878.
    9. Nana. 1882.
   10. Pot-bouille. 1882.
   11. Au bonheur des dames. 1883.
   12. La joie de vivre. 1884.
   13. Germinal. 1885.
   14. L'oeuvre. 1886.
   15. La terre. 1887.
   16. La rêve. 1888.
   17. La bête humaine. 1890.
   18. L'argent. 1891.
    Compiler's note: Sequel to 2.
   19. La débâcle. 1892.
   20. Le docteur Pascal. 1893.

  Les trois villes.
    1. Lourdes. Paris: Charpentier, 1894.
    2. Rome. Paris: Charpentier, 1896.
    3. Paris. Paris: Fasquelle, 1898.

  Les quatres évangiles. Paris: Fasquelle.
    1. Fécondité. 1899.
    2. Travail. 1901
    3. Vérité. 1903.
    4. "Justice."
  Compiler's note: Planned but not written.

Compiler's note: Translations of all the above works, with original titles, are listed in Ernest Baker and James Packman, A guide to the best fiction, English and American (London: Routledge, 1932).

ITALIAN

"Annunzio, Gabriele d'," pseud. of Gaetano Rapagnetta, 1863-1938
  I romanzi della rosa. Milan: Treves.
    1. Trionfo della morte. 1894.
    2. Il piacere. 1889.
    3. L'innocente. 1892.

  The romances of the rose. New York: Richmond.
    1. The triumph of death. Trans. by Arthur Hornblow. 1896.
    2. The child of pleasure. Trans. by Georgina Harding. 1898.
    3. The intruder. Trans. by A. Hornblow. 1898. Another translation has the title The victim.

  I romanzi del giglio.
    1. Le vergini della rocce. Milan: Treves, 1896.
  Compiler's note: An unfinished trilogy. The second and third volumes were to have titles meaning "The prodigy" and "The annunciation."

  The romances of the lily.
    1. The maidens of the rocks. Trans. by Annetta Halliday-Antona and Giuseppi Antona. New York: Richmond, 1898.

  I romanzi del melagrano.
    1. Il fuoco. Milan: Treves, 1900.
  Compiler's note: An unfinished trilogy. The second and third volumes were to have titles meaning "The dictator" and "The triumph of life."

  The romances of the pomegranate.
    1. The flame of life. Trans. by "Kassandra Vivaria." Boston: Page, 1900. Another translation has the title The flame.

Beltramelli, Antonio, 1874-1930
  Il carnevale delle democrazie. (The carnival of democracy.) Rome: Mondadori.
    1. Gli uomini rossi. (The red men.) 1904.
    2. Il cavalier Mostardo. 1921.

  La vita umile. (Humble life.) Milan: Mondadori.
    1. L'ombra del mandorlo. (The shade of the almond tree.) 1920.
    2. Ahi, Giacometta, la tua ghirlandella! (Ah, Giacometta, thy little garland!) 1921.
    3. Fior d'uliva. (Olive flower.) 1925.

Bontempelli, Massimo, 1878-
  Quattro romanzi. (Four novels.)
    1. Il figlio di due madri. (The son of two mothers.) Rome: Ediz. Sapientia, 1929.
  Compiler's note: An unfinished tetralogy. The following titles were announced: "Ramiro e la fatalità," "Tutte le donne," and "Uomo senza libri." (Ramiro and fate, All the women, Man without books.)

Bresciani, Antonio, 1797-1862
  L'ebreo di Verona; racconto storico italiano. 4 vols. Fossombrone: Società tip., 1852.
  La republica romana. 2 vols. Milan: Boniardi-Pogliani, 1855.
  Lionello. 3 vols. Milan: Guigoni, 1880. Edition number not given.

  (1) The Jew of Verona; an historical tale of the Italian revolution of 1848-49. 2 vols. Baltimore: Murphy, 1854.
  (3) Lionello. Baltimore: Hedian & Piet, 1860.

Brocchi, Virgilio, 1876-
  I romanzi dell' isola sonante. (The novels of the ringing island.)

1. L'isola sonante. Milan: Treves, 1911.
   2. La bottega degli scandali. (The shop of scandals.) Milan: Treves, 1917.
   3. Sul caval della Morte Amor cavalca. (Love rides on the horse of Death.) Milan: Treves. 1920.
   4. Il lastrico dell' Inferno, ossia Le buone intenzioni. (The pavement of Hell, or Good intentions.) Rome: Mondadori, 1920.

Il ciclo del figliuol d'uomo. (The cycle of the son of man.) Milan: Mondadori.
   1. Il posto nel mondo. (The place in the world.) 1921.
   2. Il destino in pugno. (Destiny in a fist.) 1923.
   3. La rocca sull' onde. (The rock on the waves.) 1927.
   4. Il sapore della vita. (The flavor of life.) 2 vols. 1929.

L'ansia dell' eterno. (Longing for the eternal.)
   1. Il volo nuziale. (The nuptial flight.) Milan: Mondadori, 1932.
   2. I gonfaloni di Lucifero. (Lucifer's banners.) 1933.
   3. Il roveto in fiamme. (The briar in flames.) Milan: Mondadori, 1934.

Corradini, Enrico, 1868-1921
   La patria lontana. (The distant fatherland.) Milan: Treves, 1910.
   La guerra lontana. (The distant war.) Milan: Treves, 1911.

Ferro, Guglielmo, 1871-1942
   Gli ultimi barbari. (The last barbarians.) Milan: Mondadori.
      1. La terza Roma. (The third Rome.)
         I. Le due verità. 1926.
         II. La rivolta del figlio. 1927.
      2. Sudore e sangue. (Sweat and blood.) 1930.
   Compiler's note: Announced as the third volume of a tetralogy, this volume is apparently the last one published.

      1. The seven vices; a novel of Italy in our own times. Trans. by Arthur Livingston and Elisabeth Abbott. 2 vols. New York: Harcourt, Brace, 1929.
         I. The two truths.
         II. The son's rebellion.

Fogazzaro, Antonio, 1842-1911
   Piccolo mondo antico. (Little ancient world.) Milan: Galli, 1896.
   Piccolo mondo moderno. (Little modern world.) Milan: Hoepli, 1901.
   Il santo. Milan: Baldini & Castoldi, 1905.

   (1) The patriot. Trans. by Mary Prichard-Agnetti. New York, London: Putnam's, 1906.
   (2) The sinner. Trans. by M. Prichard-Agnetti. New York, London: Putnam's, 1907.
   (3) The saint. Trans. by M. Prichard-Agnetti. New York, London: Putnam's, 1906.

   Leila. Milan: Baldini & Castoldi, 1910.
   Compiler's note: A companion novel to Il santo.

   Leila. Trans. by M. Prichard-Agnetti. New York: Doran, 1911.

Giovagnoli, Rafaello, 1838-1915
   Opimia; scene storiche del secolo IV dell' èra romana. (Historical scenes of the fourth century of the Roman era.) Rome: Capaccini, 1875.
   Plautilla; racconto storico del secolo VI dell' èra romana. (Historical tale of the sixth century of the Roman era.) 4th ed. Rome: Capaccini, 1878.
   Saturnino; racconto storico del secolo VII dell' èra romana. Milan: Carrara, 1879.
   Spartaco; racconto storico del secolo VII dell' èra romana. 2 vols. Rome: L'Italie, 1874.
   La guerra sociale; Aquilonia; racconto storico del secolo VII dell' èra romana. (The social war; Aquilonia.) Milan: Carrara, 1884.
   Messalina; romanzo storico. 2d ed. Rome: Perino, 1886.
   Faustina; scene storiche del secolo X dell' èra romana. Milan: Carrara, 1881.

ITALIAN

Giovanazzi, Giuseppe, 1885-
  La grotta dell' orso. (The cave of the bear.) Florence: Bemporad, 1936.
  La culla tra la congiura. (The cradle in the midst of the conspiracy.) Florence: Bemporad, 1938.
Gotta, Salvator, 1887-
  I Vela. (The Vela family.) Milan: Baldini & Castoldi.
    1. Pia. 1912.
    2. Il figlio inquieto. (The restless son.) 1917.
    3. La più bella donna del mondo. (The most beautiful woman in the world.) 1919.
    4. L'amante provinciale. (The provincial lover.) 1919.
    5. Tre mondi. (Three worlds.) 1921.
    6. Il prima re. (The first king.) 1922.
    7. La donna mia. (My lady.) 1924.
    8. Lula o La bufera infernal. (Lula or The infernal tempest.) 1925.
    9. Ombra la moglie bella. (Ombra the beautiful wife.) 1926.
    10. Il nome tuo. (Thy name.) 1927.
    11. La sagra della vergini. (The fair of the maidens.) 1928.
    12. Il peccato originale. (Original sin.) 1929.
    13. Tu, la mia ricchezza. (Thou, my treasure.) 1930.
    14. L'amica dell' ombra. (The friend of the shadow.) 1931.
    15. Il gioco dei colori. (The game of colors.) 1932.
    16. I figli degli amanti. (The sons of the lovers.) 1933.
    17. Lilith. 1934.
    18. Il paradiso terrestre. (The earthly paradise.) 1935.
    19. L'angelo ferito. (The wounded angel.) 1936.
    20. Portofino. 1937.
    21. I giganti innamorati. (The enamored giants.) 1938.
    22. Amina. 1929.
    23. La sposa giovane. (The young bride.) 1943.
    24. I sensitivi. (The sensitive ones.) Milan: Mondadori, 1946.
Govoni, Corrado, 1882-
  Giovinezza, fermati: sèi bella. (Youth, stay: thou art beautiful.) Milan: Mondadori.
    1. Anche l'ombra è sole. (Even the shade is sun.) 1921.
    2. La terra contro il cielo. (The earth against the sky.) 1922.
Rapagnetta, Gaetano, see "Annunzio, Gabriele d'."
Saponaro, Michele, 1885-
  Tra la vita e il sogno. (Between life and the dream.)
    1. Fiorella. Milan: Vitagliano, 1920.
    2. L'altra sorella. (The other sister.) Milan: Mondadori, 1922.

  Un uomo. (A man.)
    1. L'adolescenza. Milan: 1925.
    2. La giovinezza. (Youth.) Milan: Mondadori, 1926.
"Silone, Ignazio," pseud. of Secondo Tranquilli, 1900-
  Pane e vino. New ed. Lugano: Capolago, 1937.
  Il seme sotto la neve. Rome: Editrice Faro, 1945.

  (1) Bread and wine. Trans. by Gwenda David and Eric Mosbacher. New York, London: Harper, 1937.
  (2) The seed beneath the snow. Trans. by Frances Frenaye. New York, London: Harper, 1942.
Tranquilli, Secondo, see "Silone, Ignazio."
Verga, Giovanni, 1840-1922
  I Vinti. (The Vinti family.) Milan: Treves.
    1. I malavoglia. (Malevolents.) 1881.
    2. Maestro-don Gesualdo. 1889.
  Compiler's note: An unfinished sequence. The following titles were announced: "La contessa di Leyra," "L'onorevole Scipione," "L'uomo di Lusso."

    1. The house by the medlar tree. Trans. by Mary A. Craig. New York: Harper, 1890.
    2. Maestro-don Gesualdo. Trans. by D. H. Lawrence. New York: Boni, 1923.

SPANISH AND PORTUGUESE

Place of publication distinguishes between Spanish, Portuguese, and Latin American authors.

"Azorín," see Martinez Ruiz, José.
Baroja y Nessi, Pio, 1872-
  Tierra vasca. (Basque country.)
    1. La casa de Aizgorri. (The house of Aizgorri.) Bilboa: 1900.
    2. El mayorazgo de Labraz. (The eldest son of Labraz.) Barcelona: Henrich, 1903.
    3. Zalacain el aventurero. (Zalacain the adventurer.) Barcelona: Domenech, 1909.

    2. The lord of Labraz. Trans. by Aubrey F. G. Bell. New York: Knopf, 1926.

  La vida fantastica. (Fantastic life.)
    1. Camino de perfección. (Way of perfection.) Madrid: Rodríguez Serra, 1902.
    2. Aventuras, inventos, y mixtificaciones de Silvestre Paradox. (Adventures, inventions, and mystifications of Silvestre Paradox.) Madrid: 1901.
    3. Paradox, rey. Madrid: 1906.

    3. Paradox, king. Trans. by Neville Barbour. London: Wishart, 1931.

  La lucha por la vida. 3 vols. Madrid: 1904.
    1. La busca.
    2. Mala hierba.
    3. Aurora roja.

"The struggle for life." Trans. by Isaac Goldberg. New York: Knopf.
    1. The quest. 1922.
    2. Weeds. 1923.
    3. Red dawn. 1924.

  El pasado. (The past.)
    1. La feria de los discretos. Madrid: 1905.
    2. Los últimos romanticos. (The last romantics.) Madrid: Sucesores de Hernando, 1906.
    3. Las tragedias grotescas. (Grotesque tragedies.) Madrid: Sucesores de Hernando, 1907.

    1. The city of the discreet. Trans. by Jacob S. Fasset, Jr. New York: Knopf, 1917.

  La raza. (The race.)
    1. La dama errante. (The errant lady.) Madrid: 1908.
    2. La ciudad de la niebla. (The city of the mist.) Madrid: Sucesores de Hernando, 1909.
    3. El arbol de la ciencia. Madrid: Prieto, 1912.

    3. The tree of knowledge. Trans. by Aubrey F. G. Bell. New York: Knopf, 1928.

  Las ciudades. (The cities.)
    1. O César o nada. Madrid: Renacimiento, 1910.
    2. El mundo es así. (The world is thus.) Madrid: 1911.
    3. La sensualidad pervertida; ensayos amorosos de un hombre ingenuo en una época de decadencia. (Perverted sensuality; amorous experiments of an ingenuous young man in a decadent epoch.) Madrid: Caro Raggio, 1920.

    1. Caesar or nothing. Trans. by Louis How. New York: Knopf, 1919.

  El mar. (The sea.)
    1. Las inquietudes de Shanti Andía. (The anxieties of Shanti Andía.) Madrid: Prieto, 1911.
    2. El laberinto de las sirenas. (The labyrinth of the sirens.) Madrid: Caro Raggio, 1923.

SPANISH AND PORTUGUESE

    3. Los pilotos de altura. (The sea pilots.) Madrid: Caro Raggio, 1930.
    4. La estrella del capitán Chimista. (The star of Captain Chimista.) Madrid: Caro Raggio, 1930.

Memorias de un hombre de acción. (Memoirs of a man of action.) Madrid: Caro Raggio. Compiler's note: Listed in the order given in the Espasa-Calpe edition of Baroja, Obras completas. 19-22 were first published by Espasa-Calpe.
    1. El aprendiz de conspirador. (The conspirator's apprentice.) 1913.
    2. El escuadron del brigante. (The squadron of the brigand.) 1921.
    3. Los caminos del mundo. (The roads of the world.) 1921.
    4. Con la pluma y con el sable; crónica de 1820 a 1823. (With pen and cutlass; chronicle of 1820 to 1823.) 1921.
    5. Los recursos de la astucia. (The resources of cunning.) 1920.
    6. La ruta de aventurero. (The way of the adventurer.) 1921.
    7. Los contrastes de la vida. (Contrasts of life.) 1920.
    8. La veleta de Gastizar. (The weather vane of Gastizar.) 1918.
    9. Los caudillos de 1830. (The leaders of 1830.) 1918.
  10. La Isabelina. 1919.
  11. El sabor de la venganza. (The taste of vengeance.) 1921.
  12. Las furias. (The furies.) 1921.
  13. El amor, el dandysmo, y la intriga. (Love, dandyism, and intrigue.) 1923.
  14. Las figuras de cera. (Wax figures.) 1924.
  15. La nave de los locos. (The ship of fools.) 1925.
  16. Las mascaradas sangrientas. (Bloody masquerades.) 1928.
  17. Humano enigma. 1928.
  18. La senda dolorosa. (The painful path.) 1928.
  19. Los confidentes audaces. (Bold spies.) 1931.
  20. La venta de Mirambel. (The inn of Mirambel.) 1931.
  21. Crónica escandalosa. (Scandalous chronicle.) 1935.
  22. Desde el principio hasta el fino. (From the beginning to the end.) 1935.

Agonías de nuestra tiempo. (Agonies of our time.) Madrid: Caro Raggio.
    1. El gran torbellino del mundo. (The great whirlwind of the world.) 1926.
    2. Las veleidades de la fortune. (Inconstancies of fortune.) 1926.
    3. Los amores tardíos. (Late loves.) 1927.

La selva oscura. (The dark forest.) Madrid: Espasa-Calpe.
    1. La familia de Errotacho. 1932.
    2. El cabo de los tormentos. (The end of torture.) 1932.
    3. Los visionarios. (Visionaries.) 1937.

La juventud perdida. (Lost youth.) Madrid: Espasa-Calpe.
    1. Las noches del Buen Retiro. (Buen Retiro evenings.) 1934.
    2. El cura de Monléon. (The priest of Monléon.) 1936.
    3. Locuras de carnaval. (Carnival follies.) 1937.
    Compiler's note: Five stories.

Blanco-Fombona, Rufino, 1874-
  El hombre de hierro. (The man of iron.) 1907.
  El hombre de oro. Madrid: 1915.

  (2) The man of gold. Trans. by Isaac Goldberg. New York: Brentano, 1920.

Blasco Ibañez, Vicente, 1867-1928
  Arroz y tartana. (Rice and covered wagon.) Valencia: Sempere, 1894.
  Flor de mayo. Valencia: Sempere, 1895.
  La barraca. Valencia: Sempere, 1898.
  Entre naranjos. (Among the orange trees.) Valencia: Sempere, 1900.
  Cañas y barro. Valencia: Sempere, 1903.

  (1) The three roses. Trans. by Stuart E. Grummon. New York: Dutton, 1932.
  (2) The May flower. Trans. by Arthur Livingston. New York: Dutton, 1921.

(3) The cabin. Trans. by Dr. Francis Haffkine Snow and Beatrice M. Mekota. New York: Knopf, 1917.
(4) The torrent. Trans. by Isaac Goldberg and A. Livingston. New York: Dutton, 1921.
(5) Reeds and mud. Trans. by I. Goldberg. New York: Dutton, 1928.

La catedral. Valencia: Prometeo, 1916?
El intruso. Valencia: Prometeo, 1916.
La bodega. Valencia: Sempere, 1905?

(1) The shadow of the cathedral. Trans. by Mrs. W. A. G. London: Constable, 1909.
(2) The intruder. Trans. by Mrs. W. A. Gillespie. New York: Dutton, 1928.
(3) The fruit of the vine. Trans. by Isaac Goldberg. New York: Dutton, 1919.

Los Argonautas. Valencia: Prometeo, 1914.
La tierra de todos. (Land for all.) Valencia: Prometeo, 1922.
La reina Calafia. Valencia: Prometeo, 1923.
Compiler's note: An unfinished sequence.

(2) The temptress. Trans. by Leo Angley. New York: Dutton, 1923.
(3) Queen Calafia. New York: Dutton, 1924.

El papa del mar. Valencia: Prometeo, 1925.
A los pies de Venus. Los Borgia. Valencia: Prometeo, 1926.

(1) The pope of the sea. Trans. by Arthur Livingston. New York: Dutton, 1927.
(2) The Borgias, or At the feet of Venus. Trans. by A. Livingston. New York: Dutton, 1930.

La araña negra. (The black spider.) 10 vols. in 11. Madrid: Editorial Cosmópolis, 1928.
    1. El conde de Baselga.
    2. El padre Claudio.
    3. El señor Avellaneda.
    4. El capitán Alvarez. 2 vols.
    5. La señora de Quiros.
    6. Ricardito Baselga.
    7. Marujita Quiros.
    8. Juventud á la sombra de la vejez. (Youth in the shadow of age.)
    9. En París.
  10. El casamiento de María. (Maria's wedding.)

Viva la república. 4 vols. Madrid: Editorial Cosmópolis, 1928.
    1. En el crater del volcan.
    2. La hermosa Liejesa. (The beautiful Liejesa.)
    3. La explosión.
    4. Guerra sin cuartel. (War without quarter.)

En busca del Gran Kan. Cristobal Colon. (In search of the Great Khan.) Valencia: Prometeo, 1929.
El caballero de la Virgen. Alonso de Ojeda, 1466-1515. Valencia: Prometeo, 1929.

(1) Unknown lands; the story of Columbus. Trans. by Arthur Livingston. New York: Dutton, 1929.
(2) The knight of the Virgin. Trans. by A. Livingston. New York: Dutton, 1930.

Botelho, Abel Acácio de Almeida, 1856?-1917
  Patologia social. (Social pathology.)
    1. O barão de Lavos. (The baron of Lavos.) 1891.
    2. O livro de Alda. (The book of Alda.) 4th ed. Oporto: Chardon de Lélo, 1927. 1st edition, 1898.
    3. Amanhã. (Tomorrow.) 1902.

SPANISH AND PORTUGUESE

    4. Os lázaros; figuras de hoje. (The lepers; figures of today.) Oporto: Lello, 1904.
    5. Prospero Fortuna. Oporto: Lello, 1910.
Cuéllar, José Tomás de, 1830-94. Pseud., "Facundo"
  La linterna magica. Colección de pequeñas novelas. (The magic lantern. A collection of short novels.) 7 vols. Mexico: Cumplido.
    1. Ensalada de pollos; novela de estos tiempos que corren. (Chicken salad; a novel of these current times.) 1871.
    2. Historia de Cucho el Ninfo. (Story of Cucho the Dude.) 1871.
    3. Isolina la ex-figurante; apuntes de un apuntador. (Isolina, the ex-ballet-girl; prompt book of a prompter.) 1871.
    4. Las jamonas; secretos intimos del tocador y de confidente. (Big middle-aged women; intimate secrets of the player and confidant.) 1871.
    5. Las gentes que "son así"; perfiles de hoy. (The people that are so; profiles of today.) 2 vols. 1872.
    6. Gabriel el cerrajero, o Las hijas de mi papá. (Gabriel the locksmith, or My papa's daughters.) 1872.

  La linterna magica. Segunda época. 24 vols. Barcelona: Espasa, 1889-92.
  Compiler's note: The novels included are the first four of the above series and the three below.
    1. Baile y cochina; novela de costumbres mexicana. (Bailiff and hog; novel of Mexican customs.) 1889.
    2. Los mariditos; relato de actualidad y de muchos alcances. (The hubbies; an account of the present and of vast scope.) 1870.
    3. Los fuereños y la noche buena. (The ones from the provinces and Christmas Eve.) Santander: Imp. de el Atlantico, 1890.
"Cuevas, Plotino," see Pérez de Ayala, Ramón.
Danvila y Burguero, Alfonso, 1876-
  Las luchas fratricidas de España. (The fratricidal wars of Spain.) Madrid: Espasa-Calpe, 1926-
    1. El testamento de Carlos II. (The last will of Carlos II.) 1923.
    2. La Saboyana. Fragmentos de las memorias de Adelaida de Vaureal, condesa de Crevecoeur. (The woman of Savoy. Fragments of the memoirs of Adelaide, etc.) 1924.
    3. Austrias y Borbones. 1925.
    4. El primer Carlos III. 1925.
    5. Almansa. 1926.
    6. La princesa de los Ursinos. 1927.
    7. El archiduque en Madrid. 2 vols. 1927.
    8. El Congreso de Utrech. 2 vols. 1929.
    9-10. El triunfo de las Lises. 2 vols. 1931-32.
    11. "Aun hay Pirineso." (Yet there is Pirineso.)
  Compiler's note: Announced in preparation, 1929.
Diaz, Eduardo Acevedo, 1851-1924
  Ismael. Buenos Aires: 1888.
  Nativa. Montevideo: 1890.
  Grito de gloria. (Cry of glory.) Montevideo: 1894.
"Facundo," see Cuéllar, José Tomás de.
Fingerit, Julio
  Destinos. (Destinies.) 3 vols. Buenos Aires: Samet, 1929.
    1. Destinos.
    2. Eva Gambetta.
    3. Mercedes.
Frías, Heriberto, 1870-1928
  Tomochic. 2d ed. Rio Grande City, Texas: Recio, 1894.
  Las miserias de Mexico. (The miseries of Mexico.) Mexico: Botas, n.d.
  El triunfo de Sancho Panza. Mexico: Herrera, 1911.
Gálvez, Manuel, 1862- Full name: Manuel Gálvez Baluzera
  Escenas de la guerra de Paraguay. (1865-70.) (Episodes of the war of Paraguay.) Buenos Aires: J. Roldán.
    1. Los caminos de la muerte. (Roads of death.) 1928.

    2. Humaitá. 1929.
    3. Jornadas de agonía. (Marches of agony.) 1929.

  Escenas de la época de Rosas. (Episodes of the time of Rosas.) Buenos Aires: "La Facultad," Roldán.
    1. El gaucho de "Los Cerrillos." 1931.
    2. El general Quiroga. (1790-1835.) 1932.

Machado de Assis, Joaquín María, 1839-1908
  Memorias posthumas de Braz Cubas. Rio de Janeiro: 1881.
  Quincas Borbas. 3d ed. Rio de Janeiro: 1890.

Martínez Ruiz, José, 1876- Pseud., "Azorín"
  La voluntad. (Will.) Barcelona: Enrich, 1902.
  Antonio Azorín; pequeño libro en que se habla de la vida de este peregrino señor. (A little book in which is told the life of this wandering gentleman.) Madrid: Rodríguez Serra, 1903.

Martínez Zuviría, Gustavo Adolfo, 1883- Pseud., "Hugo Wast"
  El amor vencido. (Conquered love.) Buenos Aires: Bayardo, 1921. Republished as Los ojos vendados. (Bandaged eyes.) 1927.
  El vengador. (The avenger.) Buenos Aires: Edición Libertad, 1922.
  Compiler's note: The title of the sequel to El amor vencido was announced in advance as "El amor invencible." Apparently that title was changed to El Vengador.

  Myriam la conspiradora. 20th thous. Buenos Aires: Agencia general de librería y publicaciones, 1926?
  El jinete de fuego. (The fiery horseman.) Buenos Aires: Agencia general de librería publicaciones, 1926.
  Tierra de jaguares. (Land of jaguars.) 20th thous. Buenos Aires: L. J. Rosso, 1927.

  El Kahal, Oro. Buenos Aires: Editores de H. Wast, 1938.
    Prologo: Buenos Aires, futura Babilonia. Buenos Aires: Editores de H. Wast, 1935.
    1. El Kahal. Chile: Ercilla, 1935.
    2. Oro. (Gold.) Buenos Aires: Editores de H. Wast, 1935.

  Juana Tabor. 2d ed. Buenos Aires: Thau, 1944.
  666. Buenos Aires: Editores de H. Wast, 1942.

Mateos, Juan A., 1831-1913
  Sacerdote y caudillo. (Priest and chief.) Mexico: 1869.
  Los insurgentes. (The insurgents.) Mexico: 1869.

Miró Ferrer, Gabriel, 1879-1930
  Obras completas. Madrid: Biblioteca Nueva.
    Vol. 9. Nuestro padre san Daniel. Madrid: Imp. clásica española, 1921.
    Vol. 10. El obispo leproso. (The leprous bishop.) 1926.

    (1) Our father San Daniel; scenes of clerical life. Trans. by Charlotte Remfry-Kidd. London: Benn, 1930.

"Moreno, Bento," see Teixeira de Queiroz, Francisco.

Nabuco de Araujo, José Tito, 1832-79
  Mimi; romance brazileiro. Rio de Janeiro: 1873.
  Leões e leôas. (Lions and lionesses.) Rio de Janeiro.

Ocantos, Carlos María, 1860-
  Novelas argentinas.
    1. Léon Zalvidar. Madrid: Fortanet, 1888.
    2. Quilito. Paris: Garnier, 1891.
    3. Entre dos luces. (In the twilight.) Buenos Aires: Peuser, 1892.
    4. El candidato. Entre dos luces, II. Buenos Aires: 1893.
    5. La Ginesa. Buenos Aires: Coni, 1894.
    6. Tobi. Madrid: Villaverde, 1896.
    7. Promisión. (Promise.) Madrid: Moreno, 1897.
    8. Misia Jeromita. Madrid: Moreno, 1898.
    9. Pequeñas miserias. (Little miseries.) Madrid: Moreno, 1900.

SPANISH AND PORTUGUESE

   10. Don Perfecto. Barcelona: Montaner & Simón, 1902.
   11. Nebulosa. Madrid: Moreno, 1904.
   12. El peligro. (Peril.) Madrid: Moreno, 1904.
   13. Riquez; memorias de un viejo verde. (Memoirs of a green old age.) Madrid: Moreno, 1914.
   14. Victoria. Madrid: "Revista de archivos," 1922.
   15. La cola de paja. (The tail of straw.) Madrid: "Revista de archivos," 1923.
   16. La ola. (The wave.) Madrid: "Revista de archivos," 1925.
   17. El secreto del doctor Barbado. Madrid: Hernández & Sáez, 1926.
   18. Tulia. Madrid: Hernández & Sáez, 1927.
   19. El amboscado. (The ambush.) Madrid: Hernández & Sáez, 1928.
   20. Fray Judas. (Brother Judas.) Madrid: Hernández & Sáez, 1929.

Olavarría y Ferrari, Enrique de, 1844-1918
  Episodios nacionales mexicanos. Subtitle, some separate volumes of series one: Memorias de un criollo. (Memoirs of a creole.)
    Series one, part one. 4 vols. Mexico, Barcelona: Párres, 1886-87.
    1. Las perlas de la reine Luisa. (1808.) (Queen Luisa's pearls.)
    2. La Virgen de Guadalupe. (1809-10.)
    3. La derrota de las Cruces. (1810.) (The defeat of Las Cruces.)
    4. La Virgen de los Remedios. (1810.)
    5. El puente de Calderón. (1810-11.) (The bridge of Calderón.)
    6. Las Norias de Baján. (1811.) Mexico: Imp. del Comercio, 1880.
    7. El cura de Nucupétaro. (1811.) (The priest of Nucupétaro.) Mexico: Imp. del Camercio, 1880.
    8. El treinta de julio. (1811.) (July 30.) Mexico: Imp. del Comercio, 1881.
    9. La junta de Zitácuaro. (1811.) Mexico: Imp. del Comercio, 1881.
    Series one, part two:
    1. El sitio de Cuatla. (1812.) (The siege of Cuatla.) Mexico: Mata, 1881.
    2. Una veganza insurgente. (1812-13.) (An insurgent revenge.) Mexico: Mata, 1881.
    3. La constitución del año-doce. (1812-15.) (The constitution of the year twelve.) Mexico: Mata, 1881.
    4. El castillo de Acapulco. (1813.) (The castle of Acapulco.) Mexico: Mata, 1882.
    5. El 22 de diciembre de 1815. (1813-15.)
    6. El conde de Venadito. (1816-20.)
    7. Las tres garantías. (1820-21.) (The three guarantees.)
    8. La independencia. (1821.) Mexico: Mata, 1883.
    9. El cadalso de Padilla. (1821-24.) (The scaffold of Padilla.) Mexico: Mata, 1883.
    Series two, part one:
    1. Carne de horco. (1823-24.) (Cannon fodder.)
    2. Los coyotes. (1824.)
    3. San Juan de Ulúa. (1825.)
    4. Las gallinas. (1826-27.) (The chicken-hearted.)
    5. El motín de la Acordada. (1828.) (The insurrection of la Acordada.)
    6. La expedición de Barradas. (1829.)
    7. Los hombres de bien. (1829-30.) (Honest men.)
    8. La traición de Picaluga. (1831.) (The treason of Picaluga.)
    9. El plan de Zavaleta. (1831-32.)
    Series two, part two:
    1. El treinta y tres. (1833.) (Thirty-three.)
    2. El gobierno de Herodes. (1833.) (The government of Herodes.)
    3. La estrella de los magos. (1834.) (The star of the magi.)
    4. La tela de Penelope. (1834.) (Penelope's web.)
    5. A las puertas del cielo. (1834.) (At heaven's gates.)
    6. La aurora del centralismo. (1835.) (The dawn of centralism.)
    7. El commandante Paraja. (1836.)
    8. La vuelta de Tejas. (1836.) (The return of Tejas.)
    9. Justicia de Dios. (1836-38.) (God's justice.)

Palacio Valdés, Armando, 1853-1938
  Riverita. Madrid: Hernández, 1886.
  Maximina. 2 vols. Madrid: Hernández, 1887.

  Maximina. Trans. by Nathan Haskell Dole. New York: Crowell, 1888.

  Papeles del doctor Angélico. (Papers of Doctor Angelico.) Madrid: Suarez, 1911.
  Años de juventud de dr. Angélico; nuevos papeles del doctor Angel Jiménez. (Doctor
    Angelico's years of youth; new papers, etc.) Madrid: Suarez, 1918.
  La hija de Natalia; últimos días del dr. Angélico. (Natalia's daughter; last days of
    Doctor Angelico.) Madrid: Suarez, 1924.

Pardo Bazan, Emilia, condesa de, 1852-1921
  Los pazos de Ulloa. Madrid: Administración, 1886.
  La madre naturaleza. (Mother Nature.) Madrid: Administración, 1887?

  (1) The son of the bondwoman. Trans. by Ethel M. Hearn. London: John Lane, 1907.

  Una cristiana. Madrid: La España editorial, 1890.
  La prueba. Una cristiana, II. (The proof.) Madrid: La España editorial, 1890.

  (1) A Christian woman. Trans. by Mary Springer. New York: Cassell, 1891. A later edition
    has the title The secret of the yew tree, or A Christian woman.

  Adan y Eva.
    1. La piedra angular. Madrid: A. Perez Dubrul, 1891.
    2. Doña Milagros. Madrid: Pueyo, 1894.
    3. Memorias de un solterón. (Memoirs of a bachelor.) Madrid: Administración, 1896.

    1. The angular stone. Trans. by Mary J. Serrano. New York: Cassell, 1892.

Paz, Ireneo, 1836-1924
  Amor y suplicio. (1519-40.) (Love and anguish.) 2 vols. Mexico: Rivera, 1873.
  Doña Marina. (1519-40.) 2 vols. Mexico: I. Paz, 1883.

  Leyendas historicas de la independencia. (Historical legends of independence.) Mexico:
    I. Paz.
  First series:
    1. Le licenciado verdad. (Licensed truth.) 2d ed. 1886.
    2. La corregidora. (The mayor's wife.) 2d ed. 1887.
    3. Hidalgo. 2d ed. 1887.
    4. Morelos. 2d ed. 1889.
    5. Mina. 2d ed. 1890.
    6. Guerrero. 1894.
  Second series:
    1. Antonio Rojas. 2d ed. 1895.
    2. El tigre de Alica. (The tiger of Alica.) 2d ed. 1885. Original title: Manuel Lozada.
    3. Su Alteza Serenísima. (His Most Serene Highness.) 2d ed. 1895.
    4. Maximiliano. 1890.
    5. Juárez. 2 vols. 1902.
    6. Porfirio Diaz. 2 vols. 1911.
    7. Madero. 1914.

Pérez de Ayala, Ramón, 1881- Pseud., "Plotino Cuevas"
  Tinieblas en las cumbres; historia de libertinaje. Novela postuma de Plotino Cuevas.
    (Darkness on the crests; stories of libertinism.) Madrid: Fé, 1907.
  A. M. D. G.: la vida en un colegio de jesuitas. (To the greater glory of God: life in a
    Jesuit college.) Madrid: 1910.

SPANISH AND PORTUGUESE

La pata de la raposa. Madrid: Renacimiento, 1912.
Troteras y danzaderas. (Jig and dance tunes.) Madrid: Renacimiento, 1913.

(3) The fox's paw. Trans. by Thomas Walsh. New York: Dutton, 1924.

Luna de miel, luna de hiel. (Honey moon, bitter moon.) Madrid: Mundo latino, 1923.
Los trabajos de Urbano y Simona. (The labors of Urbano and Simona.) Madrid: Mundo latino, 1923.

Obras completas. Madrid: Pueyo, 1926.
  Vol. 18. Tigre Juan, I.
  Vol. 19. El curandero de su honra. Tigre Juan II. (His honor's quack.)

  Tiger Juan, I and II. 1 vol. Trans. by Walter Starkie. New York: Macmillan, 1933.

Pérez Galdos, Benito, 1845-1920
  Episodios nacionales. (National episodes.) 26 vols. Madrid: Administración de La Guirnalda y Episodios nacionales, 1882-1912. First and second series, 20 vols. in 10. Third and fourth series, each 10 vols. in 5. Final series, 6 vols.
  First series. Madrid: Martinez.
  1. Trafalgar. 1873.
  2. La corte de Carlos IV. 1873.
  3. El 19 de marzo y el 2 de mayo. (March 19 and May 2.) 1873.
  4. Bailén. 1873.
  5. Napoleon en Chamartin. 1874.
  6. Zaragoza. 1874.
  7. Gerona. 1874.
  8. Cádiz. 1874.
  9. Juan Martin el Empecinado. (Juan Martin the Incorrigible.) 1874.
 10. La batalla de los Arapiles. (The battle of Arapiles.) 1875.

  1. Trafalgar. Trans. by Clara Bell. New York: Gottsberger, 1884.
  2. The court of Charles IV; a romance of the Escorial. Trans. by Clara Bell. New York: Gottsberger, 1888.
  6. Saragossa. Trans. by Minna C. Smith. Boston: Little, Brown, 1899.

Second series. Madrid: Sucesores de Hernando.
  1. El equipaje del rey José. (The carriage of King José.) 1875.
  2. Memorias de un cortesano de 1815. (Memoirs of a courtier of 1815.) 1875.
  3. La segunda casaca. (The second marriage.) 1876.
  4. El grande oriente. (The great east.) 1876.
  5. El 7 de julio. (July 7.) 1876.
  6. Los cien mil hijos de San Luis. (The hundred thousand sons of Saint Louis.) 1877.
  7. El terror de 1824. 1877.
  8. Un voluntario realista. (A royalist volunteer.) 1878.
  9. Los apostólicos. 1879.
 10. Un faccioso más y algunos frailes menos. (One rebel more and some friars fewer.) 1879.
Third series. Madrid: Páez.
  1. Zumalacárregui. 1898.
  2. Mendizábal. 1898.
  3. De Oñate a la Granja. (From Oñate to La Granja.) 1898.
  4. Luchana. 1899.
  5. La campaña del maestrazgo. (The country under the grand-master's jurisdiction.) 1899.
  6. La estafeta romantica. (The romantic courier.) 1899.
  7. Vergara. 1899.
  8. Montes de Oca. (Mountains of Oca.) 1900.
  9. Los Ayacuchos. 1900.

10. Bodas reales. (Royal weddings.) 1900.

Fourth series. Madrid: Perlado, Páez.
1. Las tormentas del 48. (The tempests of 48.) 1902.
2. Narváez. 1902.
3. Los duendes de la camarilla. (The ghosts of the coterie.) 1903.
4. La revolución de julio. (The July revolution.) 1903.
5. O'Donnell. 1904.
6. Aita Tettauen. 1905-6.
7. Carlos VI en la Rápita. 1905.
8. La vuelta al mundo en La Numancia. (The return to the world in La Numancia.) 1906.
9. Prim. 1906.
10. La de los tristes destinos. (She of the sad fates.) 1907.

Final series. Madrid: Perlado, Páez.
1. España sin rey. (Spain without a king.) 1908.
2. España trágica. 1909.
3. Amadeo Primero. 1910.
4. La primera república. (The first republic.) 1910.
5. De Cartago a Sagunto. (From Carthage to Sagunto.) 1911.
6. Cánovas. 1912.

Novelas españolas contemporáneas. (Contemporary Spanish novels.)
La primera época. (The first epoch.)
1. Doña Perfecta. Madrid: 1876.
2. Gloria. 2 vols. Madrid: Obras de Pérez Galdós, 1876-77.
3. La familia de León Roch. 2 vols. Madrid: 1876-77.
4. Marianela. Madrid: Tello, 1878.

1. Doña Perfecta. Trans. by D. P. W. London: Tinsley, 1880.
2. Gloria. Trans. by N. Wetherell. 2 vols. London: 1879.
3. León Roch. Trans. by Clara Bell. 2 vols. New York: Gottsberger, 1888.
4. Marianela. Trans. by C. Bell. New York: Gottsberger, 1883.

La segunda época. (The second epoch.) 1-14, Madrid: "La Guirnalda."
1. La desheredada. (The disinherited.) 2 vols. 1881.
2. El amigo Manso. (Friend Manso.) 1882.
3. El doctor Centeno. 2 vols. 1883.
4. Tormento. 1884.
5. La de Bringas. (The woman of Bringas.) 1884.
6. Lo prohibido. (The prohibited.) 2 vols. 1885.
7. Fortunato y Jacinta; dos historias de casadas. (Fortunato and Jacinta; two stories of married people.) 4 vols. 1887.
8. Miau. 1888.
9. La incógnita. (The unknown woman.) 1889.
10. Realidad. (Reality.) 1890.
11. Angel Guerra. 3 vols. 1890-91.
12. Tristana. 1892.
13. Nazarín. 1895.
14. Halma. 1895.
15. Misericordia. (Pity.) Madrid: Tello, 1897.
16. El abuelo. (The grandfather.) Madrid: Tello, 1897.
17. Casandra. Madrid: Perlado, Páez, 1905.
18. El caballero encantado. (The enchanted cavalier.) Madrid: Perlado, Páez, 1909.

"Torquemada." Madrid: "La Guirnalda."
1. Torquemada en la hoguera. (Torquemada in the fire.) 1889.
2. Torquemada en la cruz. (Torquemada on the cross.) 1893.
3. Torquemada en el Purgatorio. (Torquemada in purgatory.) 1894.
4. Torquemada y San Pedro. (Torquemada and Saint Peter.) 1895.

Compiler's note: This tetralogy is related to Novelas españolas contemporáneas.

Rabasa, Emilio, 1856-1930. Pseud., "Sancho Polo"
La bola. (The revolution.) Mexico: 1887.

SPANISH AND PORTUGUESE

    La gran ciencia. (The great science.) Mexico: 1887.
    El cuarto poder. (The fourth estate.) 2 vols. Mexico: Spíndola, 1888.
        1. El cuarto poder.   2. Moneda falsa. (Counterfeit coins.)
Riva Palacio, Vicente, 1832-96
    Monja y casada, virgen y martir; historia de los tiempos de la Inquisición. (Nun and wife, virgin and martyr; story of the time of the Inquisition.) Mexico: Imp. de la Constitución Social, 1868.
    Martin Garatuza; memorias de la Inquisición. Mexico: Imp. de la Constitución Social, 1868.
"Sancho Polo," see Rabasa, Emilio.
Sender, Ramon José, 1901-
    Cronica del alba. Mexico: Editorial Nuevo Mundo, 1942.
    Compiler's note: First of a series of novels on modern Spain.

    Chronicle of dawn. Trans. by Willard R. Trask. New York: Doubleday, Doran, 1944.
Teixeira de Queiroz, Francisco, 1848-1919. Pseud., "Bento Moreno"
    Comedia do campo. Scenas do Minho. (Comedy of the countryside.)
        1. Os meus primeiros contos. (My first stories.) Lisbon: Mattos Moreira, 1876.
        Compiler's note: Short stories.
        2. Amor divino; estudo pathologico de uma santa. (Divine love; pathological study of a saint.) Lisbon: Pacheco & Carmo, 1877. 2d ed., completely revised, 1915.
        3. Antonio Fogueira.
        4. Novos contos de Bento Moreno. (New stories.) Lisbon: Tavares Cardoso, 1887.
        5. Amores, amores. Psychose do amor. (Love affairs. Psychosis of love.) Lisbon: A. M. Pereira, 1897.
        6. A nossa gente. (Our people.) 1900.
        7. A cantadeira. (The singer.) 1913.
        8. Ao sol e á chuva. (Under the sun and the rain.) Lisbon: A. M. Pereira, 1916.

    Comedia burgueza. (Bourgeois comedy.)
        1. Os noivos. (The betrothed.) Lisbon: D. Corazzi, 1879.
        2. O Sallustio Nogueira; estudo de politica contemporanea. Lisbon: Mattos Moreira & Cardoso, 1883.
        3. D. Agostinho. Lisbon: Tavares Cardoso, 1894.
        4. A morte de D. Agostinho. (The death of Dom Agostinho.) Lisbon: Pereira, 1895.
        5. O famoso Galrão. (The famous Galrão.)
        6. A caridade em Lisboa. (Charity in Lisbon.)
        7. Cartas d'amor. (Love letters.)
        8. A grande chimera. (The great chimera.)
Valle-Arizpe, Artemio, 1888-
    Tradiciones, leyendas, y sucedidos del México virreinal. (Traditions, legends, and events of viceregal Mexico.)
        1. Del tiempo pasado. (Concerning time past.) 1932.
        2. Amores y picardías. (Loves and knavery.) 1932.
        3. Virreyes y virreinas de la Nueva España. (Viceroys of New Spain and their wives.) 2 vols. 1933.
        4. Libro de estampas. (Book of engravings.) 1934.
        5. Historias de vivos y muertes. (Stories of the living and the dead.) 1936.
Valle-Inclan, Ramón del, 1870-1936
    Memorias del marqués de Bradomín. Madrid: Pueyo, 1907. Also published in 2 vols.
        1. Sonata de primavera. (Sonata of spring.) 1904.
        2. Sonata de estio. (Sonata of summer.) 1903.
        3. Sonata de otoño. (Sonata of autumn.) 1902.
        4. Sonata de invierno. (Sonata of winter.) 1905.
Compiler's note: This sequence is included, despite its brevity, because of its sequence structure.

    The pleasant memoirs of the Marquis of Bradomin; four sonatas. Trans. by May Heywood Broun and Thomas Walsh. 1 vol. New York: Harcourt, Brace, 1924.

    La guerra carlista. (The Carlist war.) 3 vols. Madrid: Suarez, n.d.
        1. Los cruzados de la causa. (Crusaders of the cause.) 1908.

2. *El resplandor de la hoguera*. (The splendor of the flame.) Madrid: Fé, 1909.
3. *Gerifaltes de antaño*. (Gerfalcons of long ago.) 1909.

El ruedo ibérico. (The Spanish border.) Madrid: Imp. Rivadeneyra. Vols. 21 and 22 of *Opera omnia*.
1. *La corte de los milagros*. (The court of miracles.)
2. *Viva mi dueño*. (Long live my master.) 1928.
Compiler's note: An unfinished sequence.
"Wast, Hugo," see Martínez Zuviría, Gustavo Adolfo.

Teutonic Languages

DUTCH

Ammers-Küller, Jo van, 1884-
  De opstandigen. (The rebels.) Amsterdam: Meulenhoff.
    1. De opstandigen; een familie-roman in drie boeken. 1925.
    2. Vrouwenkruistocht. (Women's crusade.) 1930.
  Author's note: "It is my intention to complete the study in a third part."

    1. The rebel generation. Trans. by M. W. Hoper. New York: Dutton, 1928.
    2. No surrender. Trans. by W. D. Robson-Scott. New York: Dutton, 1931.

  Heeren, knechten, en vrouwen; de geschiedenis van een Amsterdamsche regentenfamilie in de
    jaren 1778 tot 1813. (Masters, servants, and wives; the history of an Amsterdam govern-
    ing family in the years 1778-1813.) Amsterdam: Meulenhoff.
    1. De patriotten. (1778-87.) 1934-35.
    2. De Sans-culotten. (1792-95.) 1936.
    3. De getrouwen. (1799-1813.) (The trusty followers.) 1938.

    1-2. The House of Tavelinck. Trans. by A. v. A. van Duym and Edmund Gilligan. 1 vol. New
      York: Farrar & Rinehart, 1938.
Bosboom-Toussaint, Mevrouw Anna Louise Geertruida, 1812-86
  Leycester in Nederland. 2 vols. 1846.
  De vrouwen uit het Leycestersche tijdvak. (The women of the Leycester period.) 2 vols.
    Amsterdam: Beijerinck, 1850.
  Gideon Florenz. 2 vols. Amsterdam: Kraay, 1854.
Brouwer, Petrus van Limburg, 1798-1847
  Charicles en Euphorion. Leyden: Sijthoff, 1831.
  Diophanes. 2 vols. Leyden: Sijthoff, 1838.
Busken-Huet, Conrad, 1826-86
  Die Bruce's. 2 vols. Haarlem: H. D. Tjeenk Willink, 1898. (Written 1875-77.)
    1. Jozefine.
    2. Robert Bruce's leerjaren. (Robert Bruce's apprenticeship.)
Couperus, Louis Marie Anne, 1863-1923
  De boeken der kleine zielen. Amsterdam: Veen.
    1. De kleine zielen. 1901.   3. Zielenschemering. 1902.
    2. Het late leven. 1902.   4. Het heilige weten. (The sacred knowledge.) 1903.

  The books of the small souls. Trans. by Alexander Teixeira de Mattos. 1 vol. New York:
    Dodd, Mead, 1932.
    1. Small souls. 1914.   3. The twilight of the souls. 1917.
    2. The later life. 1915.   4. Dr. Adriaan. 1918.
Fabricius, Johan Wigmore, 1899-
  Komedianten trokken voorbij. (Comedians went past.) The Hague: Leopold, 1931.
  Melodie der verten. The Hague: Leopold, 1932.
  De dans om de galg. (The dance around the gallows.) The Hague: Leopold, 1934.

  (1-3) The son of Marietta. Trans. by Irene Clephane and David Hallett. 1 vol. Boston:
    Little, Brown, 1936.
Groenigen, August P. van
  Een nest menschen. (A nest of people.) Amsterdam: Van Looy, 1895.
  Compiler's note: The first volume of an unfinished novel cycle.

Querido, Israel, 1874-
  Amsterdamsch epos. (Epic of Amsterdam.) Amsterdam: Maatschappij voor goede en goedkoope lectuur.
    1. De Jordaan. 1912.
    2. De Jordaan: Van Nes en zeedijk. (Van Nes and the sea dike.) 1914.
Robbers, Herman, 1868-
  De roman van een gezin. (The novel of a family.) Amsterdam: Robbers.
    1. De lukkige familie. (The lucky family.) 1909.
    2. Één voor één. (One by one.) 1910.

    1. The fortunes of a household. Trans. by Helen Chilton and Bernard Miall. New York: Knopf, 1924.
Walschap, Gérard, 1898-
  De familie Roothoofd. 1 vol. Rotterdam: Nijgh & Van Ditmar, 1939.
    1. Adelaide. 1929.   2. Eric. 1931.   3. Carla. 1933.

GERMAN AND LOW GERMAN

"Alexis, Willibald," see Häring, Wilhelm.
Arnim, Ludwig Achim, Freiherr von, 1781-1831
  Die Kronenwächter. (The guardians of the crown.)
  Compiler's note: An unfinished tetralogy.
    1. Bertholds erstes und zweites Leben. (Berthold's first and second lives.) Berlin: 1817.
    2. Sämmtliche Werke, vol. 4. Berlin: 1854.
Asch, Shalom, 1880-
  Die Sintflut. (The deluge.) Trans. from the Yiddish. 1 vol. Berlin: Zsolnay, 1930. Yiddish edition: Farn mabl, 1927-32.
    1. Petersburg. 1929.   2. Warschau. 1930.   3. Moskau. 1930.

  Three cities. Trans. by Willa and Edwin Muir. 1 vol. New York: Putnam's, 1933.
    1. Petersburg.   2. Warsaw.   3. Moscow.

  Der Man fun Notseres. 1939.

  (1) The Nazarene. Trans. from the Yiddish by Maurice Samuels. New York: Putnam's, 1939.
  (2) The apostle. Trans. from the Yiddish by M. Samuels. New York: Putnam's, 1943.
  Compiler's note: Published only in English translation.
  (3) Mary. Trans. from the Yiddish by Leo Steinberg. New York: Putnam's, 1949.
Bahr, Hermann, 1863-1934
  Die Rahl. Berlin: Fischer, 1909.
  Drut. Berlin: Fischer, 1909.
  O Mensch. (O man!) Berlin: Fischer, 1910.

  Himmelfahrt. (Ascension into heaven.) Berlin: Fischer, 1916.
  Die Rotte Korahs. (Korah's gang.) Berlin: Fischer, 1919.
  Der inwendige Garten. (The inner garden.) Hildesheim: Borgmeyer, 1927.
  Compiler's note: The two trilogies are connected.
Bartsch, Rudolph Hans, 1873-
  Grenzen der Menschheit. (Limitations of humanity.) 3 vols. Leipzig: Staackmann, 1923.
    1. Der Königsgedanke. (King's thought.)
    2. Der Satansgedanke. (Satan's thought.)
    3. Erlösung. (Salvation.) First published as Er, ein Buch der Andacht. (He, a book of devotion.) 1915.
Berens-Totenohl, Josefa, 1891-
  Der Femhof. (The secret court.) Jena: Diederichs, 1934.
  Frau Magdlene. Jena: Diederichs, 1935.

GERMAN AND LOW GERMAN

Beumelburg, Werner, 1899-
  Die Gruppe Bosemüller. (The Bosemüller group.) Oldenburg: Stalling, 1930.
  Das eherne Gesetz; ein Buch für die Kommenden. (The bronze law; a book for coming generations.) Oldenburg: Stalling, 1934.
Bloem, Walter (Julius Gustav), 1868-
  Der krasse Fuchs. (The freshman.) Berlin: Vita, 1906.
  Der Paragraphenlehrling. (The law student.) Berlin: Vita, 1907.

  Das eiserne Jahr. Die Kriegsroman-Trilogie von siebzig-einundsiebzig. (The war novel trilogy of '70-71.) 1 vol. Berlin: Globus Verlag, 1940.
    1. Heer wider Heer. (Army against army.) First published as Das eiserne Jahr. Leipzig: Grethlein, 1910.
    2. Volk wider Volk. (People against people.) Leipzig: Grethlein, 1912.
    3. Die Schmiede der Zukunft. (The forge of the future.) Leipzig: Grethlein, 1913.

    1. The iron year. Trans. by Stella Bloch. London, New York: John Lane, 1914.

  Kriegserlebnis. (1914-18.) (War experiences.) 3 vols. Leipzig: Grethlein, 1934. 1 vol., without series title. Leipzig: Goten-Verlag, 1939.
    1. Vormarsch. (Advance.) Leipzig: Grethlein, 1916.
    2. Sturmsignal — ! (Charge!) Leipzig: Grethlein, 1919.
    3. Das Ganze — halt! (Company — halt!)

  Sohn seines Landes. Leipzig: Koehler, 1928.
  Held seines Landes. (Hero of his country.) Leipzig: Koehler, 1929.

  (1) A son of his country; an imaginative novel dealing with George Washington's youth. Trans. by Frederick H. Martins. New York, London: Harper, 1928.
Blunck, Hans Friedrich, 1888-
  Das werdende Volk; die Romane der nieder-deutschen Trilogie. (The evolving nation; the novels of the low-German trilogy.) 1 vol. Munich: Langen/Müller, 1934.
    1. Stelling Rotkinnsohn; die Geschichte eine Verkünders und seines Volk. (The story of a prophet and his people.) 1924.
    2. Hein Hoyer; ein Roman von Herren, Hausen, und Hagestolzen. (A novel of lords, houses, and bachelors.) 1922.
    3. Berend Fock; die Mär vom'gottabtrünnigen Schiffer. (The tale of the apostate sailor.) 1923.

  Die Urvätersage; drei Bücher aus der deutschen Frügeschichte. (The ancestral saga; three books on the early history of Germany.) 1 vol. Jena: Diederichs, 1934.
    1. Gewalt über das Feuer; eine Sage von Gott und Mensch. (Power over fire; a saga of God and man.) 1928.
    2. Kampf der Gestirne. (Conflict of the stars.) 1926.
    3. Streit mit den Göttern. (Struggle with the gods.) 1926.
Böhme, Frau Margarete, 1869-
  Tagebuch einer Verlorenen. Berlin: Fontane, 1905.
  Dida Ibsens Geschichte. (Dida Ibsen's story.) Berlin: Fontane, 1907.

  (1) The diary of a lost one. New York: Hudson Press, 1908.
Bonsels, Waldemar, 1881-
  Notizen eines Vagabunden. 1 vol. Berlin: Knaur, 1930. 3 vols. Frankfurt-am-Main: Rütten & Loening, 1922-25, and 1st ed. below.
    1. Menschenwege. 1918.
    2. Eros und die Evangelien. (Eros and the gospels.) 1921.
    3. Narren und Helden. (Fools and heroes.) 1923.

    1. Notes of a vagabond; ways of men. Trans. by J. B. Mussey. New York: Boni, 1931.
Borchardt, Georg Hermann, 1871-   Pseud., "Georg Hermann"
  Jettchen Geberts Geschichte. (Jettchen Gebert's story.) 2 vols. Berlin: Fleischel, 1907-8.

1. Jettchen Gebert. 1906. New ed., Jettchen Geberts Geschichte I, 1907.
2. Henriette Jacoby. 1908.

  1. Hetty Gebert. Trans. by Anna Barwell. New York: Doran, 1924.

Dr. Herzfeld. 2 vols. Berlin: Fleischel.
  1. Die Nacht des Dr. Herzfeld. 1912. New ed., Dr. Herzfeld I: Die Nacht. (The night.) 1922.
  2. Schnee. (Snow.) 1921.

Die steile Treppe. (The steep stairs.) 2 vols. Berlin: Deutsche Verlags-Anstalt, 1925.
  1. Einen Sommer lang. (A summer long.) Berlin: Ullstein, 1917.
  2. Der kleine Gast. (The little guest.) 1925.

November achtzehn. (November 18.) Berlin: Deutsche Verlags-Anstalt, 1930.
Ruths schwere Stunde. (Ruth's heavy hours.) Amsterdam: De Lange, 1934.
Eine Zeit stirbt. (A time dies.) Berlin: Jüdische Buch-Vereinigung, 1934.

Brehm, Bruno, 1892-
Apis und Este; ein Ferdinand-Roman. (1863-1914.) (A Ferdinand novel.) Munich: Piper, 1931.
Das war das Ende; von Brest-Litowsk bis Versailles. (1917-19.)
Weder Kaiser noch König; die Untergang der Habsburgischen Monarchie. (Neither emperor nor king; the fall of the Habsburg monarchy.) Munich: Piper, 1933.

(1) They call it patriotism. Trans. by Margaret Goldsmith. Boston: Little, Brown, 1932.
(2) That was the end. Trans by Geoffrey Dunlop. London: Hurst & Blackett, 1934.

Broch, Hermann, 1886-
Die Schlafwandler. Munich, Zurich: Rhein-Verlag.
  1. Pasenow oder Die Romantik. (1888.) 1931.
  2. Esch oder Die Anarchie. (1903.) 1931.
  3. Huguenau oder Die Sachlichkeit. (1918.) 1932.

The sleepwalkers. Trans. by Willa and Edwin Muir. 1 vol. Boston: Little, Brown, 1932.
  1. The romantic.   2. The anarchist.   3. The realist.

Bröger, Karl, 1886-
Guldenschuh. (Goldenshoe.) Berlin: Buchmeister-Verlag, 1934.
Nurnberg; der Roman einer Stadt. (The novel of a city.) Berlin: Franke, 1935.

"Burg, Paul," see Schaumburg, Paul Erich Bruno Richard.

Busse, Hermann Eris, 1891-
Bauernadel; Roman-Trilogie aus dem Schwarzwald. (Country gentry; novel trilogy of the Black Forest.) Berlin: Horen-Verlag.
  1. Das schlafende Feuer. (The dormant fire.) 1929.
  2. Markus und Sixta. 1929.
  3. Der letzte Bauer. (The last peasant.) 1930.

Colerus, Egmont, 1888-
Die neue Rasse. (The new race.) Vienna: Zsolnay, 1928.
Kaufherr und Krämer. (Merchant and shopkeeper.) Vienna: Zsolnay, 1929.

Conrad, Michael Georg, 1846-1927
Madame Lutetia! Neue Pariser Studien. Leipzig: Friedrich, 1883.
Lutetias Töchter; Pariser-deutsche Liebesgeschichten. (Lutetia's daughters; Parisian-German love stories.) Leipzig: Friedrich, 1883.

Was die Isar rauscht; München Roman-Cyklus. (What the Isar roars; Munich novel cycle.) Leipzig: Friedrich.
  1. Was die Isar rauscht. 2 vols. 1888.
  2. Die klugen Jungfrauen. (The wise virgins.) 3 vols. 1889.
  3. Die Beichte des Narren. (The fool's confession.) 1890.
Compiler's note: A longer sequence was planned but was not completed.

Conradi, Hermann, 1862-90
Phrasen. (Phrases.) Leipzig: Friedrich, 1887.
Adam Mensch. Leipzig: Friedrich, 1889.

GERMAN AND LOW GERMAN

Dahn, Felix Ludwig Sophus, 1834-1912
  Kleine Romane aus der Völkerwanderung. (Little novels of the migration of nations.) Subtitle, individual volumes: Historischer Roman aus der Völkerwanderung. Leipzig: Breitkopf & Härtel.
    1. Felicitas. (476 A.D.) 1882.
    2. Bissula. (378 A.D.) 6th ed. 1884.
    3. Gelimer. (534 A.D.) 1885.
    4. Die schlimmen Nonnen von Poitiers. (589 A.D.) (The bad nuns of Poitiers.) 1886.
    5. Fredigundis. (End of sixth century.) 1886.
    6. Attila. (453 A.D.) 1888.
    7. Die Bataver. (69 A.D.) 1890.
    8. Chlodovech. (511 A.D.) (Clovis.) 1895.
    9. Vom Chiemgau. (596 A.D.) 1896.
    10. Ebroin. 2 vols. in 1. 1897.

    1. Felicitas. Trans. by Mary J. Safford. New York: Gottsberger, 1883.
    2. A captive of the Roman eagles. Trans. by M. J. Safford. Chicago: McClurg, 1902.

Dittmer, Hans, 1893-
  Brouw Johanna. Berlin: Grote, 1919.
  Annenhof. Leipzig: Quelle & Meyer, 1922.
  Der Weg in die Stille. (The way to peace.) Halle: Heimat-Verlag, 1928.

Döblin, Alfred, 1878-
  Eine deutsche Revolution; Erzählwerk in drei Bänden. (A German revolution; narrative in three volumes.)
  Compiler's note: An unfinished trilogy on the German revolution of 1918.
    1. Bürger und Soldaten. (Citizens and soldiers.) Stockholm: Bermann-Fischer. Amsterdam: Querido, 1939.

Dörfler, Peter, 1878-
  Apollonia-Roman. Berlin: Grote.
    1. Die Lampe der törichten Jungfrau. (The lamp of the foolish virgin.) 1930.
    2. Apollonias Sommer. (Apollonia's summer.) 1931.
    3. Um das kommende Geschlecht. (Concerning the coming generation.) 1932.

  Der junge Don Bosco. (The young Don Bosco.) Freiburg: Herder, 1931.
  Der Bubenkönig; Don Bosco und seine Schlingel. (The boy king; Don Bosco and his rascals.) Freiburg: Herder, 1931.

  Allgäu-Trilogie. 3 vols. Berlin: Grote.
    1. Der Notwender. (He who averted trouble.) 1934.
    2. Der Zwingherr. (The despot.) 1935.
    3. Der Alpkönig. (The Alp king.) 1936.

Droste, Georg, 1866-
  Ottjen Alldag. 1 vol. Bremen: Schünemann, 1937.
    1. Ottjen Alldag un sien Kaperstreiche; een plattdütsch Kinnerleben an'r Waterkante. (Ottjen Alldag and his pranks; a low-German account of a child's life on the coast.) 1914.
    2. Ottjen Alldag un sien Moorher; een plattdütsch Vertellsel ut'n Kinner-un Leefsleben. (Ottjen Alldag and his mother; a low-German tale of child and love life.) 1920.
    3. Ottjen Alldag un sien Lehrtied; een Vertellsel ut'n Bremer Kopmannsleben. (Ottjen Alldag and his apprenticeship; a tale of Bremer merchant's life.) 1925.

Dwinger, Edwin Erich, 1898-
  Die deutsche Passion. Jena: Diederichs.
    1. Die Armee hinter Stacheldraht; das sibirische Tagebuch. (1915-18.) (The Siberian diary.) 1929.
    2. Zwischen Weiss und Rot; die russische Tragödie. (1919-20.) (The Russian tragedy.) 1930.
    3. Wir rufen Deutschland; Heimkehr und Vermächtnis. (1921-24.) (We call Germany, homecoming and testament.) 1932.

    1. Prisoner of war. Trans. by Ian F. D. Morrow. New York: Knopf, 1930. British title: The army behind barbed wire.
    2. Between White and Red. Trans. by Marion Saunders. New York: Scribner's, 1932.

Eckstein, Ernst, 1845-1900
  Prusias; Roman aus dem letzten Jahrhundert der römischen Republik. 3 vols. Leipzig: Reissner, 1884.
  Nero. 3 vols. Leipzig: Reissner, 1889.
  Die Claudier; Roman aus der römischen Kaiserzeit. 3 vols. Vienna: Zamarski, 1882.

  (1) Prusias; a romance of ancient Rome under the republic. Trans. by Clara Bell. 2 vols. New York: Gottsberger, 1884.
  (2) Nero. Trans. by C. Bell and Mary J. Safford. 2 vols. New York: Gottsberger, 1889.
  (3) Quintus Claudius; a romance of imperial Rome. Trans. by C. Bell. New York: Gottsberger, 1882.
Enking, Ottomar, 1867-
  Leute von Koggenstedt. (People of Koggenstedt.) Dresden: Reissner.
    1. Familie P. C. Behm. 1903.
    2. Patriarch Mahnke. 1905.
"Ernst, Otto," see Schmidt, Otto Ernst.
Ertl, Emil, 1860-
  Ein Volk an der Arbeit. (A nation at work.) Leipzig: Staackmann.
    1. Die Leute vom blauen Guguckshaus. (1809.) (The people from the blue cuckoo's house.) 1906.
    2. Freiheit, die ich meine; Roman aus dem Sturmjahr. (1848.) (Freedom, as I see it; a novel of the storm year.) 1909.
    3. Auf der Wegwacht. (1866.) (On guard along the way.) 1911.
    4. Im Haus zum Seidenbaum. (1918.) (In the house by the silk tree.) 1926.
Eulenberg, Herbert, 1876-
  Zwischen zwei Frauen; eine Schicksalsgeschichte. (Between two women; a story of destiny.) Stuttgart: Engelhorn, 1926.
  Zwischen zwei Mannern; eine Lebensdichtung. (Between two men; a fiction of life.) Stuttgart: Engelhorn, 1928.
Feuchtwanger, Lion, 1884-
  Josephus.
    1. Der jüdische Krieg. (The Jewish war.) Berlin: Propyläen-Verlag, 1932.
    2. Die Söhne. (The sons.) Amsterdam: Querido, 1935.
    3. "Der Tag wird kommen." (The day will come.)
  Compiler's note: Published only in English translation from ms.

  "Josephus." New York: Viking Press.
    1. Josephus. Trans. by Willa and Edwin Muir. 1932.
    2. The Jew of Rome. Trans. by W. and E. Muir. 1936.
    3. Josephus and the emperor. Trans. by Caroline Oram from German ms. 1942. British title: The day will come.
Findeisen, Kurt Arnold, 1883-
  Roman Robert Schumann: Du meine Seele, du mein Herz. (Robert Schumann novel: thou my soul, thou my heart.) 1 vol. Berlin: Bong, 1936. First published as Der Davidsbündler; ein Robert Schumann-Roman. (The Brotherhood of David.) 2 vols. Leipzig: Grethlein.
    1. Herzen und Masken. (Hearts and masks.) 1921.
    2. Der Weg in den Aschermittwoch. (The road to Ash Wednesday.) 1924.
Flake, Otto, 1882-
  Die Romane um Ruland. (Novels about Ruland.) Berlin: Fischer.
    1. Das Freitagskind. (Friday's child.) 1913. Reissued as Romane um Ruland I: Eine Kindheit. (A childhood.) 1928.
    2. Ruland. 1922.
    3. Der gute Weg. (The good way.) 1924.
    4. Villa U.S.A. 1926.
    5. Freund aller Welt. (Friend of all the world.) 1928.
Flex, Walter, 1887-1917
  Der Wanderer zwischen beiden Welten; ein Kriegserlebnis. (The wanderer between two worlds; a war experience.) Munich: Becksche, 1915.

GERMAN AND LOW GERMAN

Wolf Eschenlohr. Munich: Becksche, 1919.
  Compiler's note: An unfinished sequence.
Freytag, Gustav, 1816-95
  Die Ahnen. (The forefathers.) 6 vols. Leipzig: Hirzel. Vols. 1-3, 1874-75; vols. 4-6, 1880-82.
    1. Ingo und Ingraban. 1872.
    2. Das Nest der Zaunkönige. (The wren's nest.) 1873.
    3. Die Brüder vom deutschen Hause. (The brothers of the German house.) 1874.
    4. Marcus König. 1876.
    5. Die Geschwister. (Brothers and sisters.) 1878.
    6. Aus einer kleinen Stadt. (From a little city.) 1880.

  Our forefathers. Trans. by Mrs. Malcolm. 2 vols. New York: Holt, 1875.
    1. Ingo.   2. Ingraban.
Ganghofer, Ludwig Albert, 1855-1920
  Romane aus der Geschichte von Berchtesgaden. (Novels from the history of Berchtesgaden.) 1-6, Stuttgart: Bonz.
    1. Die Martinsklause; Roman aus dem Anfang des 12 Jahrhunderts. (Martin's cloister; novel of the beginning of the twelfth century.) 2 vols. 1895.
    2. Das Gotteslehen; Roman aus dem 13 Jahrhundert. (God's fief; novel of the thirteenth century.) 1899.
    3. Der Klosterjäger; Roman aus dem 14 Jahrhundert. (The cloister hunter; novel of the fourteenth century.) 1893.
    4. Der Ochsenkrieg; Roman aus dem 15 Jahrhundert. (The oxen war; novel of the fifteenth century.) 2 vols. 1914.
    5. Das neue Wesen; Roman aus dem 16 Jahrhundert. (The new order; novel of the sixteenth century.) 1902.
    6. Der Mann in Salz; Roman aus dem Anfang des 17 Jahrhunderts. (The man in salt; novel of the beginning of the seventeenth century.) 2 vols. in 1. 1906.
    7. Das grosse Jagen; Roman aus dem 18 Jahrhundert. (The great chase; novel of the eighteenth century.) Berlin: Grote, 1918.
Goedsche, Hermann Ottomar Friedrich, 1815-78. Pseud., "Sir John Retcliffe"
  Villafranca.
    1. Villafranca oder Die Kabinette und die Revolutionen; historisch-politischer Roman aus der Gegenwart. (Villafranca or Cabinets and revolutions; historico-political novel of the present.) 2 vols. Berlin: Nöhring, 1860-62.
    2. Zehn Jahre. (Ten years.) 4 vols. Berlin: Gerschel (Liebrecht), 1862-64.
    3. Magenta und Solferino. Berlin: Liebrecht, 1864. Published with Solferino in 1 vol., under the title Im Hexenkessel. (In the witches' kettle.) Radebeul: Retcliffe Verlag, 1930.
    4. Solferino. Berlin: Liebrecht, 1866.

  Biarritz. Series subtitle: Historisch-politischer Roman aus der Gegenwart. (See Villafranca.)
    Berlin: Liebrecht. Popular editions in 2 and 4 vols., 1933.
    Biarritz. 4 vols. 1868-70.
    Biarritz I: Gaeta-Marschau-Düppel. Vols. 5-8. 1871-76.
    Biarritz II: Um die Weltherrschaft. (For world dominion.) 1876.
Goethe, Johann Wolfgang von, 1749-1832
  Wilhelm Meisters Lehrjahre. (Wilhelm Meister's apprenticeship.) 1794.
  Wilhelm Meisters Wanderjahre. (Wilhelm Meister's years of travel.) 1821.
Grote, Hans Henning, Freiherr, 1896-
  Flammende Jahre. (Flaming years.) 1 vol. Braunschweig: Westermann, 1936.
    1. Heilige Saat. (Holy seed.) 1924.
    2. Führer voraus! (Leader ahead.) 1934.
    3. Eiserne Ernte. (Iron harvest.)
Haas, Rudolf, 1877-
  Der Triebl-Roman. (The Triebl novel.) Leipzig: Staackmann.
    1. Matthias Triebl; die Geschichte eines verbummelten Studenten. (The story of a student on a spree.) 1915.

2. <u>Triebl der Wanderer</u>. (Triebl the wanderer.) 1916.
3. <u>Auf lichter Höhe; ein Buch aus dunkeln Tiefen und der Menschheit Gipfelreichen</u>. (On light heights; a book from the dark depths and humanity's peak empire.) 1922.

<u>Triebl-Streiche; Geschichten vom freudigen Lebel</u>. (Triebltricks; stories of a happy life.) 1929.
Compiler's note: Short stories.

<u>Die drei Kuppelpelze des Kriminalrates. Ein fröliches Buch</u>. (The criminal magistrate's three marriage-broker's rewards. A merry book.) Leipzig: Staackmann, 1927.
<u>Die sieben Sorgen des Kriminalrats. Ein heiteres Buch</u>. (The seven cares of the criminal magistrate. A happy book.) Leipzig: Staackmann, 1930.

Hadina, Emil, 1885-
<u>Ein Theodor-Storm Roman</u>. (A Theodore Storm novel.) 2 vols. Leipzig: Staackmann, 1924-25.
  1. <u>Die graue Stadt — die lichten Frauen</u>. (The gray city — the bright women.) 1922.
  2. <u>Der Kampf mit dem Schatten</u>. (The struggle with the shadows.) 1925.

Häring, Wilhelm, 1798-1871. Pseud., "Willibald Alexis"
<u>Die Hosen des Herrn von Bredow</u>. (The trousers of Herr von Bredow.) Berlin: Adolf.
  I. <u>Hans Jürgen und Hans Jochem; vaterländischer Roman</u>. 2 vols. 1846.
  II. <u>Der Werwolf; vaterländischer Roman in 3 Büchern</u>. (The werewolf; a patriotic novel in three books.) 1848.
    1. "Hake von Stolpe."
    2. "Die Sintflut und der Tempelhofsche Berg." (The deluge and the Tempelhof Hill.)
    3. "Die Kurfürstin Elizabeth und die weise Frau." (Electoress Elizabeth and the fortune-teller.)

<u>Ruhe ist die erste Bürgerpflicht, oder Vor fünfzig Jahren; vaterländischer Roman</u>. (Calm is the first duty of the citizens, or Fifty years ago; a patriotic novel.) 5 vols. Berlin: Barthol, 1852.
<u>Isegrimm; vaterländischer Roman</u>. 3 vols. Berlin: Barthol, 1854.

Hahn-Hahn, Ida Marie Luise Sophie Fredericke Gustava, Gräfin von, 1805-80
<u>Aus der Gesellschaft</u>. Berlin: Duncker & Humblot, 1838.
<u>Der Rechte</u>. (The right one.) Berlin: Duncker, 1839.
<u>Ulrich</u>. 2 vols. Berlin: Duncker, 1841.
<u>Gräfin Faustine</u>. Berlin: Duncker, 1843.
<u>Sybilla</u>. 2 vols. Berlin: Duncker, 1846.

(1) <u>Society, or High life in Germany</u>. Trans. of "Ilda Schönholm," from <u>Aus der Gesellschaft</u>. London: Piper & Stephenson, 1854.
(3) <u>Ulrich</u>. London: Clarke, 1845.
(4) <u>Countess Faustine</u>. 2 vols. London: Clarke, 1844. U.S. translations have the titles <u>Faustina</u> and <u>Countess Obernau</u>.

Hammerstein-Equord, Hans, Freiherr von, 1881-
<u>Ritter, Tod, und Teufel; ein Bilderbuch aus dem 16 Jahrhundert</u>. (The knight, death, and the devil; a picture book of the sixteenth century.) Leipzig: Koehler & Amelang.
  1. <u>Ritter, Tod, und Teufel</u>. 1921.
  2. <u>Mangold von Eberstein</u>. 1922.

Handel-Mazetti, Enrica Ludovica Maria, Freiin von, 1871-
<u>Jesse und Maria; ein Roman aus dem Donaulande</u>. (A novel of the Danube country.) 2 vols. Kempten: Kösel, 1906.
<u>Die arme Margaret; ein Volkroman aus dem alten Steyr</u>. (Poor Margaret; a folk novel of old Steyr.) Kempten: Kösel, 1910.
<u>Meinrad Helmpergers denkwürdiges Jahr</u>. (Meinrad Helmperger's memorable year.) Stuttgart: Roth, 1900.

(1) <u>Jesse and Maria</u>. Trans. by George N. Schuster. New York: Holt, 1931.

<u>Stephana Schwertner; ein Steyrer Roman</u>. Kempten: Kösel.
  1. <u>Unter dem Richter von Steyr</u>. (Under the judge of Steyr.) 1912.

GERMAN AND LOW GERMAN

    2. Das Geheimnis des Königs. (The king's secret.) 1913.
    3. Jungfrau und Martyrin. (Virgin and martyr.) 1914.

  Sand-Trilogie. Munich: Kösel & Pustet. Earlier series title: Das Rosenwunder.
    1. Das Rosenwunder. (The miracle of roses.) 1924.
    2. Deutsche Passion. 1925.
    3. Das Blutzeugnis. (The blood testimony.) 1926.

  Frau Maria; ein Roman aus der Zeit August des Starken. (A novel of the time of August the Strong.) Munich: Kösel & Pustet.
    1. Das Spiel von dem 10 Jungfrauen. (The play of the 10 virgins.) 1929.
    2. Das Reformationsfest. (The Reformation festival.) 1930.
    3. Die Hochzeit von Quedlinburg. (The wedding at Quedlinburg.) 1931.

Hauenschild, Spiller von, 1822-55. Pseud., "Max Waldau"
  Nach der Natur; lebende Bilder aus der Zeit. (According to nature; living pictures of the time.) 3 vols. Hamburg: Hoffmann & Campe, 1851.
    1. Tyrol.   2. In Ober-Schlesien.   3. In Baden.

Hauschner, Auguste, 1862-
  Die Familie Lowositz. Berlin: Fleischel.
    1. Die Familie Lowositz. 1908.
    2. Rudolf und Kamilla. 1910.

Heinrich, Karl Borromäus, 1884-
  Karl Asenkofer. Munich: Langen, 1907.
  Karl Asenkofers Flucht und Zuflucht. (Karl Asenkofer's flight and refuge.) Munich: Langen, 1909.

"Hermann, Georg," see Borchardt, Georg Hermann.

Hohlbaum, Robert, 1886-
  Fruhlingssturm: die Romandreiheit des deutschen Menschen. (Spring storm: the novel trilogy of the German people.) Leipzig: Staackmann.
    1. Die deutsche Passion. 1924.
    2. Weg nach Emmaus. (The road to Emmaus.) 1925.
    3. Die Pfingsten von Weimar. (The Pentecost at Weimar.) 1926.

  Volk und Mann. (Nation and man.)
    1. König Volk; Roman aus der französischen Revolution. (King People; a novel of the French Revolution.) Leipzig: Staackmann, 1931.
    2. Der Mann aus dem Chaos; ein Napoleon-Roman. (The man out of chaos.) Leipzig: Staackmann, 1933.
    3. Stein; der Roman eines Führers. (The novel of a leader.) Munich: Langen/Müller, 1935.

Huch, Ricarda Octavia, 1864-
  Die Geschichten von Garibaldi. (Stories of Garibaldi.) 2 vols. Leipzig: Insel-Verlag, 1921-25.
    1. Die Verteidigung Rome. (The defense of Rome.) Stuttgart: Deutsche Verlags-Anstalt, 1906.
    2. Der Kampf um Rom. (The battle for Rome.) Stuttgart: Deutsche Verlags-Anstalt, 1907.

  Garibaldi and the new Italy. Trans. by Catherine Alison Phillips. 2 vols. New York: Knopf, 1928-29.
    1. Defeat.   2. Victory.

  Der grosse Krieg in Deutschland. (The great war in Germany.) 3 vols. Leipzig: Insel-Verlag, 1912-14.
    1. Das Vorspiel. (1585-1620.) (The prologue.)
    2. Der Ausbruch des Feuers. (1620-1632.) (The outbreak of the fire.)
    3. Der Zusammenbruch. (1633-1650.) (The collapse.)

Huna, Ludwig, 1872-
  Die Borgia-Trilogie. 3 vols. Leipzig: Grethlein, 1928.
    1. Die Stiere von Rome. 1920.

2. Der Stern des Orsini. 1921.
3. Das Mädchen von Nettuno. 1922.

"The Borgia trilogy." Trans. by Madge Pemberton. New York: Brewer & Warren.
1. The bulls of Rome. 1930. British title: The Borgian bull.
2. The star of the Orsini. 1930.
3. The maid of Nettuno. 1931.

Jansen, Werner, 1890-
Die Bücher Treue, Liebe, Leidenschaft. (The books of fidelity, love, and passion.) 3 vols. Braunschweig: Westermann, 1923.
1. Das Buch Treue; Nibelungenroman. Hamburg: 1916.
2. Das Buch Liebe; Gudrunroman. 1918.
3. Das Buch Leidenschaft; Amelungenroman. 1920.

Trilogie aus deutscher Herrenzeit. (Trilogy of the German period of dominance.) Braunschweig: Westermann.
1. Verratene Heimat. (Betrayed homeland.) 1931.
2. Heinrich der Löwe. 1923.
3. Geier um Marienburg. 1925.

Johst, Hanns, 1890-
Der Anfang. (The beginning.) Munich: Langen, 1917.
Der Kreuzweg. (The crossroad.) Munich: Langen, 1922.

"Junger, Nathanael," pseud. of (Heinrich Carl Dietrich) Johann Rump, 1871-
Hof Bokels Ende. Ein Bauernroamn aus der Lüneburger Heide zur Zeit des letzten Königs von Hannover. (The end of Hof Bokel. A peasant novel of the Lüneburger Heath at the time of the last king of Hanover.) Schönberg, Meckl.: Lehmann & Bernhard, 1908.
Heidekinds Erdenweg. Die Geschichte eines Kindes. Erzahlung aus der Lüneburger Heide um die letzte Jahrhundertwende. (Heath child's way on earth. The story of a child. Tale of the Lüneburger Heath about the turn of the last century.) Wismar, Meckl.: Hinstorffsche, 1908.
Pastor Ritgerodts Reich. Ein Roman aus der Heide. (Pastor Ritgerodt's kingdom; A novel of the heath.) Wismar, Meckl.: Hinstorffsche, 1909.

Kafka, Franz, 1883-1924
Der Prozess. Berlin: Die Schmiede, 1925.
Das Schloss. Munich: Wolff, 1926.

(1) The trial. Trans. by Edwin and Willa Muir. New York: Knopf, 1937.
(2) The castle. Trans. by E. and W. Muir. New York: Knopf, 1930.

Katz, H. W.
Die Fischmanns. Amsterdam: Allert de Lange, 1938.

(1) The Fishmans. Trans. by Maurice Samuel. New York: Viking Press, 1938.
(2) No. 21 Castle Street. Trans. from original unpublished German ms., "Schlossgasse 21," by Norman Guterman. New York: Viking Press, 1940.
Compiler's note: The first volumes of a projected series on the twentieth-century world.

Kluge, Kurt Friedrich Otto, 1886-1940
Der Herr Kortüm. 1 vol. Stuttgart: Engelhorn, 1938.
1. Die silberne Windfahne. (The silver weather vane.) 1934.
2. Das Flügelhaus. (The house with wings.) 1937.

Kneip, Jakob, 1881-
1. Porta Nigra, oder Die Berufung des Martin Krimkorn. (The calling of Martin Krimkorn.) Leipzig: List, 1932.
2. Feuer vom Himmel. (Fire from heaven.) Leipzig: List, 1936.
Compiler's note: A third volume was planned but apparently not published.

Koebner, Franz Wolfgang, 1885-
Die Nonne und der Harlekin. (The nun and the harlequin.) Leipzig: List, 1917.
Maria Evers; die Geschichte einer Komödiantin. (The story of a comedienne.) Leipzig: List, 1917.

GERMAN AND LOW GERMAN

Kolbenheyer, Erwin Guido, 1878-
  Paracelsus. Munich: Müller.
    1. Die Kindheit des Paracelsus. (The childhood of Paracelsus.) 1917.
    2. Das Gestirn des Paracelsus. (The star of Paracelsus.) 1921.
    3. Das dritte Reich des Paracelsus. (The third kingdom of Paracelsus.) 1926.
Kosel, Hermann Clemens, 1867-
  Albrecht Dürer, ein deutscher Heiland; Roman aus Nürnbergs Blütezeit. (A German savior; a novel of Nuremberg's golden age.) Berlin: Bong.
    1. Jugend und Wanderjahre. (Youth and years of travel.) 1923.
    2. Der Meister. (The master.) 1923.
    3. Der Apostel. (The apostle.) 1924.
Kotzde-Kottenrodt, Wilhelm, 1878-
  Die Wittenbergisch Nachtigall. (The Wittenberg nightingale.) Stuttgart: Steinkopf, 1917.
  Der Reiter Gottes; ein Lebensbild aus dem Glaubenskriegen. (Trooper of God; a picture of life in the wars of faith.) Stuttgart: Steinkopf, 1930.
  Wilhelmus von Nassauen; ein Mann und ein Volk. (William of Nassau; a man and a people.) Stuttgart: Steinkopf, 1933.
Kraft, Zdenko von, 1886-
  Richard-Wagner-Trilogie. Leipzig: Grethlein.
    1. Barrikaden. (Barricades.) 1920.
    2. Liebestod. (Love-death.) 1921.
    3. Wahnfried. 1922.
Krauss, Nikolaus
  Heimat; ein Romantrilogie. (Homeland.) 3 vols. Berlin: Fleischel, 1903.
    1. Lene. 1897.
    2. Die Förster von Konradsreuth. (The foresters of Konradsreuth.) 1900.
    3. Die Stadt. (The city.) 1902.
Kuchler-Ming, Rosalie
  Die Lauwiser und ihr See; Erzählung aus den Jahren 1831-36. (The Lauwisers and their lake; a tale of the years 1831-36.) Zurich: Rentsch, 1935.
  Die Lauwiser im Krieg; Erzählung aus dem Jahre 1847. (The Lauwisers in war.) Zurich: Rentsch, 1936.
Lambrecht, Nanny, 1868-
  Die eiserne Freude. (The iron joy.) Berlin: Fleischel, 1915.
  Die Fahne der Wollonen. (The banner of the Walloons.) Berlin: Fleischel, 1915.
  Der Gefangene von Belle-Jeannette. (The prisoner of Belle-Jeannette.) Berlin: Scherl, 1918.
Laube, Heinrich Rudolf Constanz, 1806-84
  Das junge Europa. (Young Europe.)
    1. Die Poeten. (The poets.) 2 vols. Leipzig: Wigand, 1833.
    2. Die Krieger. (The warriors.) 2 vols. Mannheim: Hoff, 1837.
    3. Die Bürger. (The citizens.) Mannheim: Hoff, 1837.

  Der deutsche Krieg. (The German war.) Leipzig: Haessel.
    1. Junker Hans. 4 vols. 1863.
    2. Waldstein. 3 vols. 1865.
    3. Herzog Bernhard. 2 vols. 1866.
Le Fort, Gertrud (Auguste Line Elsbeth Mathilde Petrea), Freiin von, 1876-
  Das Reich des Kindes. (The kingdom of children.) Munich: Langen/Müller, 1934.
  Compiler's note: The prologue to the following trilogy, announced in preparation.
  "Die drei Kronen; Legende de deutschen Kaiserzeit." (The three crowns; legends of the German period of empire.)
    1. "Corona argentea." Die deutsche Krone; Legende der Sachsischen Kaiser. (Silver crown. The German crown; legends of the Saxon emperors.)
    2. "Corona ferrata." Die Lombarden Krone; Legende der Salischen Kaiser. (Iron crown. The Lombard crown; legends of the Salic emperors.)
    3. "Corona aurea." Die römische Krone; Legende des Staufischen Kaiser. (Golden crown. The Roman crown; legends of the Hohenstauffen emperors.)
Lindau, Paul, 1839-1919
  Berlin. Stuttgart: Spemann.

1. Der Zug nach dem Westen. (The drive toward the west.) 2 vols. 1886.
2. Arme Mädchen. (Poor girls.) 2 vols. 1887.
Compiler's note: Continued in Felix Balden's Ledige Frauen. 1889.
3. Spitzen. 2 vols. 1888.

3. Lace; a Berlin romance. New York: Appleton, 1889.
"Lothar, Ernst," pseud. of Ernst Müller, 1890-
Macht über alle Menschen. (Power over all mankind.) Munich: Müller.
   1. Irrlicht der Welt. (Confusion of the world.) 1921.
   2. Irrlicht des Geistes. (Confusion of the spirit.) 1923.
   3. Licht. (Light.) 1925.

Der Menschenrechte. (The rights of man.) Vienna: Zsolnay.
   1. Die Mühle der Gerechtigkeit, oder Das Recht auf den Tod. (The mill of justice, or The right to die.) 1933.
   2. Eine Frau wie viele; oder Das Rechte in der Ehe. (A woman like many, or The right in marriage.) 1934.

   1. The loom of justice. Trans. by Willa and Edwin Muir. New York: Putnam's, 1935.
Lux, Joseph August, 1871-
Das Leben Anselmos. (The life of Anselm.) Leipzig: Grethlein.
   1. Amsel Gabesam, der Narr vom Kahlenberg. (The fool of Kahlenberg.) 1918. 2d and 3d ed. Berlin: Schuster & Loeffler, 1911.
   2. Auf deutscher Strasse; Amsel Gabesams Wanderjahre. (On German road; Amsel Gabesam's years of travel.) 1919.
Maas, Edgar
   1. Verdun. Berlin: Propyläen-Verlag, 1938.
   2. Werdelust. (Joy of growth.) Berlin: Propyläen-Verlag, 1938.
   3. Im Nebel der Zeit. (In the mist of the time.) Berlin: Propyläen-Verlag, 1938.
Maas, Joachim, 1901-
Zwischen den Zeiten. (Between the times.)
Compiler's note: An unfinished trilogy.
   1. Das magischen Jahr. Stockholm: Bermann-Fischer, 1945.

   1. The magic year. Trans. by Erika Meyer. New York: L. B. Fischer, 1944.
Mann, Heinrich, 1871-
Die Göttinnen, oder Die drei Romane der Herzogin von Assy. (The goddesses, or The three novels of the Duchess of Assy.) 3 vols. Munich: A. Langen, 1903. 1 vol. Munich: Wolff, 1907.
   1. Diana.   2. Minerva.   3. Venus.

   1. Diana. Trans. by Erich Posselt and Emmet Glore. New York: Coward-McCann, 1929.

Das Kaiserreich: die Romane der deutschen Gesellschaft im Zeitalter Wilhelms II. (The empire: novels of German society in the time of William II.) 2 vols. Vienna: Zsolnay, 1925, 1931.
Vol. I:
1. Der Untertan. (The subject.) Leipzig: Wolff, 1918.
2. Die Armen. (The poor.) Leipzig: Wolff, 1917.
Vol. II:
3. Der Kopf. (The head.) Vienna: Zsolnay, 1925.

   1. The patrioteer. Trans. by Ernest Boyd. New York: Harcourt, Brace, 1921. Reissued as Little superman. New York: Creative Age, 1945.

Die Jugend des Königs Henri Quatre. Amsterdam: Querido, 1935.
Die Vollendung des Königs Henri Quatre. Amsterdam: Querido, 1938.

Henri Quatre, King of France. Trans. by Eric Sutton. 2 vols. London: Secker & Warburg, 1938-39. 2 vols., without series title. New York: Knopf, 1937-39.

GERMAN AND LOW GERMAN 89

   1. King Wren: the youth of Henri Quatre. U.S. title: Young Henry of Navarre.
   2. The last days of Henri Quatre, King of France. U.S. title: Henry, King of France.
Mann, Thomas, 1875-
  Joseph und seine Brüder.
    1. Die Geschichten Jaakobs. Berlin: Fischer, 1933.
    2. Der junge Joseph. Berlin: Fischer, 1934.
    3. Joseph in Ägypten. Vienna: Bermann-Fischer, 1936.
    4. Joseph, der Ernährer. Stockholm: Bermann-Fischer, 1943.

  Joseph and his brethren. Trans. by H. T. Lowe-Porter. 4 vols. in 1. New York: Knopf, 1948.
    1. Joseph and his brethren. 1934. British title: The tales of Jacob.
    2. Young Joseph. 1935.
    3. Joseph in Egypt. 2 vols. 1938.
    4. Joseph, the provider. 1944.
"Marriot, Emil," see Mataja, Emilie.
Martens, Kurt, 1870-
  Die alten Ideale. (The old ideals.)
    1. Deutschland marschiert; ein Roman von 1813. (Germany marches; a novel of 1813.)
      Berlin: Fleischel, 1913.
    2. Pia; der Roman ihrer zwei Welten. (Pia; the novel of her two worlds.) Leipzig:
      Grethlein, 1913.
    3. Hier und drüben. (Here and yonder.) Leipzig: Grethlein, 1915.
Mataja, Emilie, 1855-   Pseud., "Emil Marriot"
  Seine Gottheit. (His divinity.) Berlin: Freund & Jeckel, 1898?
  Auferstehung. (Resurrection.) Berlin: Freund & Jeckle, 1898.
Mauthner, Fritz, 1849-1923
  Berlin W. Dresden: Minden.
    1. Quartett. 1886.
    2. Die Fanfare. 1888.
    3. Der Villenhof. 1890.
Mayer, Erich August, 1894-
  Gottfried; ein Lebensroman. (A life novel.) 2 vols. Vienna: Luser, 1929.
    1. Gottfried sucht seinen Weg. (Gottfried seeks his way.)
    2. Werk und Seele. (Work and soul.)
Mayer, Theodor Heinrich, 1884-
  Wien. (Vienna.) Leipzig: Staackmann.
    1. Der letzte Bürger. (The last burgher.) 1927.
    2. Prokop der Schneider. (Prokop the tailor.) 1927.
    3. "Menschen in Gärten." (Men in gardens.)
  Compiler's note: Announced but apparently not published.
Meding, (Johann Ferdinand Martin) Oskar, 1829-1903. Pseud., "Gregor Samarow"
  Um Szepter und Kronen. Stuttgart: Hallberger.
    1. Um Szepter und Kronen. 4 vols. 1872.
    2. Europäische Minen und Gegenminen. (European plots and counterplots.) 4 vols. 1873.
    3. Zwei Kaiserkronen. (Two imperial crowns.) 4 vols. 1874.
    4. Kreuz und Schwert. (Cross and sword.) 4 vols. 1875.
    5. Held und Kaiser. (Hero and emperor.) 4 vols. 1876.

    1. For sceptre and crown. 2 vols. London: H. S. King, 1874.

  Hohen und Tiefen. (Heights and depths.) Stuttgart: Deutsche Verlags-Anstalt, 1879-80.
    1. Verschollen. (Missing.) 4 vols.
    2. Gold und Blut. (Gold and blood.) 8 vols.
    3. Sühne und Segen. (Atonement and benediction.) 8 vols.
Meissner, Alfred, 1822-85
  Schwarzgelb; Roman aus Oesterreichs letzten zwölf Jahren. (Black yellow; a novel of
    Austria's last twelve years.) Berlin: Janke, 1862-64.
    1. Dulder und Renegaten. (Sufferers and renegades.) 2 vols.

2. Aus der Emigration. 2 vols.
　　3. Vae victis. (Woe to the vanquished.) 2 vols.
　　4. Die Opfer der Partei. (The victim of the faction.) 2 vols.

　Babel; Roman aus Oesterreichs neuester Geschichte. (A novel about Austria's most recent history.) 4 vols. Berlin: Janke, 1867.
　Compiler's note: A continuation of the above sequence.
Meyer-Meyrink, Gustav, 1868-1932
　Der Golem. Leipzig: Wolff, 1915.
　Das grüne Gesicht. (The green apparition.) Leipzig: Wolff, 1916.

　(1) The Golem. Trans. by Madge Pemberton. Boston: Houghton, Mifflin, 1928.
Moersberger, Frau Rose (Schliewen), see "Rose, Felicitas."
Molo, Walter, Ritter von, 1880-
　Die Liebes-Symphonie. (The symphony of love.) 1 vol. 5th ed. Munich: A. Langen, 1926?
　　1. Die unerbittliche Liebe. (Pitiless love.) 2d ed. Berlin: Schuster & Loeffler, 1909.
　　2. Die törichte Welt. (The foolish world.) 2d ed. Berlin: Schuster & Loeffler, 1910.
　　3. Der gezähmte Eros. (Eros tamed.) 5th ed. Berlin: Langen, 1926.
　　4. Wallfahrer zur lieben Frau. (Pilgrims to Our Lady.) Revised ed. of Wie Weibgefallen.

　Der Schiller-Roman. (The Schiller novel.) 2 vols. Munich: A. Langen, 1918.
　Vol. I:
　　1. Ums Menschentum. (For humanity's sake.) Berlin: Schuster & Loeffler, 1912.
　　2. Im Titanenkampf. (In titanic battle.) Berlin: Schuster & Loeffler, 1913.
　Vol. II:
　　3. Die Freiheit. (Freedom.) Berlin: Schuster & Loeffler, 1914.
　　4. Den Sternen zu. (Toward the stars.) 1916.

　Der Roman meines Volkes. (The novel of my people.) 1 vol. Munich: A. Langen, 1924. A revision of Ein Volk wacht auf. (A people wakes.) 3 vols. Munich: A. Langen, 1921-22.
　　1. Fridericus. 1918.
　　2. Luise. 1919.
　　3. Das Volk. Original title: Das Volk wacht auf. 1921.

　Bobenmatz. Munich: A. Langen.
　　1. Auf der rollenden Erde. (On the rolling earth.) 1923.
　　2. Bobenmatz. 1925.
　　3. Im ewigen Licht. (In the eternal light.) 1926.
Morgenstern, Soma, 1896-
　Son of the lost son. Trans. by Joseph Leftwich and Peter Gross. New York: Rinehart, 1946.
　In my father's pastures. Trans. from German ms. by Ludwig Lewisohn. Philadelphia: Jewish Pub. Soc. of America, 1948.
"Mühlbach, Luise," see Mundt, Frau Klara (Müller).
Müller, Ernst, see "Lothar, Ernst."
Müller-Guttenbrunn, Adam, 1852-1923
　Von Eugenius bis Josephus; ein deutsches Jahrhundert in Oesterreich. (From Eugene to Joseph; a German century in Austria.) 3 vols. Leipzig: Staackmann, 1918.
　　1. Der grosse Schwabenzug. (The great Swabian migration.) 1914.
　　2. Barmherziger Kaiser. (Charitable emperor.) 1916.
　　3. Joseph der Deutsche. (Joseph the German.) 1917.

　Ein Lenau-Roman. (A Lenau novel.) Leipzig: Staackmann.
　　1. Sein Vaterhaus. (His ancestral home.) 1919.
　　2. Dämonische Jahre. (Demonic years.) 2 vols. 1920.
　　3. Auf der Höhe. (On the heights.) 1921.
Mundt, Frau Klara (Müller), 1814-73. Pseud., "Luise Mühlbach"
　Friedrich der Grosse und sein Hof.
　　1. Friedrich der Grosse und sein Hof. 3 vols. Berlin: Janke, 1853.
　　2. Berlin und Sanssouci, oder Friedrich der Grosse und seine Freunde. 4 vols. Berlin: Simion, 1854.

3. Friedrich der Grosse und seine Geschwister. 3 vols. Berlin: Janke, 1855.
4. Johann Gotzkowsky, der Kaufmann der Berlin. 3 vols. Berlin: Simion, 1850. Subtitle, later editions: Friedrich der Grosse und sein Kaufmann.

"Frederick the Great and his court."
1. Frederick the Great and his court. Trans. by Mrs. Chapman Coleman. New York: Appleton, 1866.
2. Berlin and Sans Souci, or Frederick the Great and his friends. Trans. by Mrs. C. Coleman. New York: Appleton, 1867.
3. Frederick the Great and his family. Trans. by Mrs. C. Coleman. New York: Appleton, 1867.
4. Frederick the Great and his merchant. Trans. by Lady Wallace. London: Bentley, 1858. U.S. translation has the title The merchant of Berlin. 1867.

Kaiser Joseph II und sein Hof. 12 vols. Berlin: Janke, 1857.
1. Kaiser Joseph und Maria Theresia. 4 vols. 1856.
2. Kaiser Joseph und Marie Antoinette. 4 vols. 1856.
3. Kaiser Joseph als Selbstherrscher. (Emperor Joseph as autocrat.) 4 vols. 1857.

Joseph the Second and his court. Trans. by Adelaide De V. Chaudron. New York: Appleton, 1898. An earlier edition of the same translation (4 vols. in 1. Mobile, Ala.: Goetzel, 1864), may be complete; other editions apparently are not complete.
Contents: "Marie Theresa," "Isabella," "King of Rome," "Emperor of Austria," "Marie Antoinette," "The reign of Joseph."

Napoleon in Deutschland. 13 vols. Berlin: Janke, 1858.
1. Rastatt und Jena.
2. Napoleon und Königin Louise. 4 vols.
3. Napoleon und Blücher. 4 vols.
4. Napoleon und der Wiener Congress. (Napoleon and the Congress of Vienna.) 4 vols.

Napoleon in Germany. Trans. by F. Jordan. 3 vols. New York: Appleton, 1867.
1. Louise of Prussia and her times.
2. Napoleon and the Queen of Prussia.
3. Napoleon and Blücher.

Erzherzog Johann und seine Zeit. 12 vols. Berlin: Janke, 1859-63.
1. Andreas Hofer. 3 vols.
2. Erzherzog Johann und Metternich. 3 vols.
3. Erzherzog Johann und der Herzog von Reichstadt. 3 vols.
4. Erzherzog Johann als Reichsverweser. (Archduke John as imperial administrator.) 3 vols.

"Archduke John of Austria."
1. Andreas Hofer. Trans. by F. Jordan. New York: Appleton, 1868.

Prinz Eugen und seine Zeit. 8 vols. Berlin: Janke, 1864.
1. Prinz Eugen, der kleine Abbé. (Prince Eugene, the little abbé.) 4 vols.
2. Prinz Eugen, der edle Ritter. (Prince Eugene, the noble knight.) 4 vols.

Prince Eugene and his times. Trans. by Adelaide De V. Chaudron. New York: Appleton, 1869.

Der grosse Kurfürst und seine Zeit. Jena: Costenoble.
1. Der junge Kurfürst. 3 vols. 1865.
2. Der grosse Kurfürst und sein Volk. (The Great Elector and his people.) 4 vols. 1865.
3. Der grosse Kurfürst und seine Kinder. (The Great Elector and his children.) 4 vols. 1866.

"The Great Elector and his times." Trans. by Mrs. M. S. H. Smith. New York: Appleton.

1. The youth of the Great Elector. 1896.
2. The reign of the Great Elector. 1898.

Deutschland in Sturm und Drang. (Germany in storm and stress.) Jena: Costenoble.
1. Der alte Fritz und seine Zeit. 4 vols. 1867.
2. Fürsten und Dichter. (Princes and poets.) 4 vols. 1867.
3. Deutschland gegen Frankreich. (Germany against France.) 4 vols. 1868.
4. Frankreich gegen Deutschland. (France against Germany.) 5 vols. 1868.

1. Old Fritz and the new era. Trans. by Peter Langley. New York: Appleton, 1868.
2. Goethe and Schiller. Trans. by Chapman Coleman. New York: 1899.

Von Solferino bis Königgratz. (From Solferino to Königgratz.) 12 vols. Berlin: Janke, 1869.
1. Kirchenfürsten und Weltfürsten. (Prelates and princes.) 4 vols.
2. Solferino. 4 vols.
3. Die Nebenbuhler in Deutschland. (Rivals in Germany.) 4 vols.

Von Königgratz bis Chiselhurst. (From Königgratz to Chiselhurst.) Stuttgart: Simon.
1. Um Deutschlands Einheit. (For the unity of Germany.) 3 vols. 1873.
2. Wilhelmshöhe und Chiselhurst. 3 vols. 1874.

Mohammed Ali und sein Haus. 4 vols. Jena: Costenoble, 1871.
Mohammed Alis Nachfolger. (Mohammed Ali's successors.) Jena: Costenoble, 1872.
Mohammed Ali, der morgenländische Bonaparte. (The oriental Bonaparte.) Prague: Bensinger, 1872.

(1) Mohammed Ali and his house. Trans. by Chapman Coleman. New York: Appleton, 1872.

Neumann, Alfred, 1895-
Rebellen. Stuttgart: Deutsche Verlags-Anstalt, 1928.
Guerra. Stuttgart: Deutsche Verlags-Anstalt, 1928.

(1) The rebels; a romance of the Carbonari. Trans. by Huntley Paterson. New York: Knopf, 1929.
(2) Guerra. Trans. by H. Paterson. New York: Knopf, 1930.

Die Trögedie des 19 Jahrhundert. (The tragedy of the nineteenth century.) Amsterdam: De Lange.
1. Neuer Caesar. 1934.
2. Kaiserreich; der grosse Roman vom Höhepunkt und Sturz Napoleon III. (Empire; the great novel of the zenith and downfall of Napoleon III.) 1936.
3. Volksfreunden. London: Hutchinson, 1940.

1. Another Caesar. Trans. by Eden and Cedar Paul. New York: Knopf, 1934. British title: The new Caesar.
2. Gaudy empire. Trans. by E. and C. Paul. New York: Knopf, 1937. British title: Man of December.
3. Friends of the people. Trans. by Nora Wydenbruck and the author. New York: Macmillan, 1942.

Ompteda, Georg, Freiherr von, 1863-1931
Deutscher Adel um 1900. (German nobility about 1900.) Berlin: Fleischel, 1900-2.
1. Sylvester von Geyer. 2 vols. Berlin: Fontane, 1899.
2. Eysen. 2 vols. 1900.
3. Cäcile von Sarryn. 2 vols. 1902.

Paust, Otto, 1897-
Volk in Feuer. (People in the fire.) Dresden: Fischer, 1935.
Nation in Not. (Nation in distress.) Berlin: Limpert, 1936.
Land im Licht. (Land in the light.) Berlin: Limpert, 1937.

Petersen, Albert, 1883-
  Der junge Perthes. (Young Perthes.) Hamburg: Hanseatische Verlags-Anstalt, 1925.
  Perthes der Mann. (Perthes the man.) Hamburg: Hanseatische Verlags-Anstalt, 1925.

  Globe-Theater. Hamburg: Hanseatische Verlags-Anstalt.
    1. Virginia. 1926.
    2. Der Schwann vom Avon. (The swan of Avon.) 1927.

  Die Fronde; ein Mazarin-Roman. (A Mazarin novel.) Berlin: Vossische Buchhand., 1927.
  König Sonne; Roman aus der Zeit Ludwigs XIV. (The sun king; a novel of the time of Louis XIV.) Berlin: Vossische Buchhand., 1927.

  Friedrich Ludwig Schröder; der grossen Schauspielers Werdezeit. (The growing time of the great actor.) Hamburg: Alster, 1928.
  Charlotte Ackermann. Hamburg: Alster, 1929.
Pleyer, Wilhelm, 1901-
  Till Scheerauer; der Roman eines junge Deutschen. (The novel of a young German.) Weimar: Duncker, 1932.
  Der Puchner; ein Grenzlandschicksal. (A borderland destiny.) Munich: Langen/Müller, 1934.
Ponten, Josef, 1883-1940
  Volk auf dem Wege; Roman der deutschen Unruhe. (People on the road; a novel of German unrest.) Stuttgart: Deutsche Verlags-Anstalt.
  Compiler's note: An unfinished sequence, intended to include ten volumes.
    1. Die Väter zogen aus. (The fathers emigrate.) 1934.
    2. Im Wolgaland. 1933.
    Compiler's note: A revision of Wolga, Wolga, 1930, and Rhein and Wolga, 1931.
    3. Rheinisches Zwischenspiel. (Rhenish interlude.) 1937.
    4. Die Heiligen der letzten Tage. (The saints of the last days.) 1938.
    5. Der Zug nach dem Kaukasus. (The migration to the Caucasus.) 1940.
Raabe, Wilhelm, 1831-1910
  Wilhelm Raabe/Trilogie. 3 vols. Berlin: Klemm, n.d.
    1. Der Hungerpastor. 3 vols. Berlin: Janke, 1864.
    2. Abu Telfan, oder Die Heimkehr vom Mondgebirge. 3 vols. Stuttgart: Hallberger, 1867.
    3. Die Schüdderump. 3 vols. Braunschweig: Westermann, 1870.

    1. The hungerpastor. Trans. by "Arnold." 2 vols. London: Chapman & Hall, 1885.
    2. Abu Telfan; return from the mountains of the moon. 3 vols. London: Chapman & Hall, 1881.
Rainalter, Erwin Herbert, 1892-
  Die verkaufte Heimat. (The homeland sold.) Munich: Kösel & Pustet, 1928.
  Heimkehr. (Homecoming.) Leipzig: Staackmann, 1931.
Randenborgh, Frau Elisabet (Riemeier) van, 1893-
  Neu ward mein Tagewerk; Weg und Wandlung eines Frauenlebens. (My day's work became new; course and alteration of a woman's life.) Berlin: Furche, 1934.
  Die harte Herrlichkeit. (The austere splendor.) Berlin: Furche, 1935.

  Amries Vermächtnis. 1935.
  Compiler's note: A novella, concluding the novels.
Rau, Heribert, 1813-76
  Alexander von Humboldt. Culturhistorisch-biographischer Roman in sechs Theilen. (Biographical and history of culture novel in six divisions.)
    Part I:
    Die Dioskuren. (The Dioscuri.)
      1. Sonnenaufgang. Alexander von Humboldts Kindheit. (Sunrise. Childhood.) Frankfurt am Main: Meidinger, 1860.
      2. Akademisches Leben. Alexander von Humboldts Jugend. (Academic life. Youth.) Frankfurt am Main: Meidinger, 1860.

Part II:
Ueber dem Ocean. (Over the ocean.)
3-4. Humboldt und Bonpland. Alexander von Humboldts Mannesalter. (Manhood.) 2 vols. Frankfurt am Main: Meidinger, 1860.
Part III:
Im Zenith der Grösse. (At the zenith of greatness.)
5. In der Heimat. Alexander von Humboldts Mannesalter. (At home.) Leipzig: Thomas, 1860.
6. Der Stern des Jahrhunderts. Alexander von Humboldts Greisenalter. (Star of the century. Old age.) Leipzig: Thomas, 1860.

Remarque, Erich Maria, 1898-
Im Westen nichts Neues. (No news in the west.) Berlin: Propyläen-Verlag, 1929.
Der Weg zurück. Berlin: Propyläen-Verlag, 1931.

(1) All quiet on the western front. Trans. by A. W. Wheen. Boston: Little, Brown, 1929.
(2) The road back. Trans. by A. W. Wheen. Boston: Little, Brown, 1931.

Rendl, Georg, 1903-
Die Glasbläser. (The glass blowers.) Salzburg: Pustet.
1. Menschen im Moor. (People in the marshland.) 1935.
2. Die Glasbläser. 1937.
3. Das Gespenst aus Stahl. (The specter of steel.) 1938.

"Retcliffe, Sir John," see Goedsche, Hermann Ottomar Friedrich.

Reuter, Fritz, 1810-74
Olle Kamellen. Wismar: Hinstorff, 1860-64. 6-7 published in Sämmtliche Werke (Leipzig: Philipp Reclam, jun.), vols. 12-13.
1. Zwei lustige Geschichten. (Two merry tales.)
Contents: "Woans ick tau 'ne fru kamm," "Ut de Franzosentid."
2. Ut mine Festungstid. (About my time in the fortress.)
3-5. Ut mine Stromtid, I-III.
6. Dörchlauchting. (His Grace.) 1865.
7. De meckelnbörgschen Montecchi un Capuletti, oder De Reis nach Konstantinopel. (The Mecklenburg Montagues and Capulets, or The journey to Constantinople.) 1868.

"Olle Kamellen."
1. How I came by a wife. Trans. by Paul Glave. Denver: Echo Pub. House, 1883. In the year '13; a tale of Mecklenburg life. Trans. by Charles Lee Lewis. New York: Leypoldt & Holt, 1867.
2. Seedtime and harvest, or During my apprenticeship. Philadelphia: Lippincott, 1871.
3-5. An old story of my farming days. Trans. by M. W. Macdowall. 3 vols. Leipzig: Tauchnitz, 1878.

Rocco, Wilhelm, 1819-97
Vor veertig Jahre; en plattdütsche Geschichte ut'n Bremer Lanne. (Forty years ago; a low-German story from the Bremen district.) Bremen: Schünemann, 1880.
Kinner un ohle Lüde; en plattdütsche Geschichte ut'n Bremer Lanne. (Children and old people.) Bremen: Schünemann, 1882.

"Rose, Felicitas," pseud. of Frau Rose (Schliewen) Moersberger
Provinzmädel. (Provincial girl.) 10 vols.; 5 vols. Berlin: Bong, 1928.
1. Kleinstadtlust. (Small town fun.)
2. Kerlchens Lern-und Wanderjahre. (Kerlchen's years of study and travel.)
3. Kerlchen wird vernünftig. (Kerlchen becomes sensible.)
4. Kerlchen als Erzieher. (Kerlchen as teacher.)
5. Kerlchen als Anstandsdame. (Kerlchen as chaperone.)
6. Kerlchen als Sorgen-und Sektbrecher. (Kerlchen drowns care in champagne.)
7. Liebesgeschichten. (Love stories.)
8. Kerlchens Flitterwochen. (Kerlchen's honeymoon.)
9. Kerlchens Mütterglück. (Kerlchen's happiness as mother.)
10. Kerlchens Ebenbild. (Kerlchen's image.)

Rump, (Heinrich Carl Dietrich) Johann, see "Junger, Nathanael."

Salburg, Edith, Gräfin, 1868-
  Die österreichische Gesellschaft. (Austrian society.) Leipzig: Grübel & Sommerlatte.
    1. Die Exclusiven. (The exclusive set.) 1897.
    2. Papa Durchlaucht. (Serene Highness Papa.) 1897.
    3. Die Inclusiven. (The inclusive set.) 1898.

  Was die Wirklichkeit erzählt; drei Bücher die das Leben schreibt. (What reality tells; three books written by life.)
    1. Carrière; Skizzenbuch aus der grossen Welt. (Career; sketchbook of the great world.) Leipzig: Grübel & Sommerlatte, 1898.
    2. Golgatha. Dresden: Reissner, 1900.
    3. Humanitas. Dresden: Reissner, 1901.

  Seiner Majestät Strategen. (His majesty's strategists.) Dresden: Reissner, 1911.
    1-2. Königsglaube. (The king's faith.) 2 vols. 1906.
    3. Wilhelm Friedhoff. 1907.

  Dynasten und Stände; Romane aus Oesterreich-Ungarn. (Dynasties and classes; novels of Austria-Hungary.) Dresden: Reissner.
    1. Böhmische Herren. (Gentlemen of Bohemia.) 1910.
    2. Hofadel in Oesterreich. (Court nobility in Austria.) 1912.
    3. Reaktion. 1912.
    4. Revolution. 1914.
"Samarow, Gregor," see Meding, (Johann Ferdinand Martin) Oskar.
Sander, Ulrich, 1892-
  Der ewige Orlog. (The eternal campaign.) Jena: Diederichs, 1935.
    1. Jungens. (Boys.) 1935.
    2. Pioniere; ein Frontbericht. (Sappers and miners; a report from the front.) 1933.
    3. Kompost. 1934.
Schaffner, Jakob, 1875-1944
  Johannes.
    1. Johannes; Roman einer Jugend. (Novel of a youth.) 2 vols. Stuttgart: Union deutsche Verlags., 1922.
    2. Die Junglingzeit des Johannes Schattenhold. (The youth of Johannes.) Stuttgart: Union deutsche Verlags., 1930.
    3. Eine deutsche Wanderschaft. (A German tour.) Vienna: Zsolnay, 1933.
Schaumburg, Paul Erich Bruno Richard, 1884- Pseud., "Paul Burg"
  Der befreite Gott. (The liberated god.)
    1. Der Wegbereiter und die Liebe. (The forerunner and love.) Leipzig: Staackmann, 1920.
    2. Zwei Eisen im Feuer. (Two irons in the fire.) Leipzig: Koch, 1921.

  Alles um Liebe; ein Goethe-Roman. (All for love; a Goethe novel.) 6 vols. in 4. Berlin: Grass, 1930-31.
  Vol. I:
    1. Freudvoll und Leidvoll. (Joyful and sorrowful.) Leipzig: Koch, 1922.
    2. Meine Christel, I. (My Christel.) Leipzig: Koch, 1922.
  Vol. II:
    3. Christels Ehe. Meine Christel, II. (Christel's marriage.) Leipzig: Koch, 1923.
    4. Der schöne alte Herr. (The fine old gentleman.) Leipzig: Koch, 1923.
  Vol. III:
    5. Ahn und Enkel; Sie sind's die Ahnherrn meines Hauses. (Ancestor and descendant; it is they, the ancestors of my house.) Leipzig: Koch, 1924.
  Vol. IV:
    6. Der junge Goethe. (The young Goethe.)
Schickele, René, 1883-1940
  Das Erbe am Rhein.
    1. Maria Capponi. 1 vol. Munich: Wolff, 1926. First published as Ein Erbe am Rhein. 2 vols. 1925.

    2. Blick auf die Vogesen. (View of the Vosges.) Munich: Wolff, 1927.
    3. Der Wolf in der Hürde. (The wolf in the fold.) Berlin: Fischer, 1931.

"The Rhineland heritage." Trans. by Hannah Waller. New York, London: Knopf.
    1. Marie Capponi. 1928.
    2. Heart of Alsace. 1929. British title: The Rhineland Heritage.

Schlaf, Johannes, 1862-1941
  Das dritte Reich; ein Berliner Roman. (The third empire; a Berlin novel.) Berlin: Fleischel, 1900.
  Die Suchenden. (The seekers.) Berlin: Fleischel, 1902.
  Peter Bojes Freite. (Peter Boje's courtship.) Leipzig: Seemann, 1903.

  Der Kleine; ein Berliner Roman. (The little one; a Berlin novel.) Stuttgart: Juncker, 1904.
  Der Prinz. (The prince.) 2 vols. Munich: Müller, 1908.
  Am toten Punkt. (At the dead center.) Munich: Müller, 1909.

Schmidt, Otto Ernst, 1862-1926. Pseud., "Otto Ernst"
  Semper-Romane. (Semper novels.) Leipzig: Staackmann.
    1. Asmus Sempers Jugendland; der Roman einer Kindheit. (Asmus Semper's land of youth; the novel of a childhood.) 1905.
    2. Semper der Jungling; ein Bildungs Roman. (Semper the young man; a development novel.) 1908.
    3. Semper der Mann; ein Künstler- und Kämpfergeschichte. (Semper the man; a story of an artist and his struggles.) 1916-17.

    1. Asmus Semper, the story of a boyhood. Trans. by Aletheia Caton. London: Griffiths, 1909.

Schoenstedt, Walter, 1909-
  Das Lob des Lebens. New York: Farrar & Rinehart, 1938.

(1) In praise of life. Trans. by Maxim Newmark. New York: Farrar & Rinehart, 1938. Published in English and German simultaneously.
(2) The cradle builder. Trans. by Richard Winston. New York: Farrar & Rinehart, 1940.

Schuk, Pancratz, 1877-
  Die Stadt an der Donau; ein Wiener Geschichte. (The city on the Danube; a Vienna story.) Dillingen: Veduka, 1924.
  Die letzten Wiener. (The last Viennese.) Dillingen: Veduka, 1924.

Schulze-Berghof, Paul, 1873-
  Die friederizianische Trilogie. (Frederick the Great trilogy.) 3 vols. Munich: Hugo Schmidt, 1916.
    1. Die Königskerze. (The king's candle.) 1912.
    2. Der Königssohn; ein friederizianischer Roman aus der Küstriner Festungszeit. (The king's son; Frederick's time in Küstrin.)
    3. Die schöne Sabine; ein friederizianischer Roman aus den Rheinsberger Tagen. (Fair Sabine; novel of the Rhine mountain days.)

Schumacher, Heinrich Vollrat, 1861-1919
  Liebe und Leben der Lady Hamilton. (Love and life of Lady Hamilton.) Berlin: Bong, 1910.
  Lord Nelsons letzte Liebe. (Lord Nelson's last love.) Berlin: Bong, 1911.

Seeberg, Dierck
  Die Metallstadt. (The metal city.) Leipzig: Haessel.
    1. Die Mauer um die Stadt. (The wall around the city.) 1924.
    2. Unterstadt. (Lower city.) 1930.
    3. Zwischenstadt. (Middle city.) 1927.
    4. Oberstadt. (Upper city.) 1927.

Skowronnek, Fritz, 1858-
  Der Polenflüchtling; ein Roman aus dem Osten. (The refugee from Poland; a novel of the East.) Berlin: Janke, 1918.
  Pan Kaminsky. Berlin: Janke, 1920.

GERMAN AND LOW GERMAN

"Sonnleitner, A. T.," see Tluchor, Alois.
Spielhagen, Friedrich, 1829-1911
  Problematische Naturen. 2 vols. Berlin: Janke, 1863.
    1. Problematische Naturen. 4 vols. 1861.
    2. Problematische Naturen: Durch Nacht zum Licht. 4 vols. 1862.

  "Problematic characters." Trans. by Schele de Vere. New York: Leypoldt & Holt.
    1. Problematic characters. 1869.
    2. Through night to light. 1870.
Stehr, Hermann, 1864-1940
  Drei Nächte. (Three nights.) Berlin: Fischer, 1909.
  Der Heiligenhof. 2 vols. Berlin: Fischer, 1918.
  Peter Brindeisener. Treves: Linz, 1924.

  Nathanael Maechler. Berlin: Horenverlag, 1929.
  Die Nachkommen. (The descendants.) Leipzig: List, 1933.
  "Damian Maechler."
  Compiler's note: Announced in preparation.
Stilgebauer, Edward, 1868-
  Götz Krafft; die Geschichte einer Jugend. (The story of a youth.) 4 vols. Berlin: Bong, 1904-5.
    1. Mit tausend Masten. (With a thousand masts.)
    2. Im Strom der Welt. (In the current of the world.)
    3. Im engen Kreis. (In a narrow sphere.) 1905.
    4. Des Lebens Krone. (The crown of life.) 1905.

  Die Lügner des Lebens. (The liars of life.)
    1. Der Börsenkönig. (The stock king.) Berlin: Bong, 1907.
    2. Die neue Stadt. (The new city.) Dresden: Reissner, 1910.
    3. Bildner der Jugend. (Molder of youth.) Berlin: Bong, 1908.
    4. Der Eroberer. (The conqueror.) Mainz: Diener, 1909.
    5. Purpur. (Purple.) Dresden: Reissner, 1911.
    6. Pfarrer Schröder. (Parson Schröder.) Dresden: Reissner, 1912.
    7. Das Liebesnest. (The love nest.) Berlin: Bong, 1908.
Stinde, Julius Ernst Wilhelm, 1841-1905
  Die Familie Buchholz; aus dem Leben der Hauptstadt. (The Buchholz family; from the life of the capital city.) 4 vols. Berlin: Freund & Jeckel, 1893-95.
    1. Die Familie Buchholz. 1884.
    2. Die Familie Buchholz, II. 1885.
    3. Die Familie Buchholz: Frau Wilhelmine. 1886.
    4. Wilhelmine Buchholz Memoiren. 1895.
  Hotel Buchholz; Ausstellungs Erlebnisse der Frau Wilhelmine Buchholz. (Exhibition experiences of Frau Wilhelmine.) Berlin: Freund & Jeckel, 1897.
  Compiler's note: Two volumes of travel sketches, omitted here because they are not novels, also deal with the Buchholz family.

    1-2. The Buchholz family. Trans. by L. Dora Schmitz. 2 vols. New York: Scribner's, 1886.
    3. Frau Wilhelmine. Trans. by Harriet F. Powell. New York: Scribner's, 1887.
    1-4. The hausfrau rampant. Trans. and condensed by E. V. Lucas. New York: Doran, 1916.
      British title: Masterful Wilhelmine.
Stolle, Ferdinand
  Der neue Cäsar. (The new Caesar.) 3 vols. Leipzig: Meissner, 1841.
  Napoleon in Aegypten. 3 vols. Leipzig: Berger, 1844.
  Die Granitkolonnen von Marengo. (The granite columns of Marengo.) 3 vols. Plauen: Schröter, 1855.
  Boulogne und Austerlitz. 1848.
  1813. 3 vols. Leipzig: Meissner, 1838.
  Elba und Waterloo. 3 vols. Leipzig: Meissner, 1838.

Storch, Ludwig, 1803-81
  Ein deutscher Leinweber; Zeit- und Lebensbilder aus der ersten Hälfte des 16 Jahrhundert. (A German linen weaver; pictures of the life and times of the first half of the sixteenth century.) Leipzig: Weber.
    I. Philipp von Oestreich. 3 vols. 1846.
      1. Die schöne Kaufmannsfrau von Antwerp. (The Antwerp merchant's pretty wife.)
      2. Die Reise nach Spanien. (The journey to Spain.)
      3. Die Königskrone. (The king's crown.)
    II. Karl von Spanien. 3 vols. 1848.
    III. Das Haus Fugger. (The Fugger house.) 3 vols. 1850.

  Leute von Gestern; Lebensbilder aus der jüngsten Vergangenheit. (People of yesterday; pictures of life of the immediate past.)
  Compiler's note: An unfinished sequence.
    1. Aus einer Bergstadt. (From a mountain city.) 3 vols. Leipzig: Weber, 1852-53.

Stratz, Rudolph, 1864-1936
  Deutschlands Aufstieg und Niedergang. (Germany's rise and downfall.) Berlin: Scherl.
    1. Der Väter Traum; Roman aus der Zeit der Einheitsbestrebungen. (The fathers' dream; a novel of the time of efforts for unity.) 1920.
    2. Das Schiff ohne Steuer; Roman aus der Zeit nach Bismarcks Entlassung. (The ship without a rudder; a novel of the time after the dismissal of Bismark.) 1921.
    3. Der Platz an der Sonne; Roman aus wilhelminischer Zeit. (The place in the sun; a novel of Wilhelm's time.) 1921.

Strobl, Karl Hans, 1877-
  Bismarck. 3 vols. Leipzig: Staackmann, 1927.
    1. Der wilde Bismarck. 1915.
    2. Eisen und Blut. (Blood and iron.) 1917. Reissued as Mächte und Menschen. (Power and men.)
    3. Die Runen Gottes. (God's runes.) 1919.

  Die Wünschelrute, oder Das unsterbliche Deutschland. (The divining rod, or Immortal Germany.) 3 vols. Leipzig: Staackmann.
    1. Die alte Türme. (The old towers.) 1921.
    2. Wir hatten gebauet. (We had built.) 1923.
    3. Erasmus mit der Wünschelrute. (Erasmus with the divining rod.) 1927.

Stuhlen, Peter, 1900-
  Aus den schwarzen Wäldern. (From the black forests.) Berlin: Krüger, 1936.
  Compiler's note: A series note gives Eltern und Kinder as a continuation.
  Eltern und Kinder. (Parents and children.) Berlin: Krüger, 1935.
  Compiler's note: A series note lists this as the first of three volumes, to be followed by "Die Elsissträger" and "Aus der Asche." The note in Aus den schwarzen Wäldern, being the later, indicates a change in plan. Both notes refer to an intended trilogy.
  Das Erbe. (The heritage.) Berlin: Krüger, 1941.
  Compiler's note: A series note lists the two novels given above and announces the fourth. "Aus der Asche."
  Compiler's note: In preparation.

Tavel, Rudolf von, 1866-1934
  "Bern series." Bern: Francke.
  Compiler's note: Listed in order of publication.
    1. Familie Landorfer. 3 vols.
      Ja gall, so geit's; e luschtigi Gschicht us truuriger Zyt. (Well, that is how it goes; an amusing story from sad times.) 1901.
      Der Houpme Lombach. Berndeutsche Novelle. (Captain Lombach.) 1903.
      Gotti und Gotteli. Berndeutsche Novelle. (Godfather and godmother.) 1906.
    2. Der Schtärn vo Buebebärg; e Gschicht us de truebschte Tage vom alte Bärn. (The star of Bubenberg; a story from the darkest days of old Bern.) 1907.
    3. D'Frou Kätheli und ihre Buebe. (Mrs. Kathy and her little boy.) 2 vols. 1910.
    Compiler's note: A continuation of 2.

GERMAN AND LOW GERMAN

    4. Gueti Gschpane. (Good teams.) 1913.
    5. Der Donnergueg; e Liebesgeschicht us schtille Zyt. (The weatherman; a love story from quiet times.) 1916.
    6. D'Haselmuus; e Gschicht us em Undergang vom alte Bärne. (The chipmunk; a story about the downfall of old Bern.) 1922.
    7. Unspunne. (Unraveled.) 1924.
    Compiler's note: A continuation of 6.
    8. Veterane-Zyt. (Veterans' time.) 1927.
    9. Am Kaminfüür. (By the fireside.) 1928.
    10. Der Frondeur. (The rebel.) 1929.
    11. Ring in der Chetti. (The ring in the chain.) 1931.
    12. Meischter und Ritter. (Master and knight.) 1933.

Thiess, Frank, 1890-
  Jugend. 4 vols. Stuttgart: Engelhorns Nachf., 1931.
    1. Abschied vom Paradies. 1927.
    Compiler's note: A prelude to 2 and 3.
    2. Das Tor zur Welt. 1926.
    3. Der Leibhaftige. (The incarnate.) 1924.
    4. Der Zentaur. (The Centaur.) 1931. Title announced in preparation: "Die Feuersäule." (The fiery column.)
  "Youth." Trans. by H. T. Lowe-Porter. New York: Knopf.
    1. Farewell to Paradise. 1929.
    2. The gateway to life. 1927.
    3. The devil's shadow. 1927.

Tluchor, Alois, 1869-   Pseud., "A. T. Sonnleitner"
  Die Höhlenkinder. 3 vols. Stuttgart: Franckhsche Verlag, 1921-25.
    1. Die Höhlenkinder im heimlichen Grund. (The cave children in the secret ground.)
    2. Die Höhlenkinder im Pfahlbau. (In the house on stilts.)
    3. Die Höhlenkinder im Steinhaus. (In the stone house.)

  The cave children. Trans. by Winifred M. Deans. London, Glasgow: Blackie, 1935.

  Das Haus der Sehnsucht. 3 vols. Stuttgart: Franckhs. Bücher für Jüng und Alt, 1922-25.
    1. Kojas Wanderjahre. (Koja's years of travel.)
    2. Kojas Waldläuferzeit. (Koja's life in the forest.)
    3. Kojas Haus der Sehnsucht. (Koja's house of longing.)

  Die Hegerkinder. (The forester's children.) Vienna: Deutscher Verlag für Jügend und Volk.
    1. Die Hegerkinder von Aspern. 1924.
    2. Die Hegerkinder in der Lobau. 1924.
    3. Die Hegerkinder im Gamsgebirge. 1928.

Ungern-Sternberg, Alexander, Freiherr von, 1806-68
  Neupreussische Zeitbilder. (New Prussian pictures of the times.) Bremen: Schlodtmann.
    1. Die Royalisten. (The royalists.) 1848.
    2. Die beiden Schützen. (The two hunters.) 1849.

Vegesack, Siegfried von, 1888-
  Baltische Trilogie. (Baltic trilogy.) 1 vol. Berlin: Universitas, 1937.
    1. Blumbergshof; Geschichte einer Kindheit. (Story of a childhood.) 1933.
    2. Herren ohne Heer; Roman des baltisches Deutschtums. (Lords without an army; a novel of the Baltic Germans.) 1934.
    3. Totentanz in Livland. (Dance of death in Livonia.) 1935.

Volbehr, Frau Lu, 1871-
  Die neue Zeit. (The new time.) 2 vols. Dresden: Seyfert, 1909.
    1. Sebastian Rottmann. First published as Die neue Zeit. Berlin: Janke, 1905.
    2. Und alles ist Frucht. (And everything is fruit.)

"Waldau, Max," see Hauenschild, Spiller von.

Walloth, Wilhelm, 1856-
  Ovid. Leipzig: Friedrich, 1890.

Tiberius. 2 vols. Leipzig: Friedrich, 1889.
Der Gladiator; Roman aus der Zeit Kaligulas. (The gladiator; a novel of the time of Caligula.) Leipzig: Friedrich, 1888.
Oktavia; Roman aus der Zeit Neros. Leipzig: Friedrich, 1885.
Paris der Mime; realistische-historischer Roman aus der Zeit Domitians. (Paris the mime; realistic historical novel of the time of Domitian.) Leipzig: Friedrich, 1886.

(4) Empress Octavia; a romance of the reign of Nero. Trans. by Mary J. Safford. Boston: Little, Brown, 1900.

Wassermann, Jakob, 1873-1934
Christian Wahnschaffe. 2 vols. Berlin: Fischer, 1919.
  1. Eva.   2. Ruth.

The world's illusion. Trans. by Ludwig Lewisohn. 2 vols. New York: Harcourt, Brace, 1920. 1 vol. ed., 1930.

Der Wendekreis. (The tropic.) Berlin: Fischer.
  1. Der Wendekreis. 1920.
    Contents: "Der unbekannte Gast" and other stories.
  2. Oberlins drei Stufen und Sturreganz. 1922.
  Compiler's note: Novelle.
  3. Ulricke Woytich. 1923.
  4. Faber, oder Die verlorenen Jahre. 1924.

  1. World's ends. Trans. by Lewis Galantière. New York: Boni & Liveright, 1927.
  Compiler's note: "Der unbekannte Gast" is omitted.
  2. Oberlin's three stages. Trans. by Allen Porterfield. New York: Harcourt, Brace, 1925.
  3. Gold. Trans. by Louise Collier Willcox. New York: Harcourt, Brace, 1924.
  4. Faber, or The lost years. Trans. by Harry Hansen. New York: Harcourt, Brace, 1925.

Der Fall Maurizius. Berlin: Fischer, 1929.
Etzel Andergast. Berlin: Fischer, 1931.
Joseph Kerkhovens dritte Existenz. Amsterdam: Querido, 1934.

(1) The Maurizius case. Trans. by Caroline Newton. New York: Liveright, 1929.
(2) Doctor Kerkhoven. Trans. by Cyrus Brooks. New York: Liveright, 1932. British title: Etzel Andergast.
(3) Kerkhoven's third existence. Trans. by Eden and Cedar Paul. New York: Liveright, 1934.

Weiskopf, Franz Karl, 1900-
Twilight on the Danube. Trans. by Olga Marx. New York: Knopf, 1946.
Children of their time. Trans. by Ilona Ralf Sues and Heinz Norden.
Compiler's note: The first novels of a series covering the years 1913-39.

Weismantel, Leo, 1888-
Aus der Geschichte des Untergangs eines Volkes. (From the story of the fall of a nation.)
  1. Das alte Dorf; die Geschichte seines Jahres und der Menschen die in ihm gelebt haben. (The old village; the history of its year and of the people who lived in it.) Berlin: Bühnenvolksbund, 1928.
  2. Das Sterben in den Gassen. (Death in the streets.) Nuremburg: Sebaldus, 1932.
  3. Die Geschichte des Hauses Herkommer. (The story of the Herkommer house.) Nuremburg: Sebaldus, 1932.

Mathis-Nithart Roman. (Mathis Nithart novel.) Munich: Alber.
  1. Das Totenliebespaar; Roman aus der Kindheit und den Lehrjahren des Mathis Nithart, der fälschlich Mathias Grunewald genannte würde. (The dead pair of lovers; novel of the childhood and apprentice years of Mathis Nithart, who was falsely called Mathias Grunewald.) 1941.

GERMAN AND LOW GERMAN

    2. Der bunte Rock der Welt; Roman aus den Wander-und-frühen Meisterjahren des Mathis Nithart. (The soldier's uniform of the world; novel of the journeyman's years of travel and the early years as master of Mathis Nithart.) 1941.
    3. Die höllische Trinität; Roman aus den Jahren der Vollendung des Meisters Mathis Nithart. (The infernal trinity; novel of the years of perfection of Master Mathis Nithart.) 1943.

Wette, Hermann, 1857-1919
  Krauskopf. 3 vols. Leipzig: Grunow, 1903.
    1. Krauskopfs Kindheit. (Curly-head's childhood.)
    2. Vom Knaben zum Jüngling. (From boy to youth.)
    3. Vom Jüngling zum Mann. (From youth to man.)

Wichert, Ernst, 1831-1902
  Der Grosse Kurfürst in Preussen. (The Great Elector in Prussia.) 3d ed. 5 vols. in 3. Dresden: Reissner, 1897.
    1. Konrad Born. 1893.
    2. Der Schöppenmeister. (The master of the jurors.) 2 vols. 1893.
    3. Christian Ludwig von Kalckstein. 2 vols. 1896.

Wiechert, Ernst, 1887-
  Die Jeromin-Kinder. (The Jeromin children.) 2 vols. Munich: Zinnen-Verlag.
    1. Der Jeromin-Kinder. 1945.
    2. Die Furchen der Armen. (The wrinkles of the poor.) Zurich: Rascher, 1947.
    3. Announced in preparation.

Wilhelm, Hans Hermann, 1892-
  Die Frickes. Berlin: Brunnen.
    1. Das Erwachen in der Heide. (The awakening on the heath.) 1933.
    2. Das Erbe der Frickes. (The heritage of the Frickes.) 1934.
    3. Die Frickes und die Ohlhofs. 1937.

Zweig, Arnold, 1887-
  Junge Frau von 1914. Berlin: Kiepenheuer, 1931.
  Compiler's note: A prelude to the trilogy.
  Trilogie des Uebergangs.
    1. Erziehung vor Verdun. Amsterdam: Querido, 1935.
    2. Der Streit um den Sergeanten Grischa. Potsdam: Kiepenheuer, 1927.
    3. Einsetzung eines Königs. Amsterdam: Querido, 1937.

  Young woman of 1914. Trans. by Eric Sutton. New York: Viking Press, 1932.
  "A trilogy of the transition." Trans. by Eric Sutton. New York: Viking Press.
    1. Education before Verdun. 1936.
    2. The case of Sergeant Grischa. 1928.
    3. The crowning of a king. 1938.

SCANDINAVIAN

Danish

Bang, Herman Joachim, 1857-1912
  Haabløse Slaegter. (Hopeless generations.) Copenhagen: Schubothe, 1880.
  Ved Vejen. (At the road.) Copenhagen: Schubothe, 1898.
  Det hvide Hus. (The white house.) Copenhagen: Schubothe, 1898.
  Det graa Hus. (The gray house.) Copenhagen: Gyldendal, 1901.
Bruun, Laurids, 1864-1935
  Den Evige. (The eternal one.) 8 vols. in 4. Copenhagen: Gyldendal.
    1-2. Hjaerternes Møde. (The meeting of the hearts.) 1905.
    3-4. Spiring og Vaekst. (Sprouting and growth.) 1905.
    5-6. De klare Øjne. (The clear eyes.) 1906.
    7-8. Og Lyset taendtes. (And the light was lit.) 1906.

  Af Bygernes Slaegt; Roman fra Hundredsaarsskiftet. (Of the Byge family; a novel from the turn of the century.) 6 vols. in 2. Copenhagen: Gyldendal, 1909.
    Vol. I. Svend Byge. (Servant Byge.)
      1. Der laaegges ud. (The sailing out.)
      2. Under Opsejling. (During the voyage.)
      3. Paa Grund. (Aground.)
    Vol. II. Mester Byge. (Master Byge.)
      4. Mod Strøm og Vind. (Against the current and wind.)
      5. Gennem Nat til Gry. (Through night to dawn.)
      6. Braendte Skibe og nye. (Burned ships and new ones.)

  "Van Zanten trilogy." Trans. and ed. by Laurids Bruun. Copenhagen: Gyldendal.
    1. Van Zantens lykkelige Tid; Kaerlighedroman fra Pelli-Øen. (Love story from the Pelli Islands.) 1908.
    2. Det forjaettede Ø. 1910.
    3. Den glaedeløse Enke. (The joyless widow.) 1914.

  "Van Zanten trilogy." Trans. by David Pritchard. London: Gyldendal.
    1. Van Zanten's happy days. 1920.
    2. Promised isle. 1921.

  Danskernes Eventyr. (Saga of the Danes.) Copenhagen: Gyldendal.
    1. Kong Skjold. 1909.
    2. Kong Frode. 1910.
    3. Den signede Død. (The blessed death.) 1912.

  Den ukente Gud. (The unknown god.) Copenhagen: Gyldendal, 1913.
  Under Livets Trae. (Under the tree of life.) Copenhagen: Gyldendal, 1917.
Buchholtz, Johannes, 1882-
  Egholms God. Copenhagen: Gyldendal, 1915.
  Clara Van Haags Mirakler. Copenhagen: Gyldendal, 1916.

  (1) Egholm and his God. Trans. by W. W. Worster. New York: Knopf, 1922.
  (2) The miracles of Clara Van Haag. Trans. by W. W. Worster. New York: Knopf, 1922.

  Frank Dovers Ansigt. (Frank Dover's face.) Copenhagen: Gyldendal, 1933.
  Frank Dover og den lille Kvinde. (Frank Dover and the little woman.) Copenhagen: Gyldendal, 1934.

  The saga of Frank Dover. Trans. by Eugene Gay-Tifft. 1 vol. New York: Putnam's, 1938.
Gunnarsson, Gunnar, 1889-
  Af Borgslaegtens Historie. (History of the Borg family.) Copenhagen: Gyldendal.

SCANDINAVIAN

    1. Ormarr Orlygsson. 1912.
    2. Den danske Frue paa Hof. 1913.
    3. Gaest den Enøjede. 1913.
    4. Den unge Ørn. 1913.

Guest the One-Eyed. Trans. by W. W. Worster. 1 vol. New York: Knopf, 1922.
    1. Ormarr Orlygsson.   3. Guest the One-Eyed.
    2. The Danish lady at Hof.   4. The young eagle.

Livets Strand. (The shore of life.) Copenhagen, Christiania: Gyldendal, 1915.
Varg i veum. (The outcast.) Copenhagen, Christiania: Gyldendal, 1916.
Salige er de enfoldige. (Blessed are the simple.) Copenhagen, Christiania: Gyldendal, 1920.

(3) Seven days' darkness. Trans. by Roberts Tapley. New York: Macmillan, 1930.

Kirken paa Bjerget. Copenhagen: Gyldendal. Note in individual novels: "Af Uggi Greipssons
    Optegnelser." (From Uggi Greipsson's notes.)
    1. Leg med Straa. (Play with straw.) 1923.
    2. Skibe paa Himlen. 1925.
    3. Natten og Drømmen. 1926.
    4. Den uerfarne Rejsende. (The inexperienced traveler.) 1927.
    5. Hugleik den Haardtsejlende. (Hugleik the brave sailor.) 1928.

The church on the hill. Trans. by Evelyn Ramsden. 2 vols. Indianapolis: Bobbs-Merrill, 1938.
    2. Ships in the sky.   3. The night and the dream.

"Islands historie." (History of Iceland.)
    1. Edbrødre; Roman fra Islands Landnamstid. (Oath brothers.) Copenhagen, Christiania:
       Gyldendal, 1918.
    2. Jôn Arason. Copenhagen: Gyldendal, 1930.
    3. Jord. (Earth.) Copenhagen: Gyldendal, 1933.
Compiler's note: The sequence is intended to be completed in 12 volumes.

Hjortø, Knud, 1869-1931
  Stov og Stjaerner. (Dust and stars.) Copenhagen: Gyldendal, 1904.
  To Verdener. (Two worlds.) Copenhagen: Gyldendal, 1905.
  Hans Råskov. Copenhagen: Gyldendal, 1906.

Jensen, Johannes Vilhelm, 1873-
  Den lange Rejse. 2 vols. Copenhagen: Gyldendal, 1938.
    Vol. I:
    1. Det tabte Land. (The lost land.) 1919.
    2. Braen. (The ice age.) 1908.
    3. Norne-Gaest. 1919.
    Vol. II:
    4. Cimbernes Tog. (The expedition of the Cimbrians.) 1922.
    5. Skibet. (The ship.) 1913.
    6. Christofer Columbus. 1921.

  The long journey. Trans. by Arthur G. Chater. 1 vol. New York: Knopf, 1945.
    1-2. Fire and ice. 1 vol. 1923.
    3-4. The Cimbrians. 1 vol. 1923.
    5-6. Christopher Columbus. 1 vol. 1924.

Kidde, Harald, 1878-1918
  Aage og Else. Copenhagen: Gyldendal.
    1. Døden. (Dead.) 1902.   2. Livet. (Life.) 1903.

  Jaernet; Roman om Järnbäraland. (Iron; novel about iron bearing country.) Copenhagen:
  Aschehoug, 1918.
  Compiler's note: The beginning of an unfinished sequence.

Knudsen, Jakob Christian Lindberg, 1858-1917
  Gjaering. (Ferment.) Copenhagen: Gyldendal, 1902.

Afklaring. (Clarification.) Copenhagen: Gyldendal, 1902.
To Slaegter. (Two families.) Copenhagen: Gyldendal, 1910.
Rodfaestet. (Firmly rooted.) Copenhagen: Gyldendal, 1911.

Martin Luther. 1 vol. Copenhagen: Gyldendal, 1915.
    1. Angst. (Fear.) 1912.
    2. Mod. (Courage.) 1914.

Lemche, Fru Gyrithe (Frisch), 1866-
    Edwardsgave. 5 vols. Copenhagen: Gyldendal, 1920.
        1. Kjøbmaend. (Merchant.) 1901.
        2. Valeur & Krüger. 1901.
        3. Daemringstider. (Twilight days.) 1903.
        4. Naadsens Aar. (Years of grace.) 1906.
        5. Nederlagets Børn. (Children of defeat.) 1912.

    Tempeltjenere. (Temple servants.) Copenhagen: Gyldendal.
        1. Forgaarden. (Fore court.) 1926.
        2. Forsamlingens Paulun. (Pavilion of assembly.) 1927.
        3. Forhaenget. (The curtain.) 1928.

    Strømmen; kulturhistoriske Billeder fra Vandmøllernes Tid. (The river; pictures of cultural history of the time of the water mills.) Copenhagen: Gyldendal.
        1. Strømhesten. (The river horse.) 1929.
        2. Kobberkronen. (The copper crown.) 1930.
        3. De ni Møller. (The nine mills.) 1931.
        4. Baekkestrand. (Shore of the brook.) 1932.

Løkken, Thomas Olesen, 1877-
    "Niels Hald." Copenhagen: Hasselbalch.
        1. Bonden Niels Hald; en Roman om en moderne Bonde. (Farmer Niels Hald; a novel about a modern farmer.) 1920.
        2. Niels Halds Hustru; en Roman om en Kvinde. (Niels Hald's wife; a novel about a woman.) 1922.
        3. Niels Halds Hjem. (The home of Niels Hald.) 1924.

    Povl Dam. Copenhagen: Hasselbalch.
        1. Ungdom. (Youth.) 1925.
        2. Kampaar. (Years of struggle.) 1926.
        3. Sejren. (The victory.) 1927.

    Folket ved Stormosen. (People of the great swamp.)
        1. Stormosen; Billeder fra Mosens brune Land. (The great swamp; pictures from the brown land of the swamp.) Copenhagen: Hasselbalch, 1929.
        2. Mosepigens Søn; en Roman om Ungdom. (The son of the swamp girl; a novel about youth.) Copenhagen: Hasselbalch, 1931.
        3. Fra Vildmosens Land. (From the land of the wild swamp.) Copenhagen: E. V. Olsen, 1934. Compiler's note: Short stories.
        4. Drømmen om et Rige. (The dream about the kingdom.) Copenhagen: Hasselbalch, 1935.

    Guds Venner; Billeder fra Mosefolkets Liv. (Friends of God; pictures from the life of the swamp folk.) Copenhagen: Hasselbalch, 1930.
    Pigen fra Vildmosen. (The girl from the wild swamp.) 2d ed. Copenhagen: Hasselbalch, 1941.
Compiler's note: The last two novels are apparently related to the sequence but not part of it.

    En ny Baad i Hav. (The new boat at sea.)
    Bjørn Strand; en Roman om en Havn. (A novel about the harbor.) Copenhagen: Hasselbalch, 1940.

Michaelis, Karin, 1872-   Full name: Katharina Marie Bech (Brøndum) Michaelis Stangeland
  Den farlige Alder; Breve og Dagboksoptegnelser. Copenhagen: Gyldendal, 1910.
  Elsie Lindtner. Copenhagen: Gyldendal, 1912.

  (1) The dangerous age; letters and fragments from a woman's diary. New York: John Lane, 1911.
  (2) Elsie Lindtner. Trans. by Beatrice Marshall. New York: John Lane, 1912.

  Traet paa Godt og Ondt. (Tree of good and evil.) Copenhagen: Jespersen & Pio.
    1. Pigen med Glasskaarene. (The girl with pieces of glass.) 1924.
    2. Lille Løgnerske. (The little liar.) 1925.
    3. Hemmeligheden. (The secret.) 1926.
    4. Synd og Sorg og Fare. (Sin and sorrow and danger.) 1928.
    5. Følgerne. (The consequences.) 1930.

Mortenson, Enok, 1902-
  Saaledes blev jeg hjemlos; Roman fra Chicago. (Thus I became homeless; a novel from Chicago.) Holbaek: Dansk Bogsamlingsforlag, 1934.
  Jeg vaelger et Land; Roman fra Chicago. (I choose a land.) Cedar Falls, Iowa: Dansk Boghandels Forlag, 1936.

Nexø, Martin Andersen, 1869-
  Pelle Erobreren. Copenhagen, Christiania: Gyldendal. 4 vols. in 1. Copenhagen: Kunstforlaget Danmark, 1914. Not for sale.
    1. Pelle Erobreren. 1906.   3. Den store Kamp. 1909.
    2. Laereaar. 1907.   4. Gryet. 1910.

  Morten hin Røde; en Erindringsroman. (Morten the Red; a novel of recollection.) Copenhagen: Gyldendal, 1945.
  Compiler's note: A continuation of the story of Pelle, to 1918.

  Pelle the Conqueror. 1 vol. New York: Peter Smith, 1930. Reprinted by permission of Holt & Co. 4 vols. New York: Holt.
    1. Boyhood. Trans. by Jessie Muir. 1913.
    2. Apprenticeship. Trans. by Bernard Miall. 1914.
    3. The great struggle. Trans. by B. Miall. 1915.
    4. Daybreak. Trans. by J. Muir. 1917.

  Ditte Menneskebarn. (Ditte, child of man.) Copenhagen: Aschehoug.
    1. En Barndom. (Childhood.) 1917.
    2. Lillemor. (Little mother.) 1919.
    3. Syndefaldet. (The fall into sin.) 1919.
    4. Skaersilden. (Purgatory.) 1920.
    5. Mod Stjaernerne. (Toward the stars.) 1921.

  Ditte. 1 vol. New York: Peter Smith, 1931. 3 vols. New York: Holt.
    1. Girl alive! Trans. by Arthur G. Chater and Richard Thirsk. 1920.
    2. Daughter of man. Trans. by A. G. Chater and R. Thirsk. 1921.
    3. Toward the stars. Trans. by Asta and Rowland Kenny. 1922.

Pontoppidan, Henrik, 1857-1943
  Det forjaettede Land; et Tidsbillede. (The promised land; a picture of the times.) 1 vol. Copenhagen: Gyldendal, 1918.
    1. Muld. (Soil.) Copenhagen: Phillipsen, 1891.
    2. Det forjaettede Land. Copenhagen: Nordiske Forlag, 1895.
    3. Dommens Dag. (The Last Judgment.) Copenhagen: Nordiske Forlag, 1895.

    1. Emmanuel, or Children of the soil. Trans. by Mrs. Edgar Lucas. London: Dent, 1892.
    2. The promised land. Trans. by Mrs. E. Lucas. London: Dent, 1896.

  Lykke-Per. 3 vols. in 1. Copenhagen: Gyldendal, 1907.
    1. Lykke-Per, hans Ungdom. (Lucky Peter's youth.) Copenhagen: Nordiske Forlag, 1898.

2. Lykke-Per finder Skatten. (Lucky Peter finds the treasure.) Copenhagen: Nordiske Forlag, 1898.
3. Lykke-Per, hans Kaerlighed. (His love.) Copenhagen: Nordiske Forlag, 1899.
4. Lykke-Per i det Fremmede. (Lucky Peter abroad.) Copenhagen: Nordiske Forlag, 1899.
5. Lykke-Per, hans store Vaerk. (His great achievement.) 1901.
6. Lykke-Per, og hans Kaereste. (Lucky Peter and his sweetheart.) 1902.
7. Lykke-Per, hans Rejse til Amerika. (His journey to America.) 1903.
8. Lykke-Per, hans sidste Kamp. (His last struggle.) 1904.

De Dødes Rige. (The realm of the dead.) 2 vols. Copenhagen: Gyldendal, 1917. Subtitle of individual novels: En Fortaellingkres. (A cycle of tales.)
1. Torben og Jytte. 1912.
2. Storeholt. 1913.
3. Toldere og Syndere. (Publicans and sinners.) 1914.
4. Enslevs Død. (Enslev's death.) 1915.
5. Favsingholm. 1915.

Sølberg, Harry, 1880-
De Levendes Land, I-III. Christiania: Aschehoug, 1921.
1. Foran Livets Port. (Before life's portal.) 1916.
2. Lyset. (The light.) 1918.
3. De Levendes Land. (The land of the living.) 1920.

Søkongen. Oslo: Aschehoug, 1926.
Søkongens Datter. (The sea king's daughter.) Oslo: Aschehoug, 1928.
Søkongens sidste Rejse. (The sea king's last journey.) Oslo: Aschehoug, 1930.

(1) The sea king. Trans. by Edwin Björkman. New York: Morrow, 1928.

West, Johannes B., 1864-1923
Nykommerbilleder; Jonas Olsens første Aar i America. (Immigrant sketches; Jonas Olsen's first year in America.) Decorah, Iowa: Amundsen, 1920.
Hjemmet paa Praerien; Jonas Olsens første Aar i Nybygget. (The home on the prairie; Jonas Olsen's first year in the pioneer settlement.) Decorah, Iowa: Amundsen, 1921.
Jonasville; et Kulturbillede. (A picture of a civilization.) Decorah, Iowa: Amundsen, 1922

Wied, Gustav Johannes, 1858-1914
Livsens Ondskab; Billeder fra Gammelkøbing. (Life's evil; sketches from Gammelkøbing.) Copenhagen: Gyldendal, 1899.
Knagsted; Billeder fra Ind-og Udland. (Sketches from at home and abroad.) Copenhagen: Gyldendal, 1902.
Pastor Sörenson & Co.; en Redegorelse. (An explanation.) Copenhagen, Christiania: Gyldendal, 1913.

Icelandic

Gunnarsson, Gunnar, see list of novels written in Danish.
Kamban, Guðmundur, 1888-1945
Skálholt. 4 vols. Reykjavik: Isafoldarprentsmiðja, 1930-35. Danish translation, Copenhagen: Hasselbalch, 1930-32.
1. Jómfrú Ragnheiður.
2. Mala domestica. (Domestic evils.)
3. Hans herradómur. (His mastery.)
4. Quod felix. (May it be fortunate.)

1-2. The virgin of Skalholt. Trans. by Evelyn Ramsden. Boston: Little, Brown, 1935. British title: Virgin of the North.

Laxness, Halldór Kiljan, 1902-
Thu vinvidur hreini; saga ur flaeðarmálinu. (O, thou pure vine; tale from the flood shore.) Reykjavik: Acta, 1931.

SCANDINAVIAN

Fuglinn í fjörunni; politisk ástarsaga. (The bird on the beach; a political love story.)
   Reykjavik: Bokadeild Menningarsjode, 1932.
Sjálfstaett fólk; hetjusaga. 2 vols. Reykjavik: E. P. Briem, 1934-35.

(1-2) Salka Valka. Trans. from the Danish by F. H. Lyon. 1 vol. Boston: Houghton, Mifflin, 1936.
(3) Independent people. Trans. by J. A. Thompson. New York: Knopf, 1946.

"Olafur Ljósvíkingur." Reykjavik: Bókaútgáfan Heimskringla.
   1. Ljos heimsins. (The light of the world.) 1937.
   2. Höll sumarlandsins. (The chateau in Summerland.) 1938.
   3. Hús skáldsins. (The poet's house.) 1939.
   4. Fegurð himinsins. (The beauty of the sky.) 1940.

Islandsklukkan. (Bell of Iceland.) Reykjavik: Helgafell, 1943.
Hið ljøsa man. (The fair maiden.) Reykjavik: Helgafell, 1945.
Eldur í Kaupinhafn. (Fire in Copenhagen.) 1946.

Magnússon, Guðmundur, 1873-1918. Pseud., "Jon Trausti"
   Halla-Heiðarbylið. (Halla and the heath cottage.) Reykjavik: Arinbj. Sveinbjarnarson.
      1. Barnið. (The child.) 1908.
      2. Grenjaskyttan. (The foxhunter.) 1909.
      3. Fylgenið. (The hiding place.) 1910.
      4. Thorradaegur og sögulok. (Winter day and the end of the story.) 1911.

   Sögur frá Skaftáreldi á seinni hluta átjándu aldar. (Stories from the eruption of Skafta, 1783.) Reykjavik: Kristjánsson.
      1. Holt og skal. 1912.
      2. Sigur lífsins. 1913.

"Trausti, Jon," see Magnússon, Guðmundur.

Norwegian

Anker, Fru Nini (Roll), 1873-
   Huset i Søgaten. (The house on Sea Street.) Christiania: Aschehoug, 1923.
   I amtmandsgaarden. (In the magistrate's courtyard.) Oslo: Aschehoug, 1925.
   Under skraataket. (Under slanting roofs.) Oslo: Aschehoug, 1927.
Benneche, Olaf, 1883-
   Villenskov. Christiania: Aschehoug, 1905.
   Erik Rathlau. Christiania: Aschehoug, 1906.
   Udvaar fyr. (Udvaar lighthouse.) Christiania: Aschehoug, 1907.
   Henning Balg og hans datter; blade af en slegts historie. (Henning Balg and his daughter; pages from a family's history.) Christiania: Aschehoug, 1908.
   Diderik Fleming og hans hus; Kristiania-interiører fra forrige aarhundrede. (Diderik Fleming and his house; Christiania interiors from the previous century.) Christiania: Aschehoug, 1910.

   Rygnestadgutten. (The boy of Rygnestad.) Christiania: Aschehoug, 1911.
   Knekten Mundius. (Mundius the servant.) Christiania: Aschehoug, 1912.
   De bønder av raabygdelag. (The farmers of the primitive settlement.) Christiania: Aschehoug, 1913.
Bojer, Johan, 1872-
   Den store hunger. Christiania: Gyldendal, 1918.
   Det nye tempel. Oslo: Gyldendal, 1927.

(1) The great hunger. Trans. by W. J. Alexander Worster and C. Archer. New York: Century, 1919.
(2) The new temple. Trans. by C. Archer. New York: Century, 1928.

Braaten, Oskar, 1881-1929
  Ulvehiet. (The wolves' lair.) Christiania: Aschehoug, 1919.
  Mathilde. Christiania: Aschehoug, 1920.
Bull, Jakob Breda, 1853-1930
  Mørke århundreder. (Dark centuries.) Christiania: Norske Aktieforlag.
    1. Bondeoprøret. (The peasants' revolt.) 1900.
    2. Dyveke i Norge. (Dyveke in Norway.) 1901.
    3. Dyveke i Danmark. 1902.
    4. Kong Kristjern tyran. (King Christian the tyrant.) 1904.

  Hr. Samuel. Christiania: Gyldendal, 1920.
  Hr. Samuels rige. (Mr. Samuel's realm.) 1922.
Christensen, Hjalmar, 1869-
  Den gamle bygd og den nye. (The old settlement and the new.) Christiania: Aschehoug.
    1. Den gamle bygd. 1913.   2. Den nye bygd. 1914.
Christiansen, Sigurd Wesley, 1891-
  Ved Golgata. (At Golgotha.) 1 vol. Oslo: Gyldendal, 1939.
    1. Vårt eget liv. (Our own life.) 1918.
    2. Ved Golgata. 1920.

  Riket. (The kingdom.) Oslo: Gyldendal.
    1. Indgangen. (The entrance.) 1925.
    2. Sverdene. (The swords.) 1927.
    3. Riket. 1929.
Duun, Olav, 1876-1939
  Juvikfolke. 2 vols. Oslo: Norli, 1927.
    Vol. I. Fra Juvika til Håberg.
      1. Juvikingar. 1918.
      2. I blinda. 1919.
      3. Storbryllope. 1920.
    Vol. II. Odin.
      4. I eventyre. 1921.
      5. I ungdommen. 1922.
      6. I stormen. 1923.

  The people of Juvik. Trans. by Arthur G. Chater. New York: Knopf.
    1. The trough of the wave. 1930.
    2. The blind man. 1931.
    3. The big wedding. 1932.
    4. Odin in fairyland. 1932.
    5. Odin grows up. 1934.
    6. The storm. 1935.

  Medmenneske. (Fellow beings.) Oslo: Norli, 1929.
  Ragnhild. Oslo: Norli, 1931.
  Siste leveåre. (The last year of life.) Oslo: Norli, 1933.
Falkberget, Johan, 1879-
  Christianus Sextus. Oslo: Aschehoug.
    1. De første Geseller. (The first apprentice.) 1927.
    2. I hammerens tegn. (Under the sign of the hammer.) 1931.
    3. Tårnvekteren. (Tower watchman.) 1935.
Garborg, Arne, 1851-1924
  Bondestudentar. (Peasant students.) Bergen: Nygaard, 1883.
  Mannfolk. (Menfolk.) Bergen: 1886.
  Hjaa ho Mor. (At Mother's.) Bergen: Litleré, 1890.
  Traette maend. (Tired men.) 4th ed. Christiania: Aschehoug, 1897. 1st ed., 1891.

  Fred. Bergen: J. Andersen, 1892.
  Den burtkomne faderen. Christiania: Aschehoug, 1899.

SCANDINAVIAN

Heimkomin son. (The son come home.) Christiania: Aschehoug, 1908.
Compiler's note: A drama, Laeraran, 1896, deals with the same family.

(1) Peace. Trans. by Phillips Dean Carleton. New York: American-Scandinavian Foundation, W. W. Norton, 1929.
(2) The lost father. Trans. by Mabel Johnson Leland. Boston: Stratford, 1920.

Garborg, Fru Hulda (Pedersen), 1862-
Mens dansen gaar. (While the dance goes on.) Christiania: Aschehoug, 1920.
I huldreskog. (In the fairies' forest.) Christiania: Aschehoug, 1922.
Naar heggen blomstrer. (When the rowan blooms.) Christiania: Aschehoug, 1923.

Gulbranssen, Trygve, 1894-
Og bakom synger skogene; noen historier fra 1760 årene til mot 1810. Oslo: Aschehoug, 1933.
Det blåser fra Dauingfjell. Oslo: Aschehoug, 1934.
Ingen vei går utenom. (No road goes beyond.) Oslo: Aschehoug, 1935.

(1) Beyond sing the woods. Trans. by Naomi Walford. New York: Putnam's, 1936.
(2) The wind from the mountains. Trans. by N. Walford. New York: Putnam's, 1937.

Hamsun, Knut, 1859-
Under høststjaernene; en vandrers fortaelling. (A wanderer's tale.) Christiania, Copenhagen: Gyldendal, 1906.
En vandrer spiller med sordin. Christiania, Copenhagen: Gyldendal, 1909.
Den sidste glaede. (That last happiness.) Christiania, Copenhagen: Gyldendal, 1912.

Wanderers. Trans. by W. W. Worster. 1 vol. New York: Knopf, 1922.
  (1) Under the autumn star.
  (2) A wanderer plays on muted strings.
(3) Look back on happiness. Trans. by Paula Viking. New York: Coward-McCann, 1940.

Børn av tiden. Christiania, Copenhagen: Gyldendal, 1913.
Segelfoss by. 2 vols. Christiania, Copenhagen: Gyldendal, 1915.

(1) Children of the age. Trans. by J. S. Scott. New York: Knopf, 1924.
(2) Segelfoss town. Trans. by J. S. Scott. New York: Knopf, 1925.

Benoni. Christiania: Gyldendal, 1921.
Rosa; av Student Parelius papirer. Christiania: Gyldendal, 1921.

Benoni and Rosa. Trans. by Arthur G. Chater. 1 vol. New York: Knopf, 1932.
  (1) Benoni. 1925.   (2) Rosa. 1926.

Landstrykere. 2 vols. in 1. Oslo: Gyldendal, 1927.
August. 2 vols. Oslo: Gyldendal, 1930.
Men livet lever. (But life lives.) 2 vols. Oslo: Gyldendal, 1933.

(1) Vagabonds. Trans. by Eugene Gay-Tifft. New York: Coward-McCann, 1930.
(2) August. Trans. by E. Gay-Tifft. New York: Coward-McCann, 1931.
(3) The road leads on. Trans. by E. Gay-Tifft. New York: Coward-McCann, 1934.

Haukland, Andreas, 1873-
Ol-Jørgen. Copenhagen: Gyldendal.
  1. Ol-Jørgens barndom. (Ol-Jørgen's childhood.) 1902.
  2. Udvê. (Wanderlust.) 1903.
  3. Hvide naetter. (White nights.) 1904.
  4. Hjemvê. (Homesickness.) 1905.

Johnson, Simon, 1874-
Fallitten paa Braastad. (The bankruptcy at Braastad.) Minneapolis: Augsburg, 1922.
Frihetens hjem. (Freedom's home.) Minneapolis: Augsburg, 1925.

Kielland, Alexander Lange, 1849-1906
Garman & Worse. Copenhagen: Gyldendal, 1880.
Skipper Worse. Copenhagen: Gyldendal, 1882.

(1) Garman and Worse. London: Kegan Paul, 1884.

(2) <u>Skipper Worse</u>. Trans. by Henry John, Earl of Ducie. London: Low, Marston, Searle, & Rivington, 1885.

<u>Gift</u>. (Poison.) Copenhagen: Gyldendal, 1883.
<u>Fortuna</u>. Copenhagen: Gyldendal, 1884.
<u>Sankt Hans fest</u>. (The festival of Saint John.) Copenhagen: Gyldendal, 1887.

Kinck, Hans, 1865-1926
  "Herman Eek." Christiania: Aschehoug.
    1. <u>Sus</u>. (Soughing.) 1896.
    2. <u>Hugormen</u>. (The adder.) 1898.

  <u>Sneskavlen brast; bygderoman fra slutten av 70-aarene</u>. (The avalanche broke; a country novel from the end of the 70s.) Christiania: Aschehoug.
    1. <u>Storfolk og bonde</u>. (Upper class and peasant.) 1918.
    2. <u>Unge fru Sofie</u>. (Young Fru Sofie.) 1919.
    3. <u>Opover skavlen</u>. (Up over the snowdrifts.)

Løken, Haakon, 1850-1923
  <u>Anna Kathrines ungdom; hverdagsbilleder fra 1830-1840-aarene</u>. (Anna Kathrine's youth; everyday pictures from the 1830s and 1840s.) Christiania: Aschehoug, 1910.
  <u>Landsens liv; billeder fra 1850-60-aarene</u>. (Country life.) Christiania: Aschehoug, 1911.
  <u>Fra Fjordnes til Sjøvinn; billeder og minder fra 1870-aarene</u>. (From Fjordnes to Sjøvinn; pictures and memories of the 1870s.) Christiania: Aschehoug, 1912.

Prydz, Alvilde, 1848-1922
  <u>Mennesker</u>. (Human beings.) Christiania: Aschehoug, 1892.
  <u>Drøm</u>. (Dream.) Christiania: Aschehoug, 1893.

Rasmussen, Emil, 1873-
  <u>Roman fra slottene ved Dnjester</u>. (Novel from the castles at Dniester.) Copenhagen: Gyldendal.
  Compiler's note: The series title used here is the subtitle of the individual volumes.
    1. <u>Det polske blod</u>. (Polish blood.) 1918.
    2. <u>Bag gyldene mure</u>. (Behind golden walls.) 1918.
    3. <u>Paa flygtende fod</u>. (The fugitives.) 1923.
    4. <u>Mens stormene gaar</u>. (While storms gather.) 1924.
    5. <u>Det hvide orn</u>. (The white eagle.) 1926.

Rølvaag, Ole Edvart, 1876-1931
  <u>I de dage</u>. (In those days.)
    <u>I de dage; fortaelling om norske nykommere i Amerika</u>. (A tale about Norwegian newcomers in America.) Christiania: Aschehoug; Minneapolis: Augsburg, 1924.
    <u>Riket grundlaegges</u>. (The kingdom is founded.) Oslo: Aschehoug, 1925.
  <u>Peder Seier</u>. Oslo: Aschehoug, 1928.
  <u>Den signede dag</u>. (The blessed day.) Oslo: Aschehoug, 1931.

(1) <u>Giants in the earth</u>. Trans. by Lincoln Colcord and the author. New York: Harper, 1927.
(2) <u>Peder Victorious</u>. Trans. by Nora O. Solum and the author. New York: Harper, 1929.
(3) <u>Their fathers' God</u>. Trans. by Trygve N. Ager. New York: Harper, 1931.

Scott, Gabriel, 1874-
  <u>Jernbyrden; historien om Jan Vibe</u>. Fortalt av Martin Eidjord, kirketjener i Høvaag sogn. (Ordeal by fire; the story of Jan Vibe. Told by Martin Eidjord, sexton in Høvaag parish.) Subtitle, later editions: <u>En saga om faedrelandssind</u>. (A saga of patriotism). Christiania: Aschehoug, 1915.
  <u>Enok Rubens levnetsløp; en saga om faedrelandssind</u>. Fortalt av Martin Eidjord, kirketjener i Høvaag sogn. (The story of the life of Enok Ruben.) Christiania: Aschehoug, 1917.

(1) <u>The burden of iron</u>. Trans. by Käthe Miethe and Winifred Kazin. London: Hutchinson, 1935.

<u>Vignet av Harald Jordan</u>. (Portrait of Harald Jordan.) Oslo: Gyldendal.
    1. <u>Fant; et blad av de reisendes bok</u>. (Vagabond; a page from the book of travelers.) 1928.

    2. Alkejaegeren; et menneskesind. (The auk-hunter; the soul of a man.) 1933.
    3. Storebror. (Big brother.) 1934.
Singdahlsen, Ole Christopher Lie, 1877-
  Hallingdalsfortaellinger. (Tales of Hallingdal.) Christiania: Norli.
  Compiler's note: The series title used here is the subtitle of the individual volumes.
    1. Hallinger. (People of Hallingdal.) 1916.
    2. Nord i dalen. (North in the valley.) 1916.
    3. Fjeldfolk. (Mountain folk.) 1917.
    4. Folket fra Aslegaard. (People from Aslegaard.) 1918.
Skram, Fru Amalie (Alver), 1846-1905
  Hellemyrefolket. (People of Hellemyr.)
    1. Sjur Gabriel. Copenhagen: Salmonsen, 1887.
    2. "To venner." (Two friends.) Copenhagen: Salmonsen, 1887.
    3. S. G. Myre. Copenhagen: Schubothe, 1890.
    4. Afkom. (Offspring.) Copenhagen: Gyldendal, 1898.
Undset, Sigrid, 1882-1949
  Kristin Lavransdatter. Christiania: Aschehoug.
    1. Kransen. 1920.
    2. Husfrue. 1921.
    3. Korset. 1922.

  Kristin Lavransdatter. 1 vol. New York: Knopf, 1929.
    1. The bridal wreath. Trans. by C. Archer and J. S. Scott. 1923. British title: The garland.
    2. The mistress of Husaby. Trans. by C. Archer. 1925.
    3. The cross. Trans. by C. Archer. 1927

  Olav Audunssøn. Oslo: Aschehoug.
    Part I. Olav Audunssøn i Hestviken. 2 vols. 1925.
    Part II. Olav Audunssøn og hans børn. (Olav Audunssøn and his children.) 2 vols. 1927.

  The master of Hestviken. 2 vols. Trans. by Arthur G. Chater. New York: Knopf, 1932.
    Vol. I: 1. The axe. 1928.   2. The snake pit. 1929.
    Vol. II: 3. In the wilderness. 1929.   4. The son avenger. 1930.

  Gymnadenia. Oslo: Aschehoug, 1929.
  Den braendende busk. Oslo: Aschehoug, 1930.

  "The winding road." Trans. by Arthur G. Chater. New York: Knopf.
    (1) The wild orchid. 1931. British title: Gymnadenia.
    (2) The burning bush. 1932.
Uppdal, Kristofer, 1878-
  Dansen gjenom skuggeheimen. (The dance through a world of shadows.) Christiania: Aschehoug.
    1. Stigeren; Tørber Landsems far. (The master miner; Tørber Landsem's father.) 1919.
    2. Trolldom i lufta; Ølløv Skjølløgrinns ungdom. (Witchcraft in the air; Ølløv Skjølløgrinn's youth.) 1912.
    3. Vandringa; Øl-Kalles ferd. (Wandering; Øl-Kalle's journey.) 1923.
    4. Kongen; Tørber Landsems ungdom. (The king; Tørber Landsem's youth.) 1920.
    5. Dansen gjenom skuggeheimen; Sjugur Rambern. 1911.
    6. Domkyrkjebyggjaren; Tørber Landsem og Ølløv Skjølløgrinn. (The cathedral builder.) 1921.
    7. I skiftet; Tørber Landsem og Mildri'anna. (Change.) 1922.
    8. Røysingfolket; Sjugur Rambern og bøndene. (The Roysing people; Sjugur Rambern and the peasants.) 1914.
    9. Fjellskeringa; Basola Storbas og laget hans. (The mountain cutting; Boss Ola, big boss, and his team.) 1924.
    10. Herdsla; Tørber Landsem og Audun Rambern. (The tempering.) 1924.

Swedish

Bengtsson, Frans Gunnar, 1894-
   Röde Orm. Stockholm: Norstedt, 1941.
     1. Röde Orm, sjöfarare i västerled; en berättelse från okristen tid. (Red Orm; seafarers to the west; a tale from pagan times.)
     2. Röde Orm, hemma och i österled. (Home and in the east.)

     1. Red Orm. Trans. by Barrows Mussey. New York: Scribner's, 1943.
Berger, Henning, 1872-1924
   Drömlandet. (The dream country.) Vols. 1-3 of Skrifter i urval av Henning Berger. Stockholm: Bonnier, 1922.
     1. Hägringen. (Mirage.) 1909.
     2. Bendel & Co.; en chicagonovell. 1910.
     3. Fata Morgana; en stockholmsnovell. 1911.
Bergman, Hjalmar Fredrik Elgerus, 1883-1931
   Komedier i bergslagen. (Comedies in a mining district.) Stockholm: Bonnier.
     1. Två släkter. (Two families.) 1914.
     2. Dansen på Frötjärn. (The dance at Frötjärn.) 1915.
     3. Knutsmässo marknad. (Knutsmässo market.) 1916.
Didring, Ernest, 1868-1931
   Malm; skildringar nordanfrån. (Iron ore; sketches from the north.) Stockholm: Bonnier.
     1. Mannen som gjorde det. (The man who did it.) 1914.
     2. Bergets sång. (Song of the mountain.) 1915.
     3. Spelarna. (The fiddlers.) 1919.
Dixelius-Brettner, Hildur, 1879-
   Prästdottern. Stockholm: Åhlén & Akerlund, 1920.
   Prästdotterns son. Stockholm: Åhlén & Akerlund, 1921.
   Sonsonen. Stockholm: Åhlén & Akerlund, 1922.

   (1) The minister's daughter. Trans. by Anna C. Settergren. New York: Dutton, 1926.
   (2) The son. Trans. by A. C. Settergren. New York: Dutton, 1928.
   (3) The grandson. Trans. by A. C. Settergren. New York: Dutton, 1928.
Heidenstam, Verner von, 1859-1940
   Folkungaträdet. 2 vols. Stockholm: Bonnier, 1929.
     1. Folke Filbyter. 1905.   2. Bjälboarvet. 1907.

   The tree of the Folkungs. Trans. by Arthur G. Chater. 1 vol. New York: Knopf, 1925.
     1. Folke Filbyter.   2. The Belbo heritage.
Johnson, Eyvind (Olof Verner), 1900-
   Romanen om Olof. (Novels about Olof.) 4 vols. Stockholm: Bonnier, 1945.
     1. Nu var det 1914. (Now it was 1914.)
     2. Här har du ditt liv! (Here you have your life!)
     3. Se dig inte om. (Do not look back.)
     4. Slutspel i ungdom. (The last play of youth.)
Krusenstjerna, Agnes Julie Frederika von, 1894-1940
   Tonyböckerna; släktromaner. (Tony books; family novels.) Stockholm: Bonnier.
     1. Tony växer upp; scener ur ett barndomsliv. (Tony grows up; scenes from a childhood.) 1922.
     2. Tonys läroår; episoder ur un ungdom. (Tony's apprentice years; scenes from a youth.) 1924.
     3. Tonys sista läroår; resa till kejsarens hotell. (Tony's last apprentice year; trip to the kaiser's hotel.) 1924.

   Fröknarna von Pahlen. (The ladies von Pahlen.)
     1. Den blå rullgardinen. (The blue curtain.) Stockholm: Bonnier, 1930.
     2. Kvinnogatan. (Woman street.) Stockholm: Bonnier, 1930.
     3. Höstens skuggar. (Shadows of fall.) Stockholm: Bonnier, 1931.

SCANDINAVIAN

    4. Porten vid Johannes. (The gate by Johannes.) Stockholm: Spektrum & Salig, 1933.
    5. Älskande par. (Loving pairs.) Stockholm: Spektrum & Salig, 1933.
    6. Bröllop på Ekered. (The wedding at Ekered.) Stockholm: Spektrum & Salig, 1935.
    7. Av samma blod. (Of the same blood.) Stockholm: Spektrum & Salig, 1935.

Fattigadel; Viveka von Lagercronas historia. (The poor nobility; the story of Viveka von Lagercrona.) Stockholm: Bonnier.
    1. Fattigadel. 1935.
    2. Dunklet mellan träden. (Darkness between the trees.) 1936.
    3. Dessa lyckliga år. (These happy years.) 1937.
    4. I livets vår. (In the spring of life.) 1938.

Lagerlöf, Selma Ottiliana Lovisa, 1858-1940
  Jerusalem. 1 vol. Stockholm: Bonnier, 1909.
    1. I Dalarne. (In Dalarne.) 1901.
    2. I det Heliga Landet. (In the Holy Land.) 1902.

    1. Jerusalem. Trans. by Jessie Brochner. London: Heinemann, 1903.

  Jerusalem. Trans. by Velma S. Howard. New York: Doubleday, Page.
    1. Jerusalem. 1915.   2. The Holy City. 1918.

  Löwensköldska ringen. Stockholm: Bonnier, 1925.
  Charlotte Löwensköld. Stockholm: Bonnier, 1925.
  Anna Svärd. Stockholm: Bonnier, 1928.

  The ring of the Löwensköld. 1 vol. New York: Doubleday, Doran, 1931.
    (1) The ring of the Löwensköld. Trans. by Francesca Martin. 1927.
    (2) Charlotte Löwensköld. Trans. by Velma S. Howard. 1928.
    (3) Anna Svärd. Trans. by V. S. Howard.

Lidman, Sven, 1882-
  Stensborg. Stockholm: Bonnier, 1910.
  Thure-Gabriel Silfverstååhl. Stockholm: Bonnier, 1910.
  Köpmän och krigare. (Merchant and warrior.) Stockholm: Bonnier, 1911.
  Carl Silfverstååhls upplefvelser. (Carl Silfverstååhl's experiences.) Stockholm: Bonnier, 1912.
  Tvedräktens barn. (The child of disunion.) Stockholm: Bonnier, 1913.

"Martinson, Moa," pseud. of Helga (Svarts) Martinson, 1890-
  Boken om Sally. (Books about Sally.) 1 vol. Stockholm: Tidens Förlag, 1945.
    1. Kvinnor och äppelträd. (Women and appletrees.) 1933.
    2. Sallys söner. (Sally's son.) 1934.

  Mor gifter sig. (Mother marries.) Stockholm: Bonnier, 1936.
  Kyrkbröllop. (Church wedding.) Stockholm: Tidens Förlag, 1938.
  Kungens rosor. (The king's roses.) Stockholm: Tidens Förlag, 1939.

Moberg, Vilhelm, 1898-
  Knut Toring. Stockholm: Bonnier.
    1. Sänkt sedebetyg. (Low deportment grade.) 1935.
    2. Sömnlös. 1937.
    3. Giv oss jorden! (Give us the earth!) 1939.

  The earth is ours. Trans. by Edwin Björkman. 1 vol. New York: Simon & Schuster, 1940.
    1. Memory of youth. 1938.
    2. Sleepless nights.
    3. The earth is ours.

Nordström, Ludvig Anselm, 1882-1942
  Skildringar ur svenska nationens lif. (Sketches from the history of the Swedish nation.) Stockholm: Bonnier.
    1. De tolf söndagarna. (The twelve Sundays.) 1910.
    2. Ankarsparre; en fin och oskyldig roman. (An elegant and innocent novel.) 1912.
    3. Landsorts-bohème. (Country-bohème.) 1911.

4. Jobbarfamiljen Gobsman. (The Gobsmans, a speculating family.) 1913.
5. Döda världar i samhällsrymden; inledning till Petter historia. (Dead worlds on society's horizon; introduction to Peter Svensk's story.) 1920.
6. Fyrskeppet; en dagbok. (The light-ship; a diary.) 1922.
7. Landsortens problem. (The problem of the country place.) 1925.

Petter Svensks historia. (Peter Svensk's story.) Stockholm: Bonnier.
Compiler's note: See 5 above.
1. Världsstaden. (The world city.) 1923.
2. Bröderna Person i Sverge. (The Person brothers in Sweden.)
Compiler's note: A continuation of the preceding sequence.

Ossian-Nilsson, Karl Gustav, 1875-
Barbarskogen; en berättelse i klasskampens tecken. (The barbaric forest; a tale under the sign of the class struggle.) Stockholm: Bonnier, 1908.
Slätten; en berättelse från brytningstider. (The plains; a story of transition times.) Stockholm: Bonnier, 1909.
Havet. (The sea.) Stockholm: Bonnier, 1910.

Sparre, Per Georg, 1790-1871
Svenska historiska romaner. (Swedish historical novels.) Stockholm: Bonnier.
1. Den siste friseglaren. (The last free sailing ship.) 4th ed. 1892.
2. Adolf Findling. 3d ed. 1892.
3. Standaret. (The standard.) 3d ed. 1892.
4. Sjökadetten i Gustaf III:s tid. (Naval cadet at the time of Gustaf III.) 4th ed. 1893.

Starbäck, Carl Georg, 1828-85
Historiska medeltids romaner. (Historical novels of the Middle Ages.) Stockholm: Beijers, 1887.
I. Engelbrekt Engelbrektson. 2 vols.
II. Nils Bosson Sture. 3 vols.
1. Guldhalsbandet. (Gold necklace.)
2. Konungskronan. (King's crown.)
3. Testamentet. (The will.)

Historiska romaner från nyare tid. (Historical novels from the more recent times.) Stockholm: Beijers.
1. Master Olofs bröllop. (Master Olaf's wedding.) 1889.
2. Lifnektens berättelser om handelser ur Gustaf Adolfs II historia. (Reports of the bodyguards concerning events from the history of Gustaf Adolf II.) 1889.
3. Öfverste Stålhammar. (Colonel Stålhammar.) 1891.
4. Skarpskyttens ungdomsminnen. (Childhood memories of the sharpshooter.) 1891.

Stjernstedt, Marika, 1875-
Vägarne. (Highways.) Stockholm: Bonnier.
1. Landshöfdingens dotter. (The provincial governor's daughter.) 1911.
2. Daniela Hertz. 1912.

Strindberg, (Johan) August, 1849-1912
Tjänstekvinnans son. (The son of a servant.) Stockholm: Bonnier.
1. Tjänstekvinnans son; en själs utvecklingshistoria. (1849-67.) (The story of a soul's development.) 1886.
2. Jäsningstiden; en själs utvecklingshistoria. (1867-72.) (In time of fermentation.) 1886.
3. I röda rummet. (1872-75.) 1886.
4. Han och hon. (1875-76.) (He and she.) 1919.
5. Författaren. (1877-87.) (The author.) 1909.
6. Die Beichte eines Thoren. (1877-87.) Budapest: Grill, 1893. Le plaidoyer d'un fou. Paris: Langen, 1895.
Compiler's note: 6 was first published in the German and French translations listed. The first authorized Swedish edition was published in 1914. 4 and 6 above have the same sub-

SCANDINAVIAN

title as the rest of the series and are related in subject, but they are not listed with the series in Strindberg's collected works.

    1. The son of a servant; a soul's development. Trans. by Claud Field. New York, London: Putnam's, 1913.
    3. The red room. Trans. by Ellie Schleussner. New York, London: Putnam's, 1915.
    6. The confession of a fool. Trans. by E. Schleussner. London: Swift, 1912.

Topelius, Zakarias, 1818-98
  Fältskärns berättelser. Stockholm: Bonnier. Cycles I-IV published without series titles, 1854-64.
    Cycle I. Gustaf Adolf och 30-åriga kriget. 5th ed. 1872.
      1. Konungens ring.
      2. Svärdet och plogen. (Sword and plough.)
      3. Eld och vatten. (Fire and water.)
    Cycle II. Från tiden af Kristina, Carl X, och Carl XI. 5th ed. 1874.
      1. Rebell mot sin egen lycke. (Rebel against his own fortune.)
      2. Hexan. (The witch.)
      3. Majniemi slott. (Majniemi castle.)
    Cycle III. Från Carl XII:s tid. 5th ed. 1874.
      1. De blå. (The blue ones.)
      2. Flyktingen. (The fugitive.)
      3. Skuggan af ett namn. (The shadow of a name.)
    Cycle IV. Under frihetstiden. (In the time of freedom.) 2d ed. 1873.
      1. Ödemarkernas vår. (The spring of the desert districts.)
      2. Borgarekungen. (The burgher king.)
      3. Prinsessen af Vasa. (The princesses of Vasa.)
    Cycle V. Under Gustaf III:s första regeringsår. (During the first years of Gustaf III's reign.) 1867.

  The surgeon's stories; Swedish historical romance in six cycles. Chicago: Jansen, McClurg, 1884.
    Cycle I. Gustave Adolf and the Thirty Years War. (1616-48.) Trans. by Selma Borg and Marie A. Brown. New York: Carleton, 1872. Reissued as Times of Gustaf Adolf. Chicago: Jansen, McClurg, 1883.
      1. The king's ring. Boston: Page, 1901.
    Cycle II. Times of battle and of rest. (House of Vasa, 1523-1718.) 1883.
    Cycle III. Times of Charles XII. (1697-1718.)
    Cycle IV. Times of Frederick I. (1720-51.)
    Cycle V. Times of Linnaeus. (1751-71.)
    Cycle VI. Times of alchemy. (1771-72.)
    Compiler's note: There is no Swedish edition of Cycle VI. Cycles V and VI in translation may be the last part of IV and V in the original.

Wägner, Elin, 1882-
  Åse-Hanna. Stockholm: Bonnier, 1918.
  Den namnlösa. (The nameless one.) Stockholm: Bonnier, 1922.
  Svalorna flyga högt. (The swallows fly high.) Stockholm: Bonnier, 1929.

Slavic and Ugric Languages

BULGARIAN

Vazov, Ivan Minchov, 1850-1921
  Pod igoto. 1893.
  Nova semya. (The new land.) 1893.

  (1) Under the yoke. London: Heinemann, 1894.

CZECH

Capek, Karel, 1890-1938
  Hordubal. 1933.
  Povětroň. Prague: 1934.
  Obyčejný život. Prague: 1934.

  Three novels. Trans. by M. and R. Weatherall. 1 vol. New York: A. A. Wyn, 1949. Published as separate novels, London: Allen & Unwin, 1934-36.
    1. Hordubal.   2. Meteor.   3. An ordinary life.

Hasek, Jaroslav, 1883-1923
  Osody dobrého vojáka Švejka za světové valky. 4 vols. 1920-23. Published serially, beginning in 1916.
  Compiler's note: An unfinished series.

  Good soldier, Schweik. Trans. by Paul Selver. Garden City, New York: Doubleday, Doran, 1930.

Holeček, Josef, 1853-1929
  Naši. (Our people.) Prague: Topič.
    1. Úvod. Jak u nás žijou i umírají. 2d ed. Prague: Smichov, 1906. With Část II, 1 vol., 1910.
      Část II. Frantík a Bartoň. Prague: Smichov, 1901.
    2. Bartoň. 1910. Prague: Smichov, 1902.
    3. Výprava. 1912. Prague: Smichov, 1904.
    4. Boubín. 1913. 1st ed., 1906.
    5. Adamova svatba. Část I & II. 1917.
      Adamova svatba. 1907.
      Vojna I. 1909.
    6. Rok smrti. 1918. Prague: Vlastní, 1908.
    7. Mraky. Prague: Topič, 1919.
    8. Emissaři.
      Část I. 1921.
      Část II. Křtiny. 1922.
    9. Máje. 1923.

Jirásek, Alois, 1851-1930
  Mezi proudy. (Between the currents.) 3 vols. 1891.
  Proti všem. (Against the whole world.) 1894. Serially, in Zlata Praha, 1892-93.
  Bratrstvo. Tři rhapsodie. (The brotherhood; three rhapsodies.) 3 vols. Prague: Zlatá XVI, 1899.
    1. Bitva u Lučince.
    2. Mária.
    3. Žebráci.

POLISH

Muzakova, Johanna, see "Světlá, Karolina."
"Světlá, Karolina," pseud. of Johanna Muzakova (Rottova), 1830-99
  Vesnický roman. (A country story.) 1867.
  Kříž u potoka. (The cross at the brook.) 1868.
  Frantina. 1870.
  Nemodlenec. (The atheist.) 1873.
Urban, Milo, 1904-
  Živý bič. (The living scourge.) 1927.
  Hmly va úsvite. (Fogs in the dawn.) Prague: Družstevní práce, 1930.
  Vosídlach. (Trapped.) 1939.
Weiskopf, Karl, see list of novels written in German.

HUNGARIAN

Moricz, Zsigmond, 1879-
  Erdély. (Transylvania.) 3 vols. Budapest: Athenaeum, 1939.
    1. Tundérkert; történelmi regény a vii szazad elejéröl. Báthory Gábor Erdélyi fejedelemsége; Bethlen Gábor ifjúkora.
    2. A nagy fejedelem. A tündérkert viragbaborul; Bethlen Gábor dicsösége, Zsuzsanna fejedelemasszony szenvedése eljö.
    3. A nap árnyéka. Az asszonyi állat as ö uranak dicsöségében láthatatlan lesz. Minél jobb s tökéletesebb, annál jobban s tökéletesebb: ime a regény.

POLISH

Berent, Wacław, 1873-1940
  Nurt; o powiesci biograficzne. (The current; a biographical novel.)
    1. Ludzie starodawni. (People of ancient times.) Warsaw: Gebethner & Wolff, 1934.
    2. Pogrobowcy. (The gravediggers.) 1934.
    3. Diogenes w kontuszu. (Diogenes in Polish dress.) Warsaw: Gebethner & Wolff, 1937.
Dabrowska, Marja (Szumka), 1892-
  Noce i dnie. (Nights and days.) Warsaw: Mortkowicz.
    1. Bogumił i Barbara. 1932.
    2. Wieczne zmiartwienie. (Eternal grief.) 1932.
    3. Miłość. (Love.) 2 vols. 1933.
    4. Pod wiatr. (Into the wind.) 1934.
Dunin-Kozicka, M.
  Ania z Lechickich pol. (Ani from the fields of Lechickich.) Warsaw: Dom Książki Polkiej.
    1. Dzieciectwo. (Childhood.) 1931.
    2. Młodość. (Youth.) 1932.
    3. "Miłość Ani." (Ani's love.)
  Compiler's note: In preparation, 1934.
Gasiorowski, Wacław, 1869-1940
  Pułaski. Warsaw: Dom Książki Polskiej.
    1. Miłość krolewicza. (The Prince's love.) 1931.
    2. Interregnum. 1933.
    3-4. In preparation, 1934.

  Huragan. (Hurricane.) 3 vols. Warsaw: Dom Książki Polskiej, 1930.
  Rok 1809. (The year 1809.) 2 vols. Warsaw: Dom Książki Polskiej, 1928.
  Szwoleżerowie gwardji. Warsaw: Dom Książki Polskiej, 1928.
Jeske-Choinski, Teodor, 1854-1920
  Gasnace słońce. (Dimming sun.) 2 vols. Warsaw: 1895.

SLAVIC AND UGRIC LANGUAGES

Ostatni Rzymianie. (The last Romans.) 2 vols. Warsaw: 1897.
Tjara i korona. (The tiara and the crown.) 4 vols. Warsaw: 1900.

Blyskawice. (Lightning.) 1902?
Jakobini. (The Jacobins.)
Terror.

Ludzie Renesansu. (People of the Renaissance.) 1902.
Trubadurowie. (Troubadours.)
O mitre hospodarska. (About the lord's mitre.)

Kaczkowski, Zygmunt, 1826-96
  Ostatni z Nieczujów. (The last of the Nieczui.)
    1. Bitwa o chorązankę. (The battle over the daughter of the standard-bearer.) Cracow: 1852.
    2. Gniazdo Nieczjów. (Nest of Nieczui.)
    3. Starosta Holobucki. 3 vols. Warsaw: 1857.
    4. Grob Nieczui. (Grave of the Nieczui.) 4 vols. Vilno: 1858.

Kaden-Bandrowski, Juljusz, 1885-1945
  Czarne skrzydła. (Black wings.) 2 vols. Lemberg: Zakład Narodowy im. Ossolińskich, 1929.
    1. Lenora.   2. Tadeusz.

  Mateusz Bigda. 3 vols. Warsaw: "Roj," 1933.
    1. Grunt. (Soil.)
    2. Masło. (Butter.)
    3. Spizarnia. (Pantry.)

Kossak-Szczucka, Zofia, 1890-
  Krzyżowcy. (The crusaders.) 4 vols. in 2. New York: Roy Publishers, 1945.
  Krol trędowaty. New York: Roy Publishers, 1945.
  Bez oręza. (Without arms.) New York: Roy Publishers, 1945.

(1) Angels in the dust; a novel of the first Crusade. Trans. by Rulka Langer and Lola Gay-Tift. New York: Roy Publishers, 1947.
(2) The leper king. Trans. by F. S. Placzek. New York: Roy Publishers, 1945.
(3) Blessed are the meek; a novel about St. Francis of Assisi. Trans. by Rulka Langer. New York: Roy Publishers, 1944.

Kossowski, Jerzy
  Ceglany dom. (Brick house.) Warsaw: Gebethner & Wolff, 1929.
  Biały folwark. (White farmhouse.) Warsaw: Gebethner & Wolff, 1932.

Kraszewski, Josef Ignatius, 1812-87
  Series of 29 historical novels, published in 78 volumes. Warsaw: Glucksberga, 1889-91.
    1-3. Stara baśń. (An old tale.)
    4-5. Lubonie. (The loved ones.)
    6-8. Bracia zmartwychwstańcy. (Brothers risen from the dead.)
    9-10. Maslaw.
    11-12. Boleszczyce. (Followers of Bolesław.)
    13-16. Krolewscy synowie. (Royal daughters-in-law.)
    17-18. Historya prawdziwa o Petrka Włascie. (True story of Peter Własc.)
    19-22. Stach z Konar. (Stanley of Konar.)
    23-25. Waligóra.
    26-28. Syn Jazdona. (Son of Jazdon.)
    29-30. Pogrobek.
    31-32. Krakow za Łokietka. (Cracow during Łokietek's reign.)
    33-34. Jelita.
    35-38. Krol chłopów. (King of the peasants.)
    39-41. Biały ksiaże. (The white prince.)
    42-44. Semko.
    45-46. Matka królów. (Mother of kings.)
    47-48. Strzemienczyk.
    49-52. Jaska Orfanem zwanego zywota i spraw pamietnik. (Memoirs of the life and doings of John, called Orfan.)

53-55. Dwie królowe. (Two queens.)
56-58. Infantka. (Infanta.)
59-61. Banita. (The banished.)
62-64. Bajbuza.
65-67. Na królewskim dworze. (In the king's court.)
68-70. Boży gniew. (God's wrath.)
71-72. Król Piast. Michał Korybut. (King Piast.)
73-74. Adam Polanowskiego, notatki. (The notes of Adam P.)
75-76. Za Sasów. (In Saxon times.)
77-79. Saskie ostatki. (Remnants of the Saxon period.)

Krechkowiecki, Adam, 1860-1919
  O tron. (About the throne.) 4 vols. St. Petersburg: 1898-1905. Posen: Wydawnictwo Polskie.
    1. Ostatni dynasta. (The last dynasty.)
    2. Piast.
    3. Sława. (Fame.)
    4. Mrok. (Darkness.)

Krzewiński, Julyan
  Ulice i zaułki. (Streets and alleys.) Warsaw: "Roj," 1930.
  Jadźka dryndziarka. Warsaw: "Roj," 1930.

Orzeszkowa, Eliza, 1842-1910
  Collected works. Warsaw: S. Lewentala.
    Eli Makower. 3 vols. 1885.
    Meir Ezofowicz. 2 vols. 1886.

Marczynski, Antoni
  Niewolnice z Long Island. (Prisoners from Long Island.) Warsaw: "Roj," 1930.
  Przeklęty statek. (Damned vessel.) Warsaw: "Roj," 1930.
  Szlakiem hańby. (In the trail of disgrace.) Warsaw: "Roj," 1930.

Przerwa-Tetmajer, Kazimierz, 1865-1940
  Legenda Tatr. (Legends of the Tartars.) 2 vols. Warsaw: "Bibljoteka Polska," 1922.
    1. Maryna z Hrubego. (Mary from Hrubeg.)
    2. Janosik Nedza-Litmanowski.

Przybyszewski, Stanisław, 1868-1927
  Homo sapiens. 3 vols. Berlin: 1898.
  Compiler's note: First published in this German translation.
    1. Ueber Bord. 1898.
    2. Unter Weg. 1895.
    3. Im Mahlstrom. 1896.

  Homo sapiens. Lemberg: 1901.
    1. Na rozstaju. (At the crossroad.)
    2. Po drodze. (On the road.)
    3. W malstromie. (In the maelstrom.)

  Synowie ziemi. (Sons of the earth.) 3 vols. Lemberg: "Lektor," 1923.
    1. Synowie ziemi. Lemberg: 1904.
    2. Dzień sądu. (Day of Judgment.) Warsaw: 1909.
    3. Zmierzch. (Twilight.) 1911.

  Mocny czlowisk. (A strong man.)
    1. Mocny czlowisk. Warsaw: 1912.
    2. Wyzwolonie. (Deliverance.) Warsaw: 1913.
    3. Święty gaj. (Sacred grove.) Warsaw: 1913.

Reymont, Władysław Stanisław, 1868-1925
  Komedjantka. 1896. Warsaw: Gebethner & Wolff, 1927.
  Fermenty. (Ferments.) 1897. 2 vols. Warsaw: Gebethner & Wolff, 1928.

  (1) The comedienne. Trans. by Edmund Obecuy. New York: Putnam's, 1920.

  Rok 1794. (The year 1794.) 3 vols. Warsaw: Gebethner & Wolff, 1913-16.
    1. Ostatni sejm rzeczypospolitej. (The last parliament of the republic.)

    2. <u>Nil desperandum</u>. (Never despair.)
    3. <u>Insurekcya</u>. (Insurrection.)

  <u>Chłopi</u>. 4 vols. Warsaw: Gebethner & Wolff, 1921.
    1. <u>Jesień</u>.   3. <u>Wiosna</u>.
    2. <u>Zima</u>.   4. <u>Lato</u>.

  The peasants. Trans. by Michael H. Dziewicki. New York: Knopf. 4 vols., 1924-25; 1 vol., 1927.
    1. <u>Autumn</u>.   3. <u>Spring</u>.
    2. <u>Winter</u>.   4. <u>Summer</u>.

Rogala, Jan
  <u>Proba ognia</u>. (Trial by fire.) Warsaw: Gebethner & Wolff.
    1. <u>Zarzewie</u>. (Glowing coals.) 1927.
    2. <u>Płomień</u>. (Flame.) 1928.
    3. <u>Odkupienie</u>. (Redemption.) 1928.

Sienkiewicz, Henryk, 1846-1916
  "Trilogy." Warsaw: Gebethner & Wolff, 1898.
    1. <u>Ogniem i mieczem</u>. 2 vols. 1884.
    2. <u>Potop</u>. 3 vols. 1886.
    3. <u>Pan Wołodyjowski</u>. 1 vol. 1887.

  "Trilogy." Trans. by Jeremiah Curtin. Boston: Little, Brown.
    1. <u>With fire and sword</u>. 2 vols. 1890.
    2. <u>The deluge; an historical novel of Poland, Sweden, and Russia</u>. 1891.
    3. <u>Pan Michael; an historical novel of Poland, the Ukraine, and Turkey</u>. 1893.

Sieroszewski, Wacław, 1858-
  <u>Beniowski</u>. Warsaw: "Bibljoteka Polska," 1924.
  <u>Ocean</u>. Warsaw: "Bibljoteka Polska," 1924.

  <u>W szponach</u>. (In the clutches.) Warsaw: "Bibljoteka Polska," 1925.
  <u>Łancuchy</u>. (Chains.) 1926.
  <u>Topiel</u>. (The abyss.)

Strug, Andrzej
  <u>Zólty krzyz</u>. (Yellow cross.) 3 vols. Warsaw: Gebethner & Wolff, 1933.
    1. <u>Tajemnica Renu</u>. (Secret of the Rhine.)
    2. <u>Bogowie Germanji</u>. (German gods.)
    3. <u>Ostatni film Evy Evard</u>. (Last film of Eva Evard.)

Szemplinska, Elżbieta
  <u>Norodziny człowieka</u>. (Birth of man.)
    1. <u>Radosna afirmaeja</u>. (Joyful affirmation.) Warsaw: Bibljoteka Groszowa.
    2. "<u>Tonące okręty</u>." (Sinking ships.)
  Compiler's note: In preparation, 1934.

Szpotański, Stanisław, 1880-
  <u>Bez słonca</u>. (Without the sun.) 4 vols. in 2. Warsaw: Dziel Wyborowych, 1926.
  <u>Synowie klęski</u>. (Sons of defeat.) Warsaw: Gebethner & Wolff, 1928.

Tetmajer, Kazimierz, see Przerwa-Tetmajer, Kazimierz.

Wittlin, Jozef, 1896-
  <u>Powieść o cierpliwym piechurze</u>.
    1. <u>Sol ziemi</u>. Warsaw: "Roj," 1936.

  The patient infantry soldier.
    1. <u>Salt of the earth</u>. Trans. by Pauline De Chary. London: Methuen, 1939.
    2. "Healthy death."
  Compiler's note: In preparation, 1939.
    3. "Hole in the sky."
  Compiler's note: In preparation, 1939.

Wyrzykowski, Stanisław
  <u>Moskiewskie gody</u>. (Russian banquet.) 3 vols. Warsaw: Dom Książki Polskiej, 1930.

RUSSIAN

    1. Wilki pod murami Kremla. (Wolves at the walls of the Kremlin.)
    2-3. Zwycięskie słońce. Krwawy zmierzch. (Triumphant sun. Bloody dusk.)
Zapolska, Gabrjela, 1880-1921
  Sezonowa miłość. (Seasonal love.) Lemberg: "Lektor."
  Córka Túski. (Daughter of Tusk.) Lemberg: "Lektor," 1922.
Zegadłowicz, Emil, 1888-
  Żywot Mikołaja Srebrempisanego. (Life of M. S.) 3 vols. Posen: Księgarnia Św. Wojciecha.
    1. Godzina przed jutrznią. (An hour before matins.)
    2. Z pod myłńskich kamieni. (From under the stones of the mill.)
    3. Cień nad falami. (Shadow over the waves.)
Żeromski, Stefan, 1864-1925
  Walka z Szatanem. (The fight against Satan.) Warsaw, Cracow: Mortkowicz, 1921.
    1. Nawracanie Judasza. (The conversion of Judas.)
    2. Zamieć. (Storm.)
    3. Charitas.
Żuławski, Jerzy, 1874-1915
  Laus feminae. (Warsaw: "Bibljoteka Polska."
    1. Powrót. (The return.) 1914.
    2. Profesor Butrym. 1916.

  "Trilogy." Warsaw: "Bibljoteka Polska."
    1. Na srebrnym globie; rękopis z księżyca. (On the silver globe; manuscript from the moon.) 1922.
    2. Zwycięzca. (The winner.) 1921.
    3. Stara ziemia. (Old land.) 1922.

RUSSIAN

Aksakov, Sergey Timofeyevich, 1791-1859
  Semeynaya khronika i Vospominaniya. (Family chronicle and Recollections.) 2 pts. Moscow: Stepanovoi, 1856.
  Detskie godȳ Bogrova-vnuka. (The childhood of Bagrov's grandson.) Moscow: 1858.

  (1) A Russian gentleman. Trans. by J. D. Duff. New York: Longmans, Green, 1917.
  (2) A Russian schoolboy. Trans. by J. D. Duff. New York: Longmans, Green, 1917.
  (3) Years of childhood. Trans. by J. D. Duff. New York: Longmans, Green, 1916.
  Chronicles of a Russian family. Trans. by M. C. Beverley. New York: Dutton, 1924.
  Compiler's note: Includes 1 and parts of 2 and 3.
"Aldanov, M. A.," see Landau-Aldanov, Mark Aleksandrovich.
Amfiteatrov, Aleksander Valentinovich, 1862-1938
  Kontsy y nachala; khronika 1880-1918 g. g. (The end and the beginning; chronicle of men of 1880-1918.) 2 pts. St. Petersburg, 1907.
    I. Vos' midesyatniki. (The men of the eighties.) 4 pts., 2 vols.
      Vol. I. Razrushennyya voli. (Destroyed freedoms.)
        1. Molodozeleno. (Developing youth.)
        2. Svadebnyi khmyel'. (Nuptial intoxication.)
      Vol. II. Krakh dushi. (Pieces of a soul.)
        3. Vlast' tyela. (The power of the body.)
        4. Solntse zakhodit'. (The sun settles.)
    II. Devyatidesyatniki; roman o lyudyakh devyanostykh godov. (Men of the nineties; novel about people of the nineties.) 2 vols. 1911.
      Vol. I. Moskovskie oskolki. (Splinters of Moscow.)
      Vol. II. Podrugi. (Friends.)
"Bely, Andrey," pseud. of Boris Nikolayevich Bugaev, 1880-
  Vostok ili Zapad. (East or West.)
    1. Serebryanȳ golub'. (The silver dove.) 1910. 2 vols. in 1. Berlin: "Epokha," 1922.
    2. Peterburg. 1913. 2 vols. in 1. Berlin: "Epokha," 1922.

3. <u>Kotik Letayev</u>. 1920. Berlin, St. Petersburg: "Epokha," 1922.
4. <u>Kreshchenyi kitayets; prestupleni Kotika Letayeva</u>. (The baptized Chinaman; the crime of Kotik L.) Moscow: "Nikitinskie subbotniki," 1927.
5. <u>Epopea</u>. (Epic poem.)
6. <u>Moskva</u>. 2 pts., 3 vols. Moscow: "Krug," 1926.
   Pt. 1:
   <u>Moskovskiy chudak</u>. (The crank from Moscow.)
   <u>Maski</u>. (Masks.)
   Pt. 2:
   <u>Moskva pod udarom</u>. (Moscow under the blow.)

Bugaev, Boris Nikolayevich, <u>see</u> "Bely, Andrey."

Bunin, Ivan Alekseyevich, 1870-
   <u>Zhizn' Arsenieva</u>. (The life of Arseniev.)
   1. <u>Zhizn' Arsenieva; Istochki dney</u>. 1930.
   Compiler's note: The first part of an autobiographical sequence.

   1. <u>The well of days</u>. Trans. by Gleb Struve and Hamish Miles. New York: Knopf, 1933.

Chapygin, Aleksey Pavlovich, 1870-1937
   <u>Razin Stepan</u>. 3 vols. Moscow: "Krug," 1926-27.
   <u>Gulyashchiye lyudi</u>. (Idle folk.) 1936. 3 vols. Leningrad: Gikhl, 1938.
   Compiler's note: Prologue and sequel to <u>Razin Stepan</u>.

   (1) <u>Stepan Razin</u>. Trans. by Cedar Paul. London, New York: Hutchinson International Authors, 1946.

Chirikov, Evgeniy Nikolayevich, 1864-1932
   <u>Poslye 1905</u>. (After 1905.) 1911-13.
      <u>Zhizn' Tarkhanova</u>. (Life of Tarkhanova.) First three parts of <u>Poslye 1905</u>. Collected works, Vols. 13-15. St. Petersburg, 1915-16.
      1. <u>Yunost'</u>. (Youth.)
      2. <u>Izgnanie</u>. (Exile.)
      3. <u>Vozvrashchenie</u>. (Return.)
   4. <u>Sem'ya</u>. (Family.)

Danilevskiy, Grigoriy Petrovich, 1829-90. Pseud., "Skavronskiy"
   <u>Beglye v Novorossii</u>. (Fugitives in New Russia.) 1862.
   <u>Beglye vorotilis'</u>. (The fugitives have returned.) 1863.
   <u>Novye mesta</u>. (New places.) 1867.

Fedin, Konstantin, 1892-
   "The first joys." Serial version, <u>Novyi Mir</u>, No. 4, 1945.
   Compiler's note: The first volume of an unfinished trilogy.

Furmanov, Dmitry, 1891-1926
   <u>Chapaev</u>. 1925. Moscow: Gosizdat., 1929.
   <u>Myatezh</u>. (Revolt.) 1925. Moscow: Gosizdat., 1929.

   <u>Chapaev</u>. New York: International Publishers, 1935.

"Garin, N. G.," <u>see</u> Mikhailovsky, Nikolay Georgievich.

Gogol, Nikolay Vasilevich, 1809-52
   <u>Pokhozhdeniya Chichikova ili Mertvye dushi</u>. 1842. 2 vols. Moscow: Gotie, 1855-56.
   ("Waking souls.")
   Compiler's note: Not completed.
   ("Living souls.")
   Compiler's note: Not written.

   <u>Tchitchikoff's journeys, or Dead souls</u>. Trans. by Isabel Hapgood. New York: Crowell, 1886.
      Also translated under the title <u>Dead souls</u>.

"Gorkiy, Maksim," 1868-1936, pseud. of Aleksey Maksimovich Pyeshkov
   <u>Zhizn' Klima Samgina</u>. (The life of Clim Samghin.) 3 vols. 1927-28.
   Compiler's note: A fourth volume was published posthumously.

   Forty years; the life of Clim Samghin.
   1. <u>Bystander</u>. Trans. by Bernard Guilbert Guerney. New York: Cape & Smith, 1930.

RUSSIAN

    2. Magnet. Trans. by Alexander Bakshy. New York: Cape & Smith, 1931.
    3. Other fires. Trans. by A. Bakshy. New York, London: Appleton, 1933.
    4. The specter. Trans. by A. Bakshy. New York, London: Appleton-Century, 1938.
Grebenshchikov, Georgiy Dmitrevich, 1882- Pseud., "Sibiryak"
  V prostorakh Sibiri. (In Siberia's space.) 2 vols. 1914-15.
  Zmey Gorynych. 1916.
  Churaevy. (The Churaevs.) 1922.
  Rodnik v pustyne. (The well in the desert.) 1922.
  Put' chelovecheskiy. (Path of mankind.) 1922.
"Gusev, Sergey Ivanovich," see Orenburgsky, Sergey Gussiev.
Krestovski, Vsévolod, 1840-95
  Krovavȳ puff; khronika o novom' smutnom' vremeni gosudarstva Russiyskago. (The bloody puff; a chronicle about a recent disturbed time of the Russian empire.) 4 vols. St. Petersburg: 1875.
    1. Panurgovo stado. (Panurge's herd.) 1869.
    2. Dve silȳ. (Two powers.) 1874.
Landau-Aldanov, Mark Aleksandrovich, 1888- Pseud., "M. A. Aldanov"
  Myslitel. (1793-1821.) (The thinker.)
    1. Devyatoye termidora. Berlin: "Slovo," 1923.
    2. Chortov most. Berlin: "Slovo," 1925.
    3. Zagavor. (The conspiracy.) Berlin: "Slovo," 1927.
    4. Svyataya Yelena, malenkiy ostrov. Berlin: "Neva," 1923.

  The thinker. Trans. by A. E. Chamot. New York: Knopf.
    1. Ninth thermidor. 1926.
    2. The devil's bridge. 1928.
    4. Saint Helena, little island. 1924.

  Klyuch. Berlin: "Slovo," 1930.
  Begstvo. (The flight.) Berlin: "Slovo," 1931.
  Peshchera. (The cave.) 2 vols. Berlin: Petropolis, 1934-36.
  Compiler's note: This trilogy is linked by symbolic devices to The thinker and by themes and characters to The fifth seal.

  (1) The key. London: Harrap, 1931.

  Nachalo kontsa. (The beginning of the end.) Paris: Russkie Zapiski, 1939.

  The fifth seal. Trans. by Nicholas Wreden. New York: Scribner's, 1943.
Leskov, Nikolay Semenovich, 1831-95
  Starȳe godȳ v sele Plodomasove. (Old years in the village Plodomasovo.) 1869.
  Soboryane; starogorodskaya khronika. (The cathedral folk; an old town chronicle.) Moscow: V' Univ., 1872.

  (2) The cathedral folk. Trans. by Isabel Hapgood. New York: Knopf, 1924.
Markevich, Boleslav Mikhaylovich, 1822-84
  Chetvert' veka nazad. (A quarter of a century back.) 1878.
  Perelom. (Breakage.) 1880.
  Bezdna. (Abyss) 1883.
Melnikov, Pavel Ivanovich, 1819-83. Pseud., "Andrey Pecherskiy"
  V lesakh. (In the woods.) 1872. 4 vols. St. Petersburg: Vol'fa, 1881.
  Na gorakh. (On the mountains.) 2 vols. 1875-80. 4 vols. St. Petersburg: Vol'fa, 1881.
Merezhkovskiy, Dmitriy Sergeyevich, 1865-1941
  Kristos i Antikhrist.
    1. Smert bogov; Yulian otstupnik. 1896.
    2. Voskresenie bogov; Leonardo da Vinci. (The resurrection of the gods.) St. Petersburg: Klobukova, 1902.
    3. Pyotr i Aleksey. 1905.

  Christ and Anti-Christ. Trans. by H. Trench. New York, London: Putnam.
    1. The death of the gods. 1901. Also translated as Julian the Apostate.

2. The romance of Leonardo da Vinci. 2 vols. in 1. 1902. British title: The forerunner.
3. Peter and Alexis. 1905.

Pavel I. (Paul I.) 1908.
Compiler's note: Drama.
Aleksander I. 1910.
14 dekabrya. 1912.

(3) December the fourteenth. Trans. by Nathalie A. Duddington. London: Jonathan Cape, 1923.

Rozhdenie bogov; Tutankamon na Krite. (The birth of the gods; Tutankamen in Crete.) Prague: Plamia, 1925.

(1) The birth of the gods. Trans. by Nathalie A. Duddington. New York: Dutton, 1926.
(2) Akhnaton, king of Egypt. Trans. by N. A. Duddington. New York: Dutton, 1927.

Mikhailovsky, Nikolay Georgievich, 1852-1906. Pseud., "N. G. Garin"
Detstvo Tëmy. (Tioma's childhood.) 1892.
(High school boys.) 1893.
(University students.) 1895.
(Engineers.) 1897.

"Mikulich, V.," see Veselitskaya, Lydia Ivanovna.
"Ogynov, N.," see Rozanov, Mikhail Grigorevich.
Orenburgsky, Sergey Gussiev, 1867-   Pseud., "Sergey Ivanovich Gusev"
Strana ottsov. Published in Znanie, Vol. 4, 1904.
Strana detey.

(1) Land of the fathers. Trans. by Nina N. Selivanovna. New York: Dial Press, 1924.
(2) Land of the children. Trans. by N. N. Selivanovna. New York, London: Longmans, Green, 1928.

"Pecherskiy, Andrey," see Melnikov, Pavel Ivanovich.
Pomialovskiy, Nikolay Gerasimovich, 1853-
Meshchanskoye schast'e. (Citizens' luck.) 1861.
Molotov. 1861.
Prishvin, Mikhail Grigorevich, 1873-
Kashcheyeva tsep'. (Kashchey's chain.) Moscow: Gosizdat., 1928.
Pts. 1-3. Kurymushka. (Little berry.) 1924.
Pt. 4. Boi. (Battle.) 1927.
Zhuravlinaya rodina. (The house of the crane.) 1930. 3d ed. Leningrad: Izd. Pisateley, 1934.
Pyeshkov, Aleksey Maksimovich, see "Gorkiy, Maksim."
"Ropshin, V.," see Savinkov, Boris Viktorovich.
Rozanov, Mikhail Grigorevich. Pseud. "N. Ogynov"
Dnevnik Kosti Ryabtseva. (The diary of Kostya Ryabtsev.) 2 vols. in 1. Riga: Knigoizdatel'stvo "Gramatu dragus," 1928-29.
Pt. 2. Kostya Ryabtsev v vuze.
Nachalo zhizni. (The beginning of life.) Abridged edition of Dnevnik Kosti Ryabtseva. Moscow: Moskovskoe Tovarishchestvo Pisateley, 1933.
Tri ismereniya. (The three dimensions.) Moscow: Goslitizdat., 1933.
Compiler's note: A completion of the diaries.

(1) The diary of a Communist schoolboy. Trans. by Alexander Werth. New York: Payson & Clarke, 1928.
(2) The diary of a Communist undergraduate. Trans. by A. Werth. New York: Payson & Clarke, 1929.

Savinkov, Boris Viktorovich, 1879-1925. Pseud., "V. Ropshin"
Kon bledny. 1909. 3d ed. St. Petersburg: Vol'fa, 1914.
To chto ne sluchilos. 1913. Moscow: "Zadruga," 1918.

RUSSIAN

Kon voronoi. Leningrad: "Priboi," 1924.
Vospominaniya terrorista. Kharkov: "Proletariy," 1926.

(1) The pale horse. Trans. by Z. Vengerova. New York: Knopf, 1919.
(2) What never happened. Trans. by Thomas Seltzer. New York: Knopf, 1917.
(3) The black horse. Trans. by Sir Paul Dukes. London: Williams & Horgate, 1924.
(4) Memoirs of a terrorist. Trans. by Joseph Shaplen. New York: Boni, 1931.

Sergeyev-Tsenskiy, Sergey Nikolayevich, 1876-
 Preobrazhenie. (Transfiguration.)
  1. Valya. Simferopol: 1923.
  2. Obrechennie na gibel. (The doomed ones.) 1927.
  3. Kapitan Konyaev. 1926.

Brusilovskiy proryv. 2 vols. Moscow: Sovietskiy Pisatel., 1943.
 Pt. 1. Burnaya vesna. (Stormy spring.)
(The guns promote.) 1944.
Compiler's note: The sequence is still in progress; information about later volumes was not available.

Brusilov's breakthrough. Trans. by Helen Altschuler. London, New York: Hutchinson, 1945.

Sholokov, Mikhail Aleksandrovich, 1905-
 Tikhiy Don. 2d ed. 2 vols. in 1. Moscow: Moskovskiy Rabochiy, 1928-29.

The quiet Don. Trans. by Stephen Garry. 2 vols. New York: Knopf, 1941.
 1. And quiet flows the Don. 1934.
 2. The Don flows home to the sea. 1940.

"Sibiryak," see Grebenshchikov, Georgiy Dmitrevich.
"Skavronskiy," see Danilevskiy, Grigoriy Petrovich.
"Sologub, Fedor," see Teternikov, Fedor Kuzmich.
Tarasov-Rodionov, Aleksandr Ignatevich, 1885-
 Fevral. 2d ed. Moscow: Federatsiya, 1931.
 Compiler's note: Part of a cycle on the Russian Revolution.

February, 1917. Trans. by William A. Drake. New York: Covici-Friede, 1931.
Teternikov, Fedor Kuzmich, 1863-1927. Pseud., "Fedor Sologub"
 Tvorimaya legenda. (The legend in the process of creation.) 1908-12.
  1. Navyi chary. (Magic of the dead.)
  2. Kapli krovi. (Drops of blood.)
  3. Koroleva Ortruda. (Queen Ortruda.)
  4. Dym i pepel. (Smoke and ashes.)

 2. The created legend. Trans. by John Cournos. New York: Stokes, 1916.
Tolstoy, Count Leo Nikolayevich, 1828-1910
 "Trilogy." 1 vol. Petrograd: "Shizne dlya Vsyekh," 1916.
  1. Detstvo. 1852.   2. Otrochestvo. 1854.   3. Yunost'. 1856.

 1-3. Childhood, Boyhood, and Youth. Trans. by Isabel F. Hapgood. 1 vol. New York: Crowell, 1886.
Tolstoy, Aleksey Nikolayevich, 1882-1945
 Khozhdenie po mukam. (The road to suffering.) 1 and 2 in 1 vol. Moscow: Sovetskaya Literatura, 1934. Trilogy, 3 vols. in 1. Moscow: Gosizdat., 1943.
  1. Sestry. 1922.
  2. Vosemnadtsatyy god. 1934.
  3. Khmuroe utro.

The road to Calvary. Trans. by Edith Bone. 1 vol. New York: Knopf, 1946. Partial translations have the titles The road to Calvary and Darkness and Dawn.
 1. The sisters.   2. 1918.   3. Bleak morning.

Veselitskaya, Lydia Ivanovna, 1857- Pseud., "V. Mikulich"
  (Mimochka as bride.) 1883.
  (Mimochka at the Spa.) 1891.
  (Mimochka takes poison.) 1893.

  (1) Mimi's marriage. Trans. by C. Hagberg Wright. London: Unwin, 1893.

Vessyoly, Artyom, 1893-
  Strana rodnaya. (Homeland.) 1927.
  Rossiya, krov'yu umytaya. (Russia, streaming with blood.)

Virta, Nikolay E.
  Odinochestvo. (Solitude.) Moscow: Gosizdat., 1936.
  Zakonomernost. (Lawfulness.) Moscow: 1938.
  Compiler's note: The first two novels of a trilogy.

Zaitsev, Boris Konstantinovich, 1881-
  Puteshestviye Gleba. (Gleb's journey.)
    1. (The dawn.) 1937.
  Compiler's note: Apparently still unfinished.

Ref
Z
5917
S45
K4
1973

JUN 9 1976